The Reinvention of Social Practices

The Reinvention of Social Practices

Essays on Félix Guattari

Gary Genosko

ROWMAN &
LITTLEFIELD
INTERNATIONAL
London • New York

Published by Rowman & Littlefield International Ltd
Unit A, Whitacre Mews, 26–34 Stannary Street, London SE11 4AB
www.rowmaninternational.com

Rowman & Littlefield International Ltd. is an affiliate of Rowman & Littlefield
4501 Forbes Boulevard, Suite 200, Lanham, Maryland 20706, USA
With additional offices in Boulder, New York, Toronto (Canada), and Plymouth (UK)
www.rowman.com

British Library Cataloguing-in-Publication Data

A catalogue record for this book is available from the British Library

ISBN: HB 978-1-7866-0505-4
PB 978-1-7866-0506-1

Library of Congress Cataloging-in-Publication Data

Names: Genosko, Gary, author.
Title: *The reinvention of social practices : essays on Felix Guattari* / Gary Genosko.
Description: Lanham : Rowman & Littlefield International, 2018. | Includes bibliographical references and index.
Identifiers: LCCN 2017059603 (print) | LCCN 2018006210 (ebook) | ISBN 9781786605078 (electronic) | ISBN 9781786605054 (cloth : alk. paper) | ISBN 9781786605061 (pbk. : alk. paper)
Subjects: LCSH: Guattari, Felix, 1930–1992.
Classification: LCC B2430.G784 (ebook) | LCC B2430.G784 G458 2018 (print) | DDC 194—dc23
LC record available at https://lccn.loc.gov/2017059603

The paper used in this publication meets the minimum requirements of American National Standard for Information Sciences—Permanence of Paper for Printed Library Materials, ANSI/NISO Z39.48–1992.

Printed in the United States of America

Contents

Foreword

On Genosko's Method

Simon O'Sullivan

Theory should not stay in the study, seminar room, or lecture hall. Such might be the motto of Gary Genosko. Or, put differently, practice, in all its different forms, must be made to enter these often-closed spaces. Theory that does not connect to an "outside" in this sense can, at best, be condescending and elitist; at worst it can operate to obscure rather than clarify and enable. All of Genosko's work evidences this pragmatic take on conceptual (and, indeed, psychoanalytic) material: from the timely and often urgent themes and topics he focuses on to the different places the theoretical work is made to travel to.

Genosko's method is to operate "on the ground" in this sense. Theory is an immanent enquiry into various fields of practice (there is no capture of practice by a "transcendent" theory), but is also itself a practice (indeed, what else could it be?). When semiotics is not restricted to signifying regimes and "interpretosis," it names this kind of reciprocal relation. Genosko also thinks with and through very particular practices. Those which, one gets the sense, have chosen him. This is demonstrated also in the different milieux and genres which the work crosses. The method is to follow one's interests and enthusiasms and not necessarily the codes and protocols of a particular discipline (this is partly what transversality names).

Hence, of course, the interest in and attitude towards Guattari's work which is to be approached as much as a conceptual resource—a particular kind of diagram—as it is the oeuvre of a single self-contained individual. This is no "speaking for" or "in place of" Guattari. Genosko offers no secondary text—at least in the usual sense—but, rather, something that takes up the Guattarian corpus and runs further or in a different direction. Is this not what commentary is at its best? Not a homage (or, indeed, a critique) but the selection, foregrounding—even acceleration—of certain features and logics. A "clicking in" with another's way of thinking, a tracking and close attention to the rhythms and pace, and then a divergence and application elsewhere (when, again, the idea of application involves no "view from above" but the sense of a "good fit"). As such a name for Genosko's method might simply be pragmatics when this names the use of found materials in experimental encounter with the real.

Despite this "cut-loose" attitude—this invitation to borrow and apply elsewhere—Genosko's writings are also characterized by a certain rigour and attention to detail. There is a thorough immersion in Guattari's writing (and other semiotic theory) that parallels the immersion in different practices (it is partly the extensive and in-depth familiarity with Guattari's solo work—in a century of Deleuzians—that marks out Genosko's books). There is also an attention to history and to other backgrounds—a reading of a larger archive—that allows for the positioning of the different enquiries and research programmes within a broader context (in a world characterized by social media and sound bites, even within the academy, Genosko does the work as it were).

Another characteristic of the Genosko method is clarity. As the reader will discover there is, in the essays herein, an investment in pedagogy and a kind of communication (but not that which is opposed to creativity). This is also evident in the practices themselves—again, some of which Genosko is himself directly involved in—which seek to communicate but often through asignifying particles. There is a generosity to the method in this respect, an offering-up of something different: examples, yes, but also something else that invites us to enquiries we might ourselves make and speaks to something else we might ourselves become.

A key insight of Guattari's is that we are always more than one: there is a teeming molecularity—a collective of other selves—behind or beneath the molar self with which we more typically identify. Indeed, this is what "collective utterance" names: forms of expression that are both from and for a "people" yet-to-come (when this people is not only human). Writing can be a form of collaborative enunciation in this sense, attending to more molecular universes and often conducted with other individuals and groups and—why not?—other non-human forces and entities (it is this that gives the Guattarian project, which Genosko extends and expands, its science-fictional and future-orientated character).

This also goes hand in hand with a further aspect of the method: abstraction. Indeed, like Guattari, Genosko's work can be difficult (a will to clarity does not mean a flee from complexity). It is, we might say, abstract in the right way (an abstraction from the everyday and world-as-it-is in order to foster other connections). It is the particular combination of abstraction and pragmatics that further characterizes Genosko's method (as well, of course, as Guattari's). It is also the movement between these two—alongside the shuttling across other milieux and registers—that gives the particular Genosko diagram its contours and coordination points, as well as its lines of connection and lines of flight. This is evident within all the essays collected here.

Deleuze once wrote about a "style" of life which is evident in everything an individual might say and do. A certain affective—or asignifying—quality that characterizes a particular mode of being in the world. It is in this place that writing and a life connect. It seems to me that there is a certain style of life that is manifest in Genosko's method—as evidenced here but also in his talks and other involvements in and with the world. Indeed, these other forums and modes of expression are an important part of the method or what I have also called the diagram: in these direct "reports from the field" one hears Genosko's interest in the practices he is inspired by but also a certain lightness of touch—even a humour—that belies the always-serious enquiry (humour indicating here a kind of joy). One senses that the practices he looks to have opened up other universes of reference for Genosko and thus, in his hands, they do the same for us. Which is to say Genosko's method is ultimately one of affirmation: it operates to offer up other points of subjectivation around which another kind of subjectivity might begin to coalesce and cohere.

Simon O'Sullivan

Part I

IN THE SOCIAL FIELD

1. Transversality of the Oasis Skateboard Factory Alternative School
2. Informatic Striation in Indigenous Canada and Australia
3. Promises of the Post-Media Era

INTRODUCTION

The first two chapters in Part I required bringing theory into the field. A combination of theory not so much applied to situations but requiring two different kinds of access to institutions and lived experiences. The first took the form of an immersion in the life of the Oasis Skateboard Factory in Toronto, through the alternative school's Community and Parent Council, as a volunteer member specializing in language arts and publishing; the second was undertaken in Iqaluit, Nunavut, in the Canadian Arctic, by my former graduate student, Adam Bryx, under a license issued to me by the provincial authority for on-site research. Dr. Bryx conducted on the ground observations and held informal conversations with volunteers, courtesy of the local Canadian Broadcasting Corporation radio station, about local cultural practices in reusing government identifiers that Inuit were once required to bear in lieu of their names. Both of us had to parry the objections of entrenched researchers because of the incredible public freedom we gave to our interlocutors to redress wrongs. Despite political resistance to the discs that had emerged publicly by 1968 with the election of the first Inuk to the Northwest Territories council (Simonie Michael), an incredibly powerful phantasy persists in the scientific and policy communities about the programme's innocence.

The concepts that made the trips were, first, transversality and, second, an informatic model of smooth and striated. These chapters are not applications of concepts, just as Deleuze wrote of Guattari that he did not apply psychoanalysis to groups.[1] Rather, they deploy concepts in order to see how they work in new contexts. It is not possible to transfer wholesale the practical lessons of transversality from the psychiatric clinic where it was incubated and used to understand and modify group relations and the institution's analytic role, to a high school in downtown Toronto. But the concept works well there, too, as it helps to pose a certain number of key questions about the relations between the student body, teachers, and the neighbourhood they inhabit for part of their days, but also the many different kinds of relationships between the students, teachers and the businesses, graffiti artists, designers, and skateboarders who are engaged in the extended pedagogy that is structured around the construction, design, and marketing of skateboards. I have published extensively on transversality in book chapters and dictionary entries.[2] Chapter 1 does not explicate Guattari's essay but pursues the implications of transversality for the life of Oasis Skateboard Factory by emphasizing the encounters of the students with the school (to what degree does the teacher's social status rehearse the alienation that some of the students already experienced in mainstream classrooms?) and the object at its centre, the skateboard, with reference to the extra-institutional connections that help to define the school as an alternative (precisely, a credit recovery programme) and enable it to fulfil its goals with regard to the guiding themes of art and social change. To what extent is the structure of transversality that Oasis has set up maximized in its current situation, and which are the sticking points that diminish the potential for open transversal communication and self-directed movement?[3] The delicate balance that the school achieves in advancing the diagram of skateboard culture against the social identities it promotes, around gender and indigeneity, must reckon with the tendency of molar determinations to arrest becomings and the creation of the new, and the need to cultivate progressive molecular processes that everyone can affiliate with, a becoming-woman and a becoming-indigene.

Plateau 14 concerning the smooth and the striated in *A Thousand Plateaus* presents multiple models: technological, musical, maritime, mathematical, physical, and aesthetic examples of the translation of smooth into striated and reversal of striated into smooth spaces.[4] Chapter 2 adds a further model, an *informatics* of Inuit space and identity by means of striated datafication and programmes of the welfare state, but in addition reversal of striated space by means of the cultural repurposing of identifiers. The informatics model draws upon features from some of the other models. The study in Iqaluit is extended to several Australian examples in order to expand the informatics model through further indigenous references.[5] It may seem counterintuitive to align striation with datafication (personal information), new information technologies, and cellular and satellite telephony, but it is perhaps the complexity of the "simple" opposition between smooth and striated that is better illustrated. Informatics interrupts the haptic smooth space of expanses of ice and the peoples who inhabit it by introducing sedentary principles, geographic points (house numbers), and extracted properties. The ordering of intensities by the Dew Line radar early warning system simply means the occupation of smooth space can be re-smoothed by its dereliction at the end of the Cold War, so that it becomes the name of a journal (McLuhan's *Dew-Line Newsletter*), and by the proliferation of artificial oil rigs, "neonomadic" nuclear submarines of American and Russian origins, and container ships plying the melting Northwest passage. Global warming imparts a troubling smoothness to the high arctic, which is re-striated by northern scientists and their research stations, submersible probes, and ice-tethered devices.

Chapter 3 was originally my contribution to a collection of essays on post-media theory,[6] and it is adapted to include further material relating to Guattari's vision of a growing machinic orality that is de-linguistified (de-centred from a speaking subject), collectivized (de-individuated), and bestowed with a semiotic polyvocity. One of the most important and provocative dimensions of Guattari's post-media vision is his sense of machinic orality that he gained through his participation in the Paris-based Polyphonix festivals, courtesy of his friend and event co-founder Jean-Jacques Lebel, and in the Québec City–based In(ter)ventions festivals, courtesy of Richard Martel. A recording of one of Guattari's own performances was integrated into Lebel's sculptural *Monument à Félix Guattari* (1994), as his voice emanates from a gutted Renault, the same model Guattari drove. Guattari's sensitivity to the emerging machinic oral enunciative possibilities points forwards and backwards at the same time, to the need for a media archaeology of voders and vocoders, but also to the need to account for developments in AI and digital speech synthesis. Guattari wanted to separate spoken performance from written texts, and for this reason he disliked giving academic papers and lectures. In his Brazilian dialogues with Suely Rolnik, he complained of the irrevocable loss of non-written elements such as "the intrinsic rhythm, the particular sensibility, capturing the impact produced by a certain kind of problem in a certain group of people, in certain situations. . . . Really, for me, what's taking place though this journey in Brazil is a debate in twenty or thirty parts."[7] A flourishing contrapuntal enunciation exudes the energy and ingenuity Guattari associated with the most collective (multiple, machinic, impersonal, affective) spoken word performances.

Guattari's line of escape from the conservatism of postmodernism to the post-media era catapulted him into a science-fictional universe in which machinism and humanity "entertain fruitful symbiotic relations."[8] He ultimately worked out this symbiosis of machinic subjectivation in a film script, *A Love of UIQ*, in which UIQ (univers infra quark) is a subatomic alien that falls in love with a young woman who learns that there is no escape from its desire, with disastrous results.[9] The lesson of such symbiosis is tragic in Guattari's script, and it reflects his general ambivalence about the prospects for the post-media era. There is no doubt that his commitment to film was an exception.[10]

NOTES

1. Gilles Deleuze, "Three Group-Related Problems," in Félix Guattari, *Psychoanalysis and Transversality: Texts and Interviews 1955–71*, trans. A. Hodges, Los Angeles: Semiotext(e), 2015, p. 16.

2. See my first and second chapters of *Félix Guattari: An Aberrant Introduction*, London: Continuum, 2002, and chapter 2 of *Félix Guattari: A Critical Introduction*, London: Pluto, 2009; also, on transversality and architecture, my article "Transversal House: Deleuze and Guattari in Japan," *2A+P* [Rome] #1 (March 2000): 56–61; and entries on "transversality" in *The Deleuze and Guattari Dictionary*, eds. E. Young, with G. Genosko and J. Watson, London: Continuum, 2013, pp. 320–22, and an early attempt with (Adam Bryx) to address both Guattari's and Deleuze's concepts, "Transversality," in *The Deleuze Dictionary*, ed. A. Parr, Edinburgh: Edinburgh University Press, 2005, pp. 117–19 and 285–86.

3. This up-to-date version of chapter 1, based on follow-up discussions with the school, is published here for the first time. A short version appears in *Schizoanalysis and Ecosophy*, ed. C. Boundas, London: Bloomsbury, 2017.

4. Gilles Deleuze and Félix Guattari, *A Thousand Plateaus*, trans. Brian Massumi, Minneapolis: University of Minnesota Press, 1987, p. 475ff.

5. A short version of chapter 2 originally appeared with Adam Bryx, "After Informatic Striation: The Resignification of Disc Numbers in Contemporary Inuit Popular Culture," in *Deleuze and Space*, eds. I. Buchanan and G. Lambert, Edinburgh: Edinburgh University Press, 2005, pp. 109–25. The Australian material was gathered during a sabbatical year spent in Sydney in 2005–2006 and later appeared in chapter 5, "Informatic Striation" in my *Félix Guattari: A Critical Introduction*. The corrected and updated version appears here.

6. G. Genosko "The Promise of Post-Media," in *Provocative Alloys: A Post-Media Anthology*, eds. C. Apprich et al., London: MUTE and Post-Media Lab, Leuphana University, 2013, pp. 15–25.

7. Guattari and Rolnik, *Molecular Revolution in Brazil*, trans. K. Clapshow and B. Holmes, Los Angeles: Semiotext(e), 2008, p. 439.

8. Félix Guattari, *Schizoanalytic Cartographies*, trans. A. Goffey, London: Bloomsbury, 2013, p. 40.

9. Félix Guattari, *A Love of UIQ*, trans. S. Maglioni and G. Thomson, Minneapolis: Univocal, 2016.

10. See my work on minor cinema and transversal television. "Félix Guattari," in *Film, Theory and Philosophy: Key Thinkers*, ed. Felicity Colman, London: Acumen, 2009, pp. 243–52. Reprinted in J. Blankenship and T. Nagl, *European*

Visions: Small Cinemas in Transition, Bielefeld: Transcript Verlag, 2015, pp. 337–49; and "Guattari TV, By Kafka," *Deleuze Studies* [Special Issue on Guattari in the Age of Semiocapitalism] 6/2 (2012): 62–75. Reprinted with minor revisions as "Transversal Telelvision: For Guattari, by Kafka," in *Intensities and Lines of Flight: Deleuze and Guattari and the Arts*, eds. A. Calcagno, J. Vernon, and S. Lofts, London/New York: Rowman & Littlefield, 2014, pp. 149–61.

Chapter 1

Transversality of the Oasis Skateboard Factory Alternative School

Throughout his career Félix Guattari referred to the accomplishments of radical French teacher Célestin Freinet, whose work he discovered through his youthful outings in the hostelling movement with pedagogue Fernand Oury, the brother of his long-time collaborator at La Borde, Jean Oury. The institutional pedagogy movement in France dovetailed with the institutional psychotherapy practised at La Borde—paying critical attention to how institutions generate subjectivities—although the followers of Freinet and Oury were not often able to cooperate. Theory was not a strongpoint of Freinet's work, and his school's distance from the hotbed of theoretical innovation in Paris contributed to the estrangement. Nevertheless, formations of subjectivation were engendered in an original way through Freinet's use of a classroom printing press: in a way complementary to how an institution itself and its organizational diagram were foregrounded in the grid, the table of rotating duties and personnel assignments at La Borde. Inspired by Freinet, Guattari adapted practices designed for schoolchildren in rural France in the 1920s and 1930s to a psychiatric clinic specializing in the treatment of psychosis, developing the process over his career there from the mid-1950s to the early 1990s.

Looking across institutions and bringing diverse historical practices into a contemporary context, I want to report on my participation in a downtown Toronto alternative school that is built around the mediating technology of skateboards. I don't mean simply riding skateboards, although that is not a simple matter at all. I focus on the delivery of state-mandated curriculum from the ground up by means of the construction, design, and marketing of different kinds of boards and an immersion in youth street culture through the production of buttons, 'zines, graffiti, T-shirts, and of course, skateboards. I want to provide in a preliminary way a contemporary schizoanalysis of the mediations, institutional constraints, transversal extra-academic challenges and successes, as well as the prospects for its students and teachers, of this small, one room, alt-high school. I will begin with a few reflections on Freinet's techniques and methods and then turn to the skateboard factory, where I participated during 2011–2012 in the life of the school as a member of the Community Council as a specialist in publishing.[1]

SKATEBOARD PHILOSOPHY

Surfing served Marshall McLuhan well as a metaphor for riding the electronic whorl. Skateboarding is not among the sports that Deleuze and Guattari discuss, but this has not prevented their readers from linking their thought with a rhizomatics of street performances and smoothing of urban space through temporary repurposings of rails, benches, walkways, and stairs, not to mention lines of flight along a vast urban concrete phylum;[2] indeed, rhizomatic resistance is a potent theme in describing youth skateboarding against the controlled space of the skate park.[3] A study of skate punks in California is inspired by Guattari's remarks on the many kinds of deterritorialization of dominant realities that machinic intensities can provide, such as boarding in empty suburban swimming pools.[4] Yet from the time that Iain Borden published his study on architecture and skateboarding to the present, boarding has been in some cities partially integrated into urban renewal schemes, education and health curricula, adopted as a strategy for building youth social capital around the globe, and its business successes celebrated.[5] This is the broad context of my study: skateboarding's entry not so much into the mainstream, but as a controlled substance of socialization within the well-established alternative streams of high school education in Toronto. The very link between skateboarding and curriculum is an inspired Guattarian gesture of experimentation taken by founding teacher Craig Morrison, in the context of the Arts and Social Change programme he designed in the Oasis alternative school in 2006, before the programme jumped into its own "one room schoolhouse" rented in the Scadding Court Community Centre in downtown Toronto at the intersection of Dundas and Bathurst Streets in 2009. Despite its high public profile and ample positive media coverage, and the numerous awards the school has garnered, Oasis Skateboard Factory (OSF) has not been successful in acquiring a designated space of its own that doesn't require cleaning, repacking, and locking up at the end of each day, and the school must raise money through sponsorships and partnerships in order to supplement its modest official budget from the local school board. Within the past two years, however, OSF has managed to access extra funds earmarked for First Nations issues that the board has made available, and develop robust programming focused on native visual arts and culture. This has changed the cultural commitments of the school to the extent that it now features work by indigenous youth embedded in traditional visual regional styles integrated into urban street cultures and skateboarding. In 2015 the "Tkaronto" (derived from a Kanienke'haka term) Native SK8 Studies project created boards acknowledging that the school is located on traditional territories of the Wendat, Anishinabek Nation, Haudenosaunee Confederacy, Mississaugas of the New Credit First Nations, and Métis Nation, and the continuing large urban aboriginal presence in the city.

AFTER FREINET

Transiting, then, from the printing press to the skateboard, I pass through Freinet's so-called *natural method* of pedagogy that was largely a trial and error process without lessons favouring active rather than passive learning that he thought of as a "way of life."[6] Clearly in line with the active school tradition, but diverging from the more production-oriented and industrial education models, Freinet claimed that a pupil's desire for greater perfection in visual expression and power over representation could be augmented by the use of a printing press, among a whole battery of mechanical technological devices and their associated techniques; however, for schools without the requisite budget, any number of pre-digital duplicating machines would suffice, which during the period in question beginning in the 1930s, would have used a stencil, as in a mimeograph, or a limograph. Whatever the choice, getting one's hands inky was a rite of passage for Freinet's young grade school students. Stencil tech was relatively cheap and non-electrical, not to mention non-colour, delivering lines with some shadows; the copies could then be hand-coloured. The creation of copies permitted each student in the class to compile a book of his or her own work, a Book of Life, and include works by fellow classmates as well; in addition, each pupil could create a free text of their own akin to a diary, as well as contribute to the school newspaper. Individual work plans balanced with collective responsibilities. The original student publications played the role of school syllabus and attracted the wrath of both Ministry of Education officials and socialist politicians because Freinet ignored board textbooks and didn't teach the classics, either.[7] Eventually he would build one hour of mandated exercises into his daily school timetable, with the option for another hour developed to "old pedagogy" at the end of the day.[8] Freinet also developed a system of cards (*fichier documentaire*) that held information such as newspaper clippings about a variety of topics and were catalogued by subject as a classroom resource, and used in a variety of lessons.

The desire of pupils to create and to communicate their own original vision, full of their own personality and character, was at the heart of Freinet pedagogy. Freinet also promoted the use of linocut techniques of engraving and running off copies as they produced better results especially for illustrating newspaper articles.[9] Freinet used these student publications for the purpose of interscholastic communication, beginning modestly with fellow travellers, and growing as he refined his methods. Packages of Books of Life were exchanged between schools in France, and the lives of children from diverse parts of the country were shared and used as sources of materials for classroom lessons. The exchanges were regular, and they were used to deepen interest and were supplemented with maps, postcards, regional foods, and so on. At the outset, Freinet exchanged Books of Life between participating schools, formalizing the exchange with questionnaires and delivery dates, but he then wanted each school to print a high-quality illustrated newspaper for interscholastic communications. School newspapers are a staple of high school and university campuses, but Freinet believed both primary and middle years could also participate. The mature centrepiece of Freinet education is a school print shop with a movable metallic-type press; the Gutenbergian legacy is obvious without becoming a techno-fetish. He does not consider the printing press to be a panacea, but leans heavily on "modern techniques" as a source of enchantment and magic for pupils and a means to integrate them into contemporary social processes,[10] neither reducing the lessons to "education by work" nor "technical apprenticeship."[11] The production process is not manual, Freinet claimed, but "intellectual and spiritual" because it deconstructed the work-play distinction in an atmosphere that was egalitarian and democratic. The school print shop is a place of collective production.[12] It is also a place of working to a deadline as newspapers would be produced weekly. The newspaper was posted on a wall as a mural and was subject to collective review giving rise to congratulations, criticisms, and requests.

In order to facilitate group communication and collective decision making, and build the life of the school, Freinet constituted a cooperative council consisting of students and teacher—the multi-age and—ability Freinet school had only one teacher. He built this event around the posting and "common discussion" of the newspaper, but it was a democratic body with power to make decisions about certain expenditures. Although the teacher played an important role and held a veto, the formation of the assembly as a self-directed group is first and foremost at stake so that its projects may be articulated and pursued and responsibility for them taken together. The council instituted the communal life of the school. Freinet's spouse Elise introduced a vegetarian diet for the boarders and day students, including in the late 1930s refugees from the Spanish Civil War.

Freinet identified himself as a proletarian educator, joining the French Communist Party in the 1920s and participating in rural cooperatives and teacher unions; his autonomous school in Vence, a small medieval village, founded in 1936, catered to small numbers of students of different ages, many of whose parents were immigrants. Freinet believed he was operating in the Soviet Artek tradition of summer camps (with a full film studio on site)[13] and enthusiastically participated in the Youth Hostelling movement. His rural location held its own dangers when reactionary forces marshalling local anti-Soviet sentiments were able to remove him from his public post during 1932–1933. Freinet was also ill-adapted to pedagogical theories emanating from Paris, namely the institutional pedagogy movement that grew out of different conditions and adopted a highly theoretical language inherited from psychoanalysis. The fraught relationship between Freinet and institutional pedagogy—the latter recognized as a strand of the former, but without the focus on teaching materials, and more concerned with professional qualifications, academic research, and problems of urban high schools that lacked a community—yet establishes an explicit crossover between Freinet techniques and Jean Oury's experiments with adult patients at Saumery ('49–'53) and then La Borde. Experimentation necessitated by material privation is part of the standard version of this history, but so is the communist utopia of revolving intellectual and manual tasks, declassification of specialities, communitarian organization, non-hierarchical clubs, which culminates in something like the grid, the double-entry bookkeeping system that Guattari adapted to managing work assignments and durations through the categories of time and task in relation to existing role definitions (doctors, nurses, non-medical staff, patients, families).

The implementation of the grid at first placed Guattari in the role of "grid maker"[14] and expressed democratic centralism as an organizational principle, but one that would change over time as the system mutated and became more sophisticated, that is, less logical and rational, and more subject to distributed monitoring and decision making. For Guattari, "the grid is a double-entry table that allows for the collective management of individual assignments in relation to tasks. It is a kind of regulatory device for the necessary deregulation of the institution."[15] This abstract machine that is expressed on paper bears little overt relation to the printing press as a concrete object, but both are machines that articulate affects and assignments, by exposing resistances, enabling recognition of limitations, requiring negotiation, heightening shifting valorizations, and emergent singularities, towards the production of new kinds of subjectivities and the collective auto-engendering of institutional life with various degrees of formation.

Complementary forms of transversal experimentation exist between the Freinet classes articulated around concrete machines and the collectively produced journals and newspapers and the grid at La Borde (rewriting the doctor–patient relationship), in as much as they enabled the formation of subject groups, in addition to the multilevel communication opened up by the cooperative council that rewrote the student–teacher relationship by centring the classroom around the press itself rather than orienting itself to the teacher and his lecture podium. Individual and collective auto-engenderings of the institution do not necessarily result in archivable artefacts, but these are durable records of desiring-productions.[16]

The situation at OSF is not so far removed from these concerns. The position and authority of the teacher is not decentred, but remains intact, although traditional performances at the head of the class are minimized. Reliance on invited experts from the skateboarding world, from the arts, and from professional design firms makes the classroom a place of heterogeneity, not just at the level of content, but also at the level of exterior contact. The introduction of new technologies into the classroom, as well as access to laser cutting at other sites, has changed the relationship of the students to the materials at hand, especially the maple veneer strips with which they build boards, and at the same time entangled the professional/manual distinction within a lesson that is not fully deliverable in the class itself. The presence of the founding figure also poses a quandary about succession should either Craig Morrison or the co-teacher Lauren Hortie depart. A similar quandary about whether anyone practises schizoanalysis may be posed after Guattari and Jean Oury's deaths; is the idea of an "institutional cure" offered by analyses emerging on a contingent basis from non-specialists and collective assemblages still a possibility?[17]

EVERYDAY LIFE AT THE SKATEBOARD FACTORY

Within the board system, a standard curriculum must be delivered, a daily schedule made available for parents and for purposes of transparency and accountability; occasional disciplinary problems do arise with a class consisting of around 20–25 students of ages 16–20. But the challenges faced by at-risk, marginal youth are multiple—homelessness, poverty, hunger, mental and physical health issues directly and regularly affect OSF students in some measure, although the class composition of a given cohort varies. Grades must be assigned and submitted according to the requisite achievement-level scales and learning outcomes, not even Freinet could swerve around such requirements. Yet the OSF is, as co-teacher Lauren Hortie observes, "not in a school building. . . . There's no bell. We do not sing the national anthem."[18] The setting in a community centre with its diverse all ages clientele in an impoverished neighbourhood next to a large and notorious public housing estate, social services, a pool and skating rink, as well as the lively small food businesses outside on the sidewalk (a new and welcome development), is a far cry from a school layout in which the distance between any point on the property to the principal's office may be the measure of an alienated student's life. OSF caters to re-engagement students who are short of high school credits and cannot graduate, which does not mean that they can graduate from OSF, since they may lack credits that are not available there. As a result, only a portion of the class graduates directly from OSF each year, an event that is treated as a special honour and held at Toronto skateboard design shop and long-standing partner, Roarockit. OSF students are said to be with tenderness "misfits" who have either dropped out of mainstream schools or are currently faltering in some manner. OSF has an enviable success rate when it comes to students earning class credits in English, art, and business, but it does not offer a full range of high school subjects. The recent trend is that greater numbers of OSF students are receiving their high school diplomas from OSF, rather than having to re-enter a more traditional high school environment in order to earn missing credits. The idea that skateboarding is an activity that may satisfy physical science requirements is still radical and has broad appeal!

The site of the rented one-room school, the downtown Scadding Court Community Centre, is scheduled for closure and on the redevelopment block, a predicament that makes OSF's thus far unsuccessful search for a suitable new location more urgent. It is not that there is a shortage of unused school properties in the city; on the contrary, many schools stand empty as the board has pursued a low enrolment closure policy that has gutted neighbourhood institutions. Although a few basement locations have been dangled before OSF, they are unsuitable for an outward-looking school that needs a visible presence at street level to meet its goals of community engagement.

And an entirely different object mediates school life—the skateboard. The cultural status of the board remains linked with a subcultural ensemble signifying rebellion, despite its accommodations and services performed in the name of socializing youth. This is how Morrison and Hortie get "buy-in" from the students by putting them into contact with the subculture many live, or at least emulate, and translating the conflict with law enforcers and property owners most urban boarders have experienced into a model of how to succeed in the spirit of cooperative associations, for instance, in the Student Design Team which does work with community partner-clients like Kensington Market retailer Longboard Living and, ultimately, by establishing sole proprietorships of some size and shape, although this is not a guarantee but a tactic of passage into adulthood. However, the object is not given, preformed, and readymade. It must be created from kits provided by partner Roarockit design. This is the DIY ethos at play in delicate balance with the entrepreneurial mission of the school. Yet DIY is filtered through a careful lesson plan in skateboard design and art history and technique development.

There is open recognition that OSF teaches entrepreneurial skills. This is a bulwark against high youth employment rates. While Morrison admits "we are really about products," he qualifies this with the observation that "for at-risk youth, that product allows for opportunity for engagement. If you're without a product you don't have a feedback loop." Student success is OSF success and vice versa, but this success for a large measure takes place by means of contingent arrangements with outside sponsors. Part of the public face of this success is that it is embedded in business, which is ironic, as Morrison comments: "Why this is a moment when we're popular and supported, it's because we teach business . . . I frickin' hate business." Hortie explains that by business what is meant is the development and marketing of a "personal brand." Design has the flavour less of an order word that freezes and more of a password that unthaws. For Morrison, students design their lives and worlds; they sell their boards and their services, not to mention their 'zines, buttons, and T-shirts; they make contracts and fulfil them. They learn to pass by transforming intensity into extensivity. They are mentored by volunteers in the advertising sector, by artists, and by designers. For instance, a much-publicized mentoring arrangement with global ad agency Anomaly in 2013 provided direct feedback about pitching proposals and business strategies.[19] Yes, OSF students make products and sell them, just as Freinet did when he developed a printing press and sold it to his followers, publishing instructions in his journal on how to assemble it, and neither are anti-capitalist projects. But OSF teachers and students engage in critiques of consumerism and dominant norms, including local political issues, and gender biases in skateboarding culture.

OSF has refocused itself on deploying the skateboard as an "engagement tool for girls," as Morrison puts it, and the gender imbalances in classes have dramatically improved from the early years that were dominated by teenage boys. A leadership project undertaken by three OSF students in 2011 ("Heels on Wheels") was funded by an external grant from Change Our World (Ministry of Education, Ontario) and was primarily educational, addressing girls' empowerment through skateboarding within the alternative school system (http://changeourworld.ca/submissions/category/9) in Toronto. The self-determined presence of young women in skateboarding magazines is still marginal, but reports about women's organizations and events are more regular, and women's histories in skate communities provide missing reference materials that can be existentially impactful.

The self-entrepreneurial subject is produced by finance capital in the wake of the evacuation of social supports, precarization, and immaterialization of labour. Is the skateboard school caught up in this process? It would seem so, yet entrepreneurialism does not generate a monolithic subject, because the process that is initiated contains components that also characterize subject groups, namely, openness and assumption of risk, and the successful confrontation with alterity; we see this in the aesthetic and political confrontations with the enemies of the subculture in the guise of powerful civic politicians who scapegoat urban youth (skateboarders, graffiti artists, bicycle messengers, squeegee kids). The construction of the mayor as a castrating master whose blind demands and punishments one cannot evade teaches only passivity and capitulation, and does not as Guattari insists allow one to get past such "pseudo-phallic" phantasies and gain critical insight into the gender dynamics and economic interests structuring political life. To have the students acknowledge the socio-economic forces impinging upon their decision making, and thus to see that they are also subjugated groups waiting to be heard but by whom exactly remains unknown. OSF is not, of course, an analytic milieu, so these lessons are not on the table alongside the spray paint cans and tubs of wood glue, yet they are glimpsed through the many ways that social life explicitly finds its way into their classroom, and how the leading groups of "seniors" manage it, responding by imprinting onto successes or by retreating into silence, avoidance, disappearance, drug use, and so on. Early in the reign of "crackhead" mayor Rob Ford, OSF students contributed a lively flow of street art mocking him and at least one student even built their personal brand around quite-pointed political mockery.[20] This aesthetic and subcultural resistance to mystification was evidence that OSF had managed at some level to outflank "blind" social demands for respectful attitudes towards leaders and political hierarchy, a staple of typical civics lessons.

In the pages of *Concrete Wave*, a local Toronto magazine and OSF partner in which students have published their written and graphic work describing links between boarding and creativity ("Lost in Translation," 2012), we see an example of how consumption of style within the subculture is modified by a collective contribution that contains ideas first tried out in classroom 'zines and visual design exercises. Publishing in a magazine is productive work that reflects shared interests in the culture, even though writing is a challenge for many students. Connecting with the skateboarding print universe, and taking responsibility beyond an assignment, a move towards a new becoming writer and contributor was initiated by modifying their position as audience/readership, in which many of the students counted themselves and their friends. Although this material is not reintegrated into the classroom as the foundation for lessons in the Freinet tradition, it is evidence of the strong connections that the students build with subcultural vehicles and various community organizations, for instance, the local downtown independent businesses where their non-riding boards are hung by clients as signage and wall art. A recent OSF exhibition ("Youth Are Revolting") and auction of boards at the gallery space in the Gladstone Hotel on Queen Street West combined fundraising for a school trip and school promotion of its mentorship programmes with local artists.

On any given day when class is in session, at the centre of the makeshift classroom may be found a portable sawhorse, with a vise holding on to a recently glued seven-ply maple skateboard. Rough edges are hand sanded. Running commentary is provided by fellow students. Sawdust is in the air and on the floor. Turpentine bristles nose hairs; spray paint cans, tubs of wood glue, styrofoam board moulds litter the tables—not single desks and seating plans, but shared, movable tables. Painter's tape is being pulled off boards at some tables, stencils refined and applied, and spray paint applied out of doors. Over in the "kitchen" area, the toaster trips a breaker and the ancient computers crash. For certain groups, power tools are devalued, and hand-sanding is a preference for small-scale production. There is a story here, and it has to do with prevalence of broken equipment in middle school and high school woodworking shops. Lunch suddenly appears in the hands of a student's grandmother. Some kids go out for a cigarette. A visiting graffiti artist shows up and commences work with a student on a new design. It is always quiet when sharp knives are in use. Full-scale diagrams are spread out on the tables. Portraits on bits of broken skateboards are stored in a milk carton, awaiting up-cycling. The soundtrack of the classroom is scraping and sanding, with occasional bursts of music from portable personal music systems. In full swing the classroom is not centred on a teacher at the front of the room. Interactions with Morrison and Hortie are sporadic, individual and problem-based, but consultations are scheduled, and progress towards set goals is emphasized and monitored. There is up to a point an unpredictable nature to class time, subject to tangents, diversions, debates, peccadilloes. Yet one-on-one consultations are taking place between teachers and artists and other guests. Projects tend to be layered and overlap. Students are taking time out to write their contributions to the school's *Slo Skate* zine. Often this is a painful, academic process, but some of the students are highly skilled writers and advance rapidly. Most figure out that the desire to interview a skate or art star is risky. Requests are e-mailed. Anxiousness and disappointment are inevitable, but these too are usable. The best approach is to request an interview with someone they believe will respond. Non-responses are sometimes integrated into the report as badges of honour: "As you can image, Shepard Fairey [OBEY] is currently over-booked. . . . Regrettably he must decline your invitation to participate." Some connections in the skate and street art worlds are forged, questions sent, and answers read, and rewritten in a report format about a person, an organization, an event. The zine eventually comes together. The process is low-tech, classic alt-press production techniques, maybe without the waxing and porcelain rollers! Not everything is like this.

OSF has a manual screen-printing station. It can screen on grip tape and offers this service through a local board shop.

A skateboard is not a printing press! There are many skateboards in various states of composition and decomposition in OSF on any given day. A skateboard is a diagram and not a code. It is exploratory, whether in production or on the street. In passing from the virtual to the actual, the diagrammatic function of the skateboard is filtered by a gamut of factors from the curriculum to its layers of veneer, but taken together they are productive of new realities. OSF itself changes in relation to the skateboards made in and for it, and for others outside, both lost and found, force new sensations together all across the city. Every skateboard begins with a package of raw materials and is conjoined to a sketch for a brand that travels along a pedagogical passage all the way from warm-up work to the finished board and beyond into the streets or onto the walls of small shops, art galleries, and private homes. Students at OSF are transmitters of a skateboard's potentialities. Their rhizomes extend well beyond the classroom's walls and are thrown outward by curricular prerogatives such as seeking sponsors for boards, negotiating designs, gaining an honorarium on sales participating in pop-up shops; or instead of cash, donations are brokered, and philanthropic giving by students or sponsor is encouraged. The entrepreneurial skills acquired at OSF do not reduce a skateboard's diagram to education as work. As Morrison observes: "We're reframing hands-on skills so that they're not just a working class characteristic." Freinet's critique of "education by work" struggled against its utilitarian framing and denigration of manual labour with its "potential for an ulterior social production."[21] Instead, he considered his goal to be "schooling by life, for life, by work," an achievement in which each child would make the school his or her own. Here, OSF wants to distinguish itself from tech-training or vocational training that overcodes social subjects as non-academic tradespeople, despite the intense machinism that crosses both work and play. The "victory lap" phenomenon, according to which local high school students take a fifth year to refocus themselves into a non-professional career, often involves a proto-apprenticeship in the trades, often with strong artisanal dimensions. But OSF does not position itself to feed into this practice.

OSF focuses on materials, their manipulation, and transformation into products. It plays on the myth of the one-room schoolhouse with a rented room, but its marginality is never in doubt as it still has to hope that the yearly budget process will actually guarantee that enough wood will be available to build skateboards. Let's not forget these boards are canvases for young designers. OSF is not a segregated school as it is open to the outside and has complex relations with many social scenes and actors, including major institutions. In 2012 a group of OSF students were artists-in-residence in the after-school programme at the Art Gallery of Ontario where they staged skateboard construction workshops. This kind of relationship with a mainstream, establishment institution modifies their role as students and opens them to a variety of novel encounters. However, the school term and the various deadlines that have to be met are constraints of the skateboard diagram that set up the conditions for exploration. A new diagrammatic extension is the annual NYC school field trip, which exploits industry contacts, opportunities for pop-up shops, and fundraising.

OSF students are academically successful with high class pass rates (between 90 and 100%). The courses offered across grades 9–12 in a typical slate (2015–2016) include Youth and Culture Studies; Skateboard Design; Creativity and Social Entrepreneurship; DIY Media and Publishing; Street Art. These may be taken for credit in specific areas (history, geography, English, business, art) or on a credit recovery basis, in whole or in part, on an individualized basis or in a remedial cluster. These designations are part of the school board's prerogative to assist struggling students without forcing them to repeat the same courses they have already failed. Every new cohort poses new challenges as the working relationships within the class have a tendency to decay into non-attendance, and this can be detrimental to individual and group opportunities, especially when the stakes are high (i.e., when attendance is poor for invited guests).

OSF helps students to take advantage of interactions with the outside and in doing so attempts to maximize its transversality and organizational complexity. Transversality is known to exist in every institution; although it is not quantified, it is a "coefficient" that modifies local variables. As a coefficient, transversality is linked to degrees of blindness within an organization, and what it takes to calibrate it may be considered put in its service. Transversality always runs up against institutional inertia, primarily with reference to school board politics around curriculum, and a given cohort can choose social regression. The fact of the non-school property location of OSF, which is seen by both teachers and students as high in transversality, also necessitates that nothing is left in place at the end of the day, limiting project continuity and therefore introducing another pressure of conformity from the many layers of the outside, not only the local centre, but the board, and the city of Toronto.

The figures of the entrepreneur and leader are deployed against inclinations to retreat from encounters with openness, with all of their contingencies, as threat management and preservation of scarce resources. Over the course of a year, and from year to year, relational configurations change and new challenges arise, while some conditions linger. The negotiation of otherness is a core requirement of success at the school, and in this it needs to be recognized that traumas, such as deaths, do arise within the skateboarding community in

Toronto.[22] How such an event mobilizes the class and its subgroups to reaffirm their existence in the group or face decaying into alienation in a hostile environment that lessens feelings of security will shape outcomes during that period of crisis and for sometime after.

The spatial independence of the school, the flexible cultural affinities between teachers and students, the unfurling diagram of the skateboard as a means of enhancing encounters establish new points of reference, and reduce inhibitions, while not reducing all such encounters to exchange values—although this is an ever-present mono-dimensionalizing threat even when it is a necessity of survival—together constitutes the transversality of the OSF. Skateboards that are not for riding but for visual and sculptural expression are not so easily captured by a skills discourse because, after all, the manual skills required to assemble a skateboard kit are not especially advanced but, instead, de-reify subcultural commodities for the students with the lessons that they can themselves make the signs of the subculture they desire; yet, skateboards retain some elements of uncontainability when and if they are put back on the streets, but always in the shifting contexts of political representations for the public control of youth subcultures. As an abstract diagram, the skateboard is not exhausted by its riding, and it is embedded in a formal and informal assemblage of teachables like street art and self-publishing, but also sharable musical, food, and fashion choices, and all of the practices within the alt-arts universe including tattooing, piercing and other body modifications, and small-scale craft production (even broken boards are recycled as canvases for new expressions). As a transversal tool, skateboard subculture in the broadest sense in its academic context within OSF and beyond its walls provides students with much more than entrepreneurial self-management skills, but serves as a metamodel not only for a participatory critique of skateboard subculture, in other words, as acumen that is carried through a self-invented creative but institutionally structured entry point into the very subculture already inhabited in a variety of ways by OSF students and teachers. Yet as Guattari recognized, in taking into account the analyses of early education by Anne Querrien and Liane Mozère, the issue is how capitalist labour power is manufactured through compliance, acceptance, and pleasure, appropriately tooled (he did not mention entrepreneurism, but it is worthwhile underlining).[23] While Guattari was ever watchful for phallocratic and other forms of repressive sexuality, at the very least it may be said that OSF not only takes a critical position on gender politics, but is less in the business of forbidding anything, but probably just as guilty, and just as susceptible, on the question of how funding is used as a disciplinary device cultivating dependency on contingent windfalls. Finally, it is appropriate to think of a double re-entry at play: returning to school but also re-entering the subculture with new critical goals and conditions of contact. OSF doesn't flirt with a failure-based entrepreneurial wisdom, because most of the class has already known rejection and its deleterious consequences. Skateboards provide existential supports for subjectivity's enrichment and reinvention, yet must grapple with the calculated deployment of entrepreneurism that simultaneously threatens and promotes transversal relations with an outside that is paradoxically both active and passive in its influences, both welcoming and risky, and displaying an ambivalence articulated by the teachers themselves; indeed, the collective phantasies (of the anti-teacher and sometimes peer) attached to the teachers and the mystifications of the school board must be flushed out, and the mixing of teenage molecules in the many temporary reassurances of sex, drugs, and rock and roll is full of lessons whose value is accessible only for those prepared not to evade them.[24]

NOTES

1. In addition to my own experiences during 2011–2012, and my attendance at the 2015 fundraiser at the Gladstone Hotel "The Youth Are Revolting," I make extensive use of an interview conducted by Ariel Fieldin and Michael Barker with OSF teachers Craig Morrison and Lauren Hortie, "The Innovators: Interview with Craig Morrison and Lauren Hortie," *Notes from the Field* (2015). http://notesfromthefield.ca/talking-with-teachers-in-alternative-schools/oasis-skateboard-factory/. I am grateful for the invitation of Craig Morrison to participate in the communal life of the school and to lend a hand to the students and to the Community Council's activities, especially around field trip planning and graduation celebrations.
2. Hunter H. Fine, "The Skateboard Dérive: A Poststructuralist Performance of Everyday Urban Motility," *Liminalities: A Journal of Performance Studies* 9/3 (June 2013): 1–20.
3. Sherri Leafgren, *Reuben's Fall: A Rhizomatic Analysis of Disobedience in Kindergarten*, Walnut Creek, CA: Left Coast Books, 2009, pp. 180–81.
4. Konstantin Butz, *Grinding California: Culture and Corporeality in American Skate Punk*, Bielefeld: Verlag, 2012, p. 212.
5. Iain Borden, *Skateboarding, Space and the City: Architecture and the Body*, London: Bloomsbury, 2003.
6. Célestin Freinet, *La méthod naturelle 1. L'apprentissage de la langue*, Neuchatel: Delachau and Niestlé, 1968, p. 120.
7. Victor Acker, *The French Educator Célestin Freinet (1896–1966): An Inquiry into How His Ideas Shaped Education*, Lanham, MD: Lexington Books, 2007, p. 60.
8. Nicholas Beattie, *The Freinet Movements of France, Italy, and Germany 1920–2000*, New York: Edwin Mellen Press, 2002, p. 22ff.
9. Freinet, *La méthod naturelle*, p. 123.
10. Ibid., p. 309.
11. Ibid., pp. 251–53.
12. Ibid., p. 174.

13. Beattie, *Freinet Movements*, p. 140.

14. François Dosse, *Deleuze and Guattari: Intersecting Lives*, trans. D. Glassman, New York: Columbia University Press, 2011, p. 57.

15. Guattari, "La grille," *Chimères* 34 (1998): 4.

16. Through the diverse fields of anti-psychiatry, David Cooper's experiments in the ward known as Villa 21 in Shenley Hospital during the mid-1960s are representative of how the prospects of diffusing psychiatric roles come up against the entrenched authority of physicians, as well as demands by patients that those who provide care are qualified. Breaking what Franco Basaglia called the "circle of power" in the psychiatric institution, in which power and aggression are internalized by doctors, passed along to nurses, and then turned against patients, requires recognition of how the cycle reproduces itself and how it may be broken through a common struggle in which there is solidarity between the "healthy and the sick." Basalgia's development of a staff and patient's daily assembly at the psychiatric hospital at Gorizia reduced formal distinctions by giving patients a voice, with a rotating chair selected from elected patients, and collectivized responsibility for finding solutions to a number of issues in the institution that were no longer perceived as individual. Marked by spontaneity and disorganization, the assembly helped to realize Basagalia's negation of the institution as an overturning that called it into question and forced it into crisis. The central strand that crosses anti-psychiatry, Freinet pedagogy as well as institutional pedagogy and analysis such as it was practised at La Borde, is the displacement of the authority of the doctor and teacher (see Basaglia, *Psychiatry Inside Out: Selected Writings of Franco Basaglia*, trans. N. Scheper-Hughes and Anne M. Lovel, New York: Columbia University Press, 1987).

17. Jean-Claude Polack, "Analysis, between Psycho and Schizo," in *The Guattari Effect*, eds. E. Alliez and A. Goffey, London: Continuum, 2011, p. 60.

18. Unless otherwise indicated, quotes from Hortie and Morrison are from the Ariel Fielding and Michael Barker interview, no page numbers.

19. Susan Krashinsky, "A Different Kind of School Board," *The Globe and Mail* (December 7, 2013): M4.

20. Guattari wrote of the non-effects of male idols outside of the sphere of mystification: "This is especially evident in phases of social regression, as for instance when fascist, dictatorial regimes or regimes of personal, presidential power give rise to imaginary phenomena of collective pseudo-phallicization that end in a ridiculous totemization by popular vote of a leader: the leader actually remains essentially without any real control over the signifying machine of the economic system, which still continues to reinforce the power and autonomy of its functioning" (Guattari, "Transverality," in *Psychoanalysis and Transversality*, trans. Rosemary Sheed, Los Angeles: Semiotext(e), 2015, p. 105).

21. Freinet, *La méthod naturelle*, p. 252.

22. Wendy Gillis and Betsy Powell, "Cabbie Charged in Skateboarder's Death," *The Toronto Star* (May 15, 2012) and Erin Anderssen, "Skateboarders Becoming a Force to Reckon with on Streets," *The Globe and Mail* (May 16, 2012).

23. Félix Guattari, *Lignes de fuite: Pour une autre monde possible*, La Tour d'Aigues: Editions de l'Aube, 2011, pp. 68–69.

24. I am grateful for the invitation of Hélene Frichot to the Deleuze Camp 2015 Daughters of Chaos on the island of Utö in the Stockholm archipelago where I taught a course on How to Build an Institution and presented a section of an earlier version of this chapter. The graduate students who were attending the camp lectures and credit class in transversal writing not only accepted my challenge to assemble a skateboard kit in a very compressed time frame and without really knowing one another, but also to reflect upon the exercise as an organizational event in private conversations and public demonstrations, not to mention carefully articulated remonstrations. It seems that for architecture students the task was too simple, yet they struggled to grasp that their resistance to it was a key aspect of the exercise. One innovative solution offered by the students was to "fold" their design into the layers of the board so it remained buried until such a time that it was scraped enough or broken. This re-embedded resistance longitudinally and exposed the role broken boards play in the decorative recycling economy of Oasis.

Chapter 2

Informatic Striation in Indigenous Canada and Australia

There is a dimension of Guattari's conceptual arsenal that is especially promising in diagnosing the technomaterial and cultural conditions of information society. This constitutes an investigation of a phenomenon I call, after Guattari, *informatic striation*: a concept that identifies a complex communication between two kinds of spaces: smooth and striated within the networking of society.[1] Generally, informatic means that administrative codings are deployed in order to translate smooth cultural practices considered ambiguously heterogeneous or nonformal into a formally organized, manageable collection of distinct, yet homogeneously coded data; the striation of smoothness by informatic means also effects a new smoothing operation in the ease with which files and data sets are compared, contrasted, and combined in novel ways. Striation has the aim of identifying and (in)dividuating otherwise-unidentifiable persons; yet the combination of databases containing such information, by means of abstract operations and creative extrapolations from existing attributes, forges new classifications and identities that do not readily map back onto persons.

My hypothesis is that there are elements of smoothness in First Nations, Inuit, and Australian Aboriginal cultures that are an affront to state bureaucrats and lawmakers. Although this hypothesis remains problematic in many of its details, it is less an attempt to name an originary element than an effort to find a starting point that can adequately explain the conditions to which vast administrative sweeps and social sortings have been historically applied. Striation captures through the imposition of criterial discernment derived from a shared grid; however, a striated space may be smoothed over or dissolved by the discontinuation of a certain coding operation or by the reintroduction of smooth elements resisting containment or evading certain subordinations. I am introducing into the discussion of the smooth-striated relation an informatic model of social sorting as it pertains to indigenous experience, using comparative material from Canada and Australia.

The context for this approach was set in motion by Paul Patton's book *Deleuze and the Political*. Patton understands the war machine—the creative assemblage that brings about metamorphoses in the face of state forces to which it is exterior and resistant to the latter's apparatuses of capture and colonization by means of sedentarity—as a propagator of smoothings of all sorts.[2] Patton's insight is that it is possible to make smoothing useful in terms of understanding the dynamic and transformative work of Australian Aboriginal peoples in resisting and transforming the sovereign, colonizing settler state by means of jurisprudence. The emergence in both Australia and Canada of native title to land and resources otherwise previously transformed by law into the property of white settlers or "Crown land" shows great potential and "expresses a novel kind of right which opens up a smooth space in between indigenous and colonial law."[3] What is accomplished by Aboriginal law in this smoothing is a deterritorialization of the judicial means of colonial capture; likewise, the latter comes to recognize another body of law, having a degree of uncertainty about whether Australia was settled or conquered, Patton concludes, and this troubles the Crown's sovereignty. At the basis of this smoothing is an assertion by native peoples of customary tribal practices hitherto not and/or insufficiently acknowledged by so-called settlers: contrary to the discriminatory doctrine of *terra nullius*, the land was not empty (uninhabited, lawless) when Australia was captured by the Crown; it was not a vast lack, and it was not striated with reference to an abstract, fixed grid of quantitative assessment (time zones, state boundaries, geometries of location, and all non-local parameters, including ownership of land).

Concepts like smoothing and deterritorialization are useful in describing how tourism and cultural appropriations of difference work: traditional practices such as ceremonial dances may be deterritorialized from their living matrices of meaning and authority and recoded or resignified as a touristic spectacle in a marketplace of entertainments from which one may choose on any given vacation. In this context smoothing accomplishes the production of equivalence—culture is no more than a commodity and has no other existence outside the market. Smoothing here is a process of naturalization of cultural difference as commodity.[4] However, what is at stake here is that deterritorialization has transformative effects both positive and negative: touristic simulacra of traditional practices have the power to offer a glimpse into an otherwise-occluded world of non-market symbolic relations that may be personally transformative, and even contribute to the survival and intergenerational dissemination of some practices among indigenous persons themselves.

DISC NUMBERS

The history of disc numbers and their replacement by other systems, in addition to the perspective on contemporary redeployments of older, out-of-official-use systems in contemporary Inuit popular culture, centred on Iqaluit,[5] involves passages between, mixtures of, fixing and unfixing smooth and striated informatic sortings. This study mixes historical and contemporary examples, with the latter focusing on resignification of old and out-of-date informatic striations.

It is interesting to note that until 1967 all Inuit (formerly Eskimos) in the Yukon and Northwest Territories were identified by numbers:

> . . . imprinted on tags worn around the neck. Not surprisingly the Eskimos objected to the system and, in preparation for its abandonment, during the four years from 1967 to 1971 the Eskimos selected their own surnames which are now used in lieu of numbers. Neither the old disc-number files nor the new registry of names contain data other than that normally recorded at birth.[6]

What is remarkable about this passage is that the few, rather vague, details provide for a dramatic tension between rejection and remedy, from the alleged perspective of the Inuit themselves: they rejected the disc numbering system (and the "dog tag" technology) and then selected a new system that permitted the choice of surnames. The sense of empowerment is undeniable, if illusory, and is at least as strong as the government's desire to exonerate its past practices.

The issue of rejection or even of the replacement of one striating governmental practice for another does not reach far enough into the reappearance and myriad reuses of disc numbers and the discs themselves, although it has been flagged by some of those directly involved in its justification. For instance, a long-time Arctic researcher, John MacDonald, director of the Igloolik Research Centre, has maintained that "a more practical employment of disc numbers recently came to my attention. There's a man in Igloolik . . . who always uses his E-number on combination locks and even on his banking access card because . . . it's the only number he'll remember all his life."[7] The question here concerns not only the long-lasting effects of striations but whether everyday redeployments of them after the life of the disc number programme are in fact (re)smoothings and, if so, do these have a softly subversive (without ever believing they "suffice to save us," as Deleuze and Guattari remind their readers)[8] rather than an adaptive dimension?

The context of the transformation of striated to smooth capital is central to the analysis of Deleuze and Guattari and is, as they put it, the "essential thing."[9] The resignification of striations like the disc numbers in a post-classical smoothed space of integration and control, a smooth capitalist space, seems on the one hand a moot point considering the inevitability of the conclusion: reuses of disc numbers after the fact of the programme merely participate in the new networked relations whose transversal flows are smooth, with provisos—that remote and sparsely populated regions still have less dense information networks, that telephone companies still own the lines used by Internet service providers, and so on. Yet the interesting question concerns the "necessity and uncertainty"[10] of such passages. The refloating of disc numbers in such a semi-smooth, semi-striated space (depending on one's level of analysis) of computer-assisted mediation suggests that no amount of bureaucratic striation could contain the smooth elements of Inuit culture that survive and which, in fact, counter-conquer the renaming regime of old by reinvention or (re)smoothing.

Deleuze and Guattari's formulations of smooth igloos and nomads and Eskimo ice space in *A Thousand Plateaus*, drawn from cultural anthropologist Edmund Carpenter, remain a matter of some import and contention.[11] It would seem here that what is at issue is less a space than a set of cultural practices in relation to striations and smoothings sponsored by federal and territorial governments (and crossing into personal security and systems security in commercial transactions) in dynamic centrifugal movement from centre to periphery, finally sufficiently smoothed to translate and engage the flows of the information economy (circulation in remote and anonymous systems of verification), and partially refloated in creative productions (conversely, under which conditions they are not refloatable). "Eskimo space" is introduced in the aesthetic model rather than in the maritime model by Deleuze and Guattari, yet it is a vast frozen ice sea at issue, and the melting of the polar cap is a perilous striating of non-visual haptic vision by exposing natural orienting markers (it is the opposite of what Deleuze and Guattari state, as the smooth disappears in catastrophic warming).[12] They do not mention Inuit inukshuks as examples of cultural markers that pertain to vision at a distance.

The debts of Deleuze and Guattari to Carpenter, while not counting among their explicitly named models, are sufficient to ask after, among the many anthropological source materials in *A Thousand Plateaus*, since they help give definition to nomad thought. Unlike Christopher L. Miller who reads the anthropological source materials of nomad thought as "foreign to nomadology itself,"[13] while skipping over the material borrowed from Carpenter, the idea of "Eskimo space" is recast, not to criticize either Carpenter's enthusiasms for so-called Eskimo Realities (his praise of "great" documentary filmmaker Robert Flaherty, director of *Nanook of the North* [1922], rekindles a kind of prototypical act of cinematic primitivism—noble, happy subjects in an ethnographically thin drama set in the cinematographic present) or his omissions (e.g., disc numbers, despite an acute sensitivity to the inauthenticity of governmental policies and the effects of the welfare state). Indeed, Carpenter's role as founding editor of what would become Canadian media guru Marshall McLuhan's famous journal of the 1950s *Explorations*, the final instalment of the original series which featured a special issue "Eskimo" by Carpenter and Flaherty and painter Frederick Varley in 1959, makes clear that the decisive influence of McLuhan on Carpenter's vision of Eskimo society as implosive, anindividual, auditory-tactile, haptic-close, non-optical, non-linear, non-nominal—in short, smooth. Deleuze and Guattari's heavily ellipsized quotation[14] from Carpenter runs together paragraphs from pages 20 and 25 on orientation and igloos creating an "intricated aggregate" in words perhaps adequate to Carpenter's descriptions of Eskimo language as consisting of independent "tight conglomerates, like twisted knots." There is a tension between the knots of weaving and the entanglements of felt; would a *felt* language be anti-imperial?[15] These examples of poetic anthropology settle within the same model: that there is something smooth about Inuit life that keeps issuing challenges to the self-appointed bestowers of names and number crunchers in state bureaucracies and elsewhere (churches, mining companies, etc.). Felt (smooth) and weaving (striated) belong to the technological model, which is indexed on fabric rather than language. Language does not figure in Deleuze and Guattari's models.

One of the oddities of Inuit art in Canada is that art historians and curators are perhaps most familiar with disc numbers since they work with them every day. Most museum and gallery collections hold sculptures and prints "signed" with disc numbers, often but not always in lieu of names. The compilation of a given Inuit artist's biography is a complex affair involving up to six different names: commonly known name, its various spellings, a surname (if one of the above is not such), nickname, baptismal name, and disc number.[16] Names, then, multiply and bureaucrats lose their bearings. Drift was arrested by the "decisive striation" of the disc number, but not even it could hold the incipient smoothness that would escape from it. So the bureaucrats asked again: how do we contain Inuit names in the little spaces on our forms and documents? By 1970 a new plan of attack called Project Surname was launched. This was a sponsored (Northwest Territories Commissioner) census-like, self-identification project in which Inuit could "choose" surnames, even though they had not used them before; they could also have first names as long as these "could be written in Roman Script or English letters,"[17] like the "southern readers" for schoolchildren introduced into the government schools for Inuit in the 1950s.[18] First and last names are ordered in the standard last-name-first-first-name-last routine and semiologically subjected by imperial language, linking the requirement of the form-fillable response to another national project, the issuing of Social Insurance Numbers (SIN) to all citizens, including Inuit, who were not yet included when the programme was introduced in 1964, but who would be issued the springboard for dataveillance that is the Canadian Social Insurance Number.

The issue of contemporary "Eskimo space" poses a problem of how to study its informatic striation and (re)smoothing and, despite severe criticisms, remains relevant. For example, in many far northern communities such as the aforementioned Igloolik, at one time houses had no street numbers as most do today: "One occupies without counting," to refocus an example from the musical model of Deleuze and Guattari.[19] This is quite common in small communities in rural and remote Canada (i.e., in unorganized municipalities). What happens when populations diversify and grow and new services appear such as taxi cabs and other delivery vehicles? Then, "one counts in order to occupy," if you will, so that deliveries can be made. Which numbering system is used? In some instances, it isn't a system at all but a matter of personal choice. Some houses in Igloolik bear the disc numbers of their inhabitants.[20] This is a good example of melding smooth and striated, of an impure intermixture, a Brownian street address. The challenge here is to grasp the tone of the example. In which register is it to be understood: parody of street numbers? Probably. I will return to this because understanding the tone is key to what resignification communicates. In the meantime, it is worth noting that Google didn't send its cartographers to Iqaluit until 2013. Street view in winter is a kind of holey mesh between smooth and striated spaces.

ADMINISTRATIVE CONVENIENCE AS ENDOCOLONIALIST VIOLENCE

The imposition of disc numbers, sometimes referred to misleadingly and unintentionally ironically as E-numbers (just why will be easy to appreciate shortly), dates from the 1940s. The first date of note is 1941, which was a census year in Canada. National census taking occurred during this period every ten years. One of the typical methodological challenges facing census statisticians was the under-enumeration of First Nations peoples, as well as inaccuracies in the collection of personal information about them that skewed the official data (the category "Indian" was created in 1851 in Canada but in subsequent decades the explicit policy goal became the assimilation into the general population of any person who could still be defined this way). Mid-way between census years, then, government bureaucrats in the Departments of Indian Affairs and Natural Resources began to initiate changes that would address a variety of issues around identification and enumeration of First Nations. The need for this had been developing throughout the 1930s through parallel and complementary identificatory acts of "cultural inscription"[21] aimed at Inuit that ranged from standardization of spelling of names adapted with difficulty for English pronunciation (above and beyond a missionary naming regime inscribed in baptismal certificates that reproduced redundancy in the proliferating Johns and Marys and Pauls and Davids), fingerprinting, imposition of surnames, discussions of the appropriate model for the disc numbers systems (i.e., military dog tags bearing individual and unit numbers), and a range of related issues driven forward by the collection of reliable vital statistics as well as policing issues in what was then known as the Northwest Territories (i.e., it was the responsibility of the Royal Canadian Mounted Police to update the lists, therein making their presence felt in outlying communities, and making it possible for them to identify individuals; especially, in some instances, in order to place them under arrest).[22] In a sense striation is precisely the practice of identifying individuals for the dual purposes of enabling and constraining them: for, on the one hand, delivering welfare cheques to them and, on the other hand, arresting them.

This general situation was exacerbated in the case of Inuit because of cultural naming practices in which many persons might very well have the same name, of a great hunter, for instance; all of those bearing the name would be connected with the ancestor and embody the soul of their namesake, a condition for his or her resting in peace, even though not everyone bearing the name would have the same intimacy with the deceased.[23] The fact that Inuit names were genderless and without surnames, and that many different persons had the same name, even Christian names, not to mention that there could be a different spelling and pronunciation of the same name in every colonial institution present in the north, defined a local smoothness based on intensities of spiritual affiliations that aggravated the search for viable models of striation. Even animals could temporarily hold a name until a new human birth occurred.

Personal names are my concern, but it is easy to appreciate the politics of naming as it relates to toponymy by considering that the place known since 1987 as Iqaluit, an Inuktitut word meaning the "place of fish [arctic char]," had been known since the late sixteenth century as Frobisher Bay, after its so-called discoverer Martin Frobisher. The Department of Natural Resources has authority over the geographical names of Canada system of authorization and assigns its own imprimatur—Unique Identifier codes—to official names. Dating from the late nineteenth century, the Canadian "Names Board" is a state apparatus of capture, a machinic enslavement to official geography and cartography, and it consolidates endocolonial assertion of sovereignty over the territory it appropriates in its names (containing the name "Iqaluit" in brackets on older maps below Frobisher Bay), but also entails a social subjection of Inuit to an "exterior object,"[24] that is, entering processes of statistical subjectivation. Indeed, the process of endocolonization, which turns processes of colonialist domination inward on targeted groups of a given state's population within its national boundaries, makes a subject (loyal, beholden, captured) who is a part of an inverted colonial machine (hence we can speak of national-imperial subjectivation). Resistance to the imposition of external over indigenous names has gained immense ground since the 1980s. A strong example of southern academic and Inuit collaboration towards regaining place names is found in the work of geographer Ludger Müller-Wille on Nunavik.[25] The rich gazetter of place names that he produced in collaboration with Inuit elders reveals the uniqueness and subtlety of naming within oral tradition. Müller-Wille's project not only countered the erasure of cultural tradition carried out by machinic enslavement with the reinstatement of such names, whose specificity right down to the shore, dune, point, and line was remarkable, but also provided energy for renewing bonds with the land.

Machinic enslavement has been, however, advancing and mutating with computerization in the society of surveillance; this generalized, networked enslavement[26] accelerated in the years of the Second World War before passing into the postmodern forms of control with their distinct textures of modulation and flexibility. The "list-form" catches up Inuit peoples in Canada through the disc numbers scheme, but this is not unique for First Nations in Canada have been since the mid-nineteenth century subjected to regimes of registration for the purposes of the construction of "Status" as Indians in the Indian Register, maintained by DIAND, and subject to shifts in policy (dominated at one time by the principle of assimilation, then amended by expanding entitlement through the reintroduction of hitherto excluded categories of persons determined through political positions taken on lines of descent) and thus in legislation defining conditions of inclusion or exclusion (known during the assimilationist period as "enfranchisement," doublespeak for disenfranchisement from status or forced integration into white mainstream culture) for the sake of registration. The Indian Register and the Band Lists comprising it intersects with another register—Reserve Land entitlements administered through Location Tickets (until 1951) and thereafter Certificates of Occupation. These dense striations of identity and location are linked to exterior objects, as they are in the case of the Inuit, because "Status" confers rights to federally administered benefit programmes (specific tax exemptions, etc.). The Certificates of Indian Status or "Status Cards" are no-tech paper identity cards produced by the Bands themselves and include a registration number with vital statistics (date of birth, height, weight, eye colour, sex, band name, and number) and a photograph.[27] "Status" is the product of a history of superfine bureaucratic striations of the welfare state in concert with crude endocolonialist racism still active today in the constructions of health knowledge about First Nations peoples (e.g., the diabetes "epidemic").[28]

The politics of the erasure of personal names and their renumbering for official purposes has been described as an exercise in "administrative convenience."[29] It produced individually identifiable bodies ("tagged") through a process of animalization, the wearable fibre disks for hanging around the neck or attached to the wrist; this "taxonomic" strategy was done in the interest of "good administration," thereby "transform[ing] Inuit society into a more manageable entity."[30] The discs themselves were rich in semiotic overcoding. Small, circular, and fibrous, they bore the stamp of the Crown on the centre of one side around which the words "Eskimo Identification Canada" turned (an icon of semiotic enslavement). All lettering was in English (national or official languages are one of the examples Guattari used to illustrate the semiological economies of power that set the parameters of competence and set the means for comportment and communication)[31] and syllabics were disregarded. The reverse side held a sequence of letters and numbers. The discs were not a unanimous choice of interested state representatives, but they won out over identity cards. The initial programme of disc design and distribution of discs in the early 1940s used individual identification numbers on each disc of up to four digits. In addition to semiological subjection through the symbol of state authority, official language, and numerical code, there is a social subjection initiated through taxonomic capture and classification. Importantly, this social subjection merely meant that "classification preceded experimentation."[32] The subjection to an exterior object was renewed, this time during 1944–1945 with the introduction of the Family Allowance Program, then a universal system of monthly payments to families with children under the age of sixteen years. This was the occasion for the revision of the disc number protocol to include geographic/spatial identifiers prior to the personal identifiers: twelve districts and two regions segmented the Arctic—initially nine in the East and three in the West; they grew to fourteen in the 1950s.[33] These identification districts were represented in the form of E or W–dash–1–12 before personal identifiers indicating place of birth ("E" is neither electronic nor Eskimo). The aforementioned Frobisher Bay was E7. Geographic striation into registration districts created manipulable categories (abstract placeholders) open to experimental combinatorics that accelerated during the 1950s (actual population relocations to bleak locations being the most severe). These were subjections to disciplinary calculations of federal welfare expenditures—rising—in relation to alleged sites of employment opportunities—falling—conceived with complex references to Cold War technological development (and earlier, such as the landing strip at Frobisher Bay built in 1941 as a stopover point for US military flights to Europe); and specifically, Distant Early Warning Systems installations in Canada's Arctic, opportunities for resource extraction and geological surveys, livestock raising schemes (a steady stream of sheep and pigs went north in the 1950s, but livestock farming simply didn't work in the Arctic), art commodification programmes, sovereignty jitters in Canada's north, and estimations of fluctuating game reserves, to name only a few.[34] The salient point is that the technical machines of the state shift enslavement to subjection.[35] Inuit were subjected to the technical machines of capitalist expansion in the north, with humanist apologies provided by the State's welfare policies and "well-intentioned" experiments (during the 1920s "confusion" reigned about who was responsible for the Inuit;[36] it was in 1939 that the federal government assumed "responsibility" for Inuit, a Supreme Court decision that did not go down well, and in the 1951 and 1970 Indian Acts, Inuit were excluded).[37] Even today, the pollution from the Second World War and Cold War militarization is bringing federal government remediation money and short-term employment to the Arctic. It is not unusual to peer into the waters around Iqaluit and see a submerged parking lot of military vehicles.

The militarization of the Arctic in the 1940s and 1950s by the US Air Force and RCAF was the most important factor in the introduction of a historic striation, the temporary wage economy. Deleuze and Guattari explicitly link work to military organization, both through the appropriation of the war machine and the "nullification of smooth space"[38] but also the state organization of armies and the production of surpluses in the form of stockpiles—weapons industries. In the case of the Inuit the link is incomplete. On top of traditional range patterns of Inuit groups (not strictly nomadic but structured by base camps and trap lines and shifting hunting groups), the clusterings produced by the locations of missions and trade posts, free or forced adjustments to trapline patterns and locations, not to mention the centralizing influences of earlier whaling stations, the military installations created significant contractions that were at odds with existing policies of population dispersal advocated by the Hudson's Bay Company at least from the 1920s to the 1950s before forced relocation became a government policy where state welfare could be thus administered (further, the residential school system was created in 1840 as a disciplinary technology for the state and church's Christian civilizing mission that in 1886 became legally compulsory for parents to send their children, fearing fines and imprisonment). Pressures from federal welfare programmes such as the Old Age Pension Act (1927) were not felt in the Arctic until decades later due to uneven distributions of funds. The overwhelming evidence is of a policy cluster against the settlement of Inuit, despite the pressures for "in-gathering" that had been building for decades. Paternal visions of "native life," supported by epidemiological worries about Inuit health amid the squalor around the bases, as well as the spectre of post-construction unemployment in settlements around military and other installations, RCMP concerns about social instabilities, continued to "discourage aggregations," despite the effects of the wage economy at such places as Frobisher Bay, Cambridge Bay, and elsewhere and, by the 1960s, the centralizations of populations produced by government welfare, loans, housing (the DEW Line brought subsidized housing with it, even if the housing consisted of styrofoam igloos, that is, simulated igloos),[39] health programmes and resource extraction of the so-called Diefenbaker vision (Canadian prime minister from 1957 to 1963).[40] Aggregation was necessary for population surveillance and efficient programme delivery and administration. Aggregation, one might say, is space-time striation, on its way to generalized machinic enslavement whose perfection and "absolute speed," in turn, is to be reconstituted as smooth capitalist space.

DE- AND RE-CODED FLOWS

All apparatuses of capture release "decoded flows." Such flows are overflows or escape-flows appearing beside and beyond the codes that give rise to them.[41] But the flows do not simply escape for they are knotted together (conjoined, recoded, netted, determinate), and then in turn escape once more out of the holes in the nets. The distinction between the conjoining of topical becomings and an abstract, generalized conjunction—the general axiomatic of decoded flows that is capitalism—is decisive for a new threshold is thus reached.[42]

This process is evident in the case of disc numbers: the subordination of Inuit cultural naming practices to administrative overcodings—capturing them by making naming functional, that is, regularizing naming, for bureaucratic sorts—in the form of the disc numbering and related systems that synthesize identity in new and bizarre connections (i.e., personal numbers with their geographic striations are connected with estimates of shrinking caribou populations and thus groups were forcibly relocated from one place to another regardless of other considerations, including long-term survival). Resignification slips through the nets of overcoding.

Resignifications of disc numbers arise because the codes that created them can no longer contain them. The overcodings that gave rise to disc numbers were displaced by a new overcoding called Project Surname, and this was a scattering force because no collection for disposal of discs was undertaken; anyway, a molar injustice of the disc system was that the number remained in the memories of each and circulated with them, finding new referential materials with which to freely attach. Some call the power of resignification cultural reappropriation.[43] The issue is that decoding is already in resignification linked to new recodings. The pertinent examples are all from the 1990s and after. The correlative decodings that undoubtedly arose prior to this time are less vivid than those that are available for scrutiny today, largely because these are tied to material recodings that circulate widely. The question of the rarity of such recodings cannot be definitively solved. They are limited in their effects, in the same sense that smoothings do not in themselves suffice to liberate and, with respect to Patton's interpretation, necessitate going before the court with the confidence of having made something actionable but with few means to determine the outcome.

An example is in order. In 1991 a promotional activity was staged in Iqaluit as a fundraising event for the Elders' Society that featured the issuing of mock discs—Q-numbers and registration certificates—aimed at Qallunaat (white people) and signed by Abe Okpik, the Inuk originally hired to undertake Project Surname.[44] The parodic tone of these mock discs constitutes smoothings that communicate new values of cultural becoming. Hence, decoding attaches to mimetic recoding in parodic mode that issues from the Inuit-initiated Quallunaat Registry. This Registry, unlike the DIAND-controlled and -maintained Indian Registry, does not transform the identity of the white celebrities (actors, politicians, artists, journalists, and hockey players) who participated in it, except in as much as it occurs in a different space, that of becoming—temporary, semiotically disruptive, less an exact value that commands the tools of the informatics revolution in a countervailing fashion than a refloating of hand-inscribed artefacts embedded in a site-dependent locale where the stakes have been reconstituted and redirected.

Decoded flows are rather quickly attached to recodings. The touristic artefact is a good example. The Q-certificate is politically pointed, quite unlike most tourist art; it sends a message about the ridiculousness of disc numbers to visitors who may otherwise not know the history. Some recodings succumb more readily to imposed forms and thus to a limiting practicality than others. There are music industry product recodings. In 1999 and 2002, two songs of note appeared on compact discs: Susan Aglukark's "E186" and Lucie Idlout's "E5–770, My Mother's Name." Both CDs graphically reproduce original discs and run strings of E-numbers as borders or frames around the artwork and lyric sheets. Both Aglukark and Idlout have family roots in Nunavut and are well known, but neither lives there today, pursuing careers elsewhere. Both singers make disc numbers the subject of songs and deliver criticisms of E-numbers as theft. However, the fury with which Idlout delivers her message of animalization ("cattled E") in a clanking machinic redundancy of the government "farming" of "name numbers"—the same background recitation of strings of E-numbers is used by Aglukark—is dismissed in some quarters as "youthful radicalism" since she was not old enough to have received a disc number, unlike Aglukark, for example.[45]

In music, storytelling, cultural geography reporting, the sculptural arts, and documentary filmmaking, the reclaiming of disc numbers is under way. Surely, this was an effect of the optimism and pride in the success of the land claims process that led to the creation of the territory of Nunavut in 1999. The most significant shift is that disc numbers have become integrated into the subject matters of various works. In addition to song titles and film titles, sculptures bearing the disc numbers of their sculptors, but not as signatures, have been noted in popular publications.[46] These artistic recodings only tell part of the story, even if they are far from the overcodings that separated "right" from "wrong" names and used numbers in lieu of names. This phenomenon and its alleged corrections in Project Surname have also become a subject of interest for the Nunavut Law Review Commission's attempt to correct the corrections of Project Surname in Project Correction: not only misspellings but also missed registrations that snarl due bureaucratic processes (i.e., ineligibility for old age pension benefits due to lingering uses of disc numbers on birth certificates as a result of being overlooked during Project Surname), incorrect birthdates, and mismatches between pieces of ID.[47] Compared with a use of substitute names in legal discourse in, for example, the famous adoption case "Deborah E4–789,"[48] the work of the current law commission is confronting head-on the obstacles of the intensive violence of the past. Re-smoothings have the salutary effect of exposing lingering effects of striations across generational divides.

The problem is the emission of smoothings from striations. That is the release of decoded flows beside and beyond the imprisoning striations and overcodings of informatic impositions, and the recoding of these. The decoded flows are not free in the sense that when Inuit regain cultural naming practices and in the process resignify disc numbers, new attachments to cultural products and informations systems are made and hence new subjugations arise (i.e., to commodity forms, to music product formats, etc.). Yet there is an indeterminacy to the flight of decodings. When an Inuk uses a disc number on a snowmobile bib, as an e-mail address, as a PIN number at a cash machine, as a house number, as part of the subject of a work of art, in short, when such a number is deployed in any instance requiring a personal identifier (but not exclusively since a personal identifier, which is partially striating, is not necessary in many potential reuses of disc numbers such as in the purchase of lottery tickets), there is a positive and enabling engagement existing between flight and (re)capture. This is precisely how surveillance resembles stratification: both are ambivalently enabling and restrictive, beneficial and unfortunate, as Deleuze and Guattari state.[49] When informatic striations are embedded in the memories of individuals and intersect with cultural naming practices, disc numbers are externalized and find new attachments. If Inuit names are points of transition that carry some values (inspiration, fear) while erasing other specificities (holding in abeyance the recipient's gender specificity until puberty while carrying that of the previous owner), and disc numbers, despite their "functional" and unfortunate histories, are regained in the field of this cultural practice, they, too, communicate and constellate and connect, often with the values of irony and parody, enabling the transit of individuals into informatic matrices.

After all, as Guattari reminds us, transits-transformations between striated ontological functions—for instance, in passing from Territories to Universes, the subject in the world, existentially incarnated and grasped, takes flight into incorporeal universes of one's own self-definition—constitute smoothing operations par excellence and possess the power to effect "ontological conversions." The initial hypothesis was of a smoothness that was then striated by disc numbers and further re-smoothed with qualifications. The punchline, as one Inuk put it in terms of a redundancy full of irony, is this: "I am seeking the right government agency to apply to renew my disk!" exclaimed Jaipiti Nungak, E9–1956.[50] So often laughter accompanies the contemporary mentions of disc numbers—the humour having a local inflection such as the person who was an "E1"—"only 1"—or had an "E6" but attended school in a differently numbered region and was out of sorts from the shuffling. Although many of the discs themselves have been lost over time to all but memory, today surviving discs are reappearing as personal accessories, affixed to hats and coats as pendants, and worn as a kind of jewellery with pride.

In a time of cultural renewal and innovation, resignification of disc numbers is itself a cultural smoothing marking transits, real changes of direction, intensities of tradition and its multiple interruptions, into the new social flows of Integrated World Capitalism. As these transits proliferate, smoothness homogenetically emerges. The question is no longer or so much that of intergenerational resurrection through names, but a general, largely passive process in which the striations of discontinued disc numbers find new manifestations through resignifying attachments as linear strings of identifying letters and numbers, that is, as individual or personal identifiers for the purpose of engaging pervasive machinic networks of computer-mediated communication, which are retained and reproduced and compared in ways not so far removed from their original usage. This is largely passive because it is not a question of development or intensification in the fields of possibility as the pure potential of decoded flows passes into actual recodings but, rather, it is more a matter of their reinsertion for pragmatic purposes in everyday transactions and activities, a point underlined by Inuit today. Still, even here there are subtle explorations of fields of possibility in parody and humour, and in the laughter they can still elicit interpersonal communication among Inuit (it is, after all, still quite laughter-provoking to refer to someone by his or her disc number), indeed, in the injustices they revisit in protest, even in the small acts of experimenting with disc and number in different contexts. The resignification of disc numbers in contemporary Inuit popular culture effects displacements, not a global overcoming, of semiotic subjections and machinic enslavements, and is not a coherent subcultural, oppositional practice. Rather, today, disc numbers are viable and concrete subject matters for creative adventures of cultural self-reference. Naming is not merely a subset of informatic striation, but it is a metamodel that flows through resignifying practices and deciphers models by sharing affects hitherto not associated with the discs.

DISORGANIZED INFORMATIC SUBJUGATIONS OF AUSTRALIAN ABORIGINES

Social control of Aboriginal populations by means of narcotic dependency, especially alcohol, is perhaps as old as the Australian nation. Historical research in Queensland, for instance, reveals that during the nineteenth century alcohol was used to manage and manipulate the Aboriginal workforce (a misnomer because wages for Aboriginals remained discretionary) because it was cheap (especially when offered in lieu of wages and contracts) and could be controlled surreptitiously by a cabal of publicans, magistrates, and police at the local and state levels with interests in generating a network of dependents and informers. This was done in support of the state's policy of disconnecting federal agencies from local Aboriginal councils, thus ensuring the "almost monopoly control over all aspects of Aboriginal life" enjoyed by state departments in charge of Aboriginal affairs.[51]

Alcohol's handmaiden was bureaucratic inscription of Aboriginal identities. In eighteenth- and nineteenth-century New South Wales, the politics of inclusion and exclusion of Aboriginal communities in official statistical constructions based on data collection in the state were not easily decodable: inclusion in law did not entail counting, and exclusion resulted in the partial absence of official records. Data collection was fickle and often subject to the whims of local clerks. However, state interests were served by selective bureaucratic inscriptions since the absence of officially recorded life events helped to not only support the thesis that the Aboriginal race was disappearing but also the breaks in the official historical record made it difficult for Aboriginal activists to establish ancestry and thus to ground any sorts of claims for services and recognition based on heritage.[52]

One of many clear expressions of this official erasure at the federal level was the infamous section 127 of the Australian Constitution of 1901 (not repealed until 1967) that spelled out in no uncertain terms that "Aboriginal natives should not be counted" in the final numbers. Demographic blankness is one thing (officially addressed by statisticians only in the early 1970s), but the relatively recent intentional destruction of existing administrative files on Aboriginal families and individuals within the Department of Indigenous Affairs is another. The "collateral damage" caused by the disposal of large numbers of archival materials is easily appreciated for their usefulness in claims to Native Title since "the files that remain form the back-bone of evidential records for expert witness reports" in just such cases.[53]

This is not so much an informatic extension of *terra nullius*, but a contingent social informatics of Aboriginal subjugation, a disorganized bureaucratic inscription of identity, which gave rise, however slowly and unevenly, to pernicious metonyms attached to Aboriginal rights. These are noted by Tim Rowse, among others: alcohol and cash (welfare) became metonyms for the ambiguous citizenship offered to Aboriginals.[54] Further, "citizenship through assimilation" was a metonym for acquiring a dog license.[55]

It is worth exploring in greater depth these connections: alcohol-dog license-citizenship. Australian alcohol researcher Maggie Brady has collected first-hand accounts from Aboriginal interlocutors about when the "grog" became available, and its disastrous consequences. A commonality in the reflections of Aboriginal witnesses is the connection between citizenship rights and legal access to alcohol: "citizenship to drink"; "citizenship came in and that's the reason I had to go and drink."[56]

In her introductory overview to the works of artist Sally Morgan, whose screen print *Citizenship* (1987) visualizes the connection between citizenship for Aboriginals and the collaring and registration of dogs under legislative threat, Jill Milroy explains:

> Aboriginal peoples had to apply to become "citizens" in their own country under the Native Citizenship Rights Act (1944). Strict conditions applied requiring Aboriginal peoples to prove that they lived like "whites." They were not allowed to associate with other Aboriginal people. Citizenship papers looked similar to a passport, containing a photograph and signature. The papers had to be carried at all times and could be easily revoked. As Jack McPhee recalls: "we used to joke about the whole thing among ourselves. . . . We all called our papers a Dog License. We thought that was a better name for it than citizenship."[57]

The dog license or dog tags animalized Aboriginals in a specific way. The counter-term adopted by Aboriginals for these tags was, of course, derogatory and critical of discriminatory policies aimed against them, but also revealed the implicit assumption about how citizenship was applied to them as a form of domestication—they were made into pets of the Australian family of man. That is, those who held citizenship papers were "civilised" and "Europeanised" and thus whitened and kept on an informatic leash. In other words, they could legally access alcohol and thus their social worlds expanded to the extent that they were permitted entry (unevenly) into hotels and bars. Hence the idea of citizenship as a passport to white society and the purity rules that prevented newly minted Aboriginal citizens from "consorting" with other Aboriginals, sometimes even their own siblings and parents, under threat of revocation. Even the metonym (citizenship = alcohol) could be cancelled if an Aboriginal citizen shared alcohol with non-citizen Aboriginals. In essence, the conception of citizenship at play worked on negation: in order to become a citizen, one had to renounce Aboriginality, and hence the name "exemption certificate" that was also applied to the dog license. The exemption was one's Aboriginality; one was exempt from treatment as a non-citizen and, hence, one was supposed to enjoy the rights of white Australians (social security benefits) but only by means of renouncing one identity and assuming another even if bureaucratic recategorization could not ameliorate troubles encountered in everyday life. The effects, as noted earlier, were at best "ironic"[58] but on the plane of everyday life inflicted "a daily turn of slights and tacit exclusions."[59] The removal of the exemption certificate in the late 1950s and the invitation to apply the benefits of the post-war welfare state to all Aborigines still involved exclusion on the grounds of the lingering thought of "the other" of the domestic—nomadic and primitive Aborigines would not enjoy state benefits like pensions and maternity benefits.

The parallels with Canada in the field of informatic subjugation are striking: Australian dog licenses and Canadian Inuit dog tags; exemption is a species of "enfranchisement," a form of assimilation and loss of indigeneity by First Nations. As far as the surveillance of First Peoples in Canada and Australia is concerned (even in the case of the administration of the use of alcohol as a form of social control), the histories of the two countries dovetail even against the stark contrasts of the former's treaty-based political history of Crown-tribal nation relations and the latter's very late recognition of title and land rights. This is not the place to compile a list of the comparative colonial miseries of Aboriginal and First Nations experience in their respective countries.

GORGETS

The salient comparison between Canada and Australia is that informatic striation is historically tied to naming and stratifying gifting practices. The historical material concerns the practice of awarding decorative gorgets to Aboriginals both as rewards for services rendered to various branches of the government and as awards for special achievements and demonstration of skills, but just as often as a strategy for building alliances with reliable informants. The crescent-shaped metal plates were worn around the neck on a chain and bore inscriptions that bestowed a fictitious title on the wearer, most often "King" or "Chief," as well as a transliterated name or invented English first name linked to an anglicized place name ("King Billy"). Although clearly implicated as an informatic inscriptive practice of an expanding endocolonialist administration throughout the century, the common use of colonial icons (emu and kangaroo) on the gorgets (as well as the coronet) also made them signifiers of imperial power. The bestowal of fictitious titles has been recoded from an Aboriginal perspective not as an emblem of ridicule (mock aristocracy) and interpellation of manipulable foreign hierarchies (tools for social disorganization), but as real indicators of leadership and strength especially under the duress of invasion: "the 'fictitious' titles were incorporated by Aboriginal people into their own language and culture"[60] in positive ways because they confirmed the power of certain individuals. This was not always the case as undeserved titles left some open to ridicule. Although self-appointed Aboriginal leaders and self-nominated "kings" may have been granted some authority by white officials, this did not translate into credibility within Aboriginal communities where the sobriquet really needed a real foundation.

The ability of Aboriginal cultures to absorb and resignify informatic striations like the disc numbers and gorgets by recoding them in meaningful ways is evident in the work of contemporary self-identified Aboriginal artists like Treahna Hamm (of the Yorta Yorta clan) whose zinc breastplates (another common word for the gorgets and king plates) with sedge fringes recode significations of oppression and annihilation (gorgets were sometimes awarded to those believed the last of their kind) because they offer valuable, sometimes the only, material link to lost figures, specific places, and family members. The genealogical value of the gorgets for Aboriginal self-understanding of family, community, and place—in this case an "Aboriginal heritage site" Barmah Forest breastplate (2005)[61]—cannot be underestimated in the context of the disorganized destruction and re-presentation by the state of material evidence of Aboriginal history: evidence, that is, that would enhance the actionability of Aboriginal claims on territory and resources in the present and future tenses. Hamm's design work on the crescent plates evokes living forms but also turns around the object's function as a stratifying distinction, at one time a death watch,[62] into a vehicle of cultural presence and survival. Moreover, the aesthetic and symbolic recodings stand over and against the official collection of and display in museological contexts of genuine "heritage" items and the state's protection of them against their auction and sale on the shifting winds of the open antiques market.[63]

With the example of Australian gorgets it is once again possible,[64] as was the case with disc numbers, to appreciate the movements of striations and smoothings as indeterminate passages affecting mutations between heterogeneous and homogeneous domains of manifestation and possibility. In this chapter smoothings are positioned prior to the imposition of state striations, and some of these latter are re-smoothed through acts whereby autochthones regain and reinvent artefacts of endocolonial subjugation, new cultural possibilities, themselves constrained by the fields in which they intersect (the art market, music industry, administrative surveillance systems, legal struggles, etc.), each with their own striations and smoothnesses. The originary smoothness corresponds to nomadism (outside the state, and about which the latter is suspicious, wants to repress, but can't do without as a source of innovation) and not to romanticism or to primitivism. Deleuze scholars working on Australian themes have been careful to emphasize the mutual pressures of nomad and state, of smooth and striated, desert (nomos) and city (polis), rapidity as opposed to gravity; indeed, nomadism is not a racial category.[65] Recall Guattari's suggestion that when striations are smoothed, a passage from one ontological function to another takes place; resignification is regained by artists and activists even if this ends up among a variety of other striations and smoothings in the intersecting registers of contemporary global network society: the traffic engineer and the jaywalker, the systems security analyst and hacker. The point to hold on to is that smoothings and striations are always in process (they are like passages between active and passive states), whether the passage is apprehended in terms of synchronic and diachronic temporalities, or instantiation and abstraction, manifestation and potentialization. Canadian examples of First Nations' modifications of technologies of registration and control include beaded deerhide treaty ticket pouches (prior to the Status Card), and the decoration (mostly painting) of the recto sides of ledgers by band elders; ledgers were used by Indian agents to document the movement of people and goods in and out of reserves and were an illegally enforced control technology that First Nations actively resisted.[66] These small acts show how smooth spaces are exuded from the most striated circumstances. They are traces of invention showing mastery of materials in ongoing struggles against systems of capture and containment.

NOTES

1. Deleuze and Guattari, *A Thousand Plateaus*, p. 474ff.
2. Paul Patton, *Deleuze and the Political*, Oxford: Blackwell, 2000, p. 114.
3. Ibid., p. 129.
4. Deborah Root, *Cannibal Culture: Art, Appropriation, and the Commodification of Difference*, Boulder, CO: Westview, 1996, p. 86.
5. The bulk of the on-site research for this project in Iqaluit was undertaken by a former graduate student Adam Bryx, who received his doctorate in drama at the University of California under Bryan Reynolds.
6. Department of Communications and Department of Justice, *Privacy and Computers: A Report of a Task Force,* Ottawa: Government of Canada, 1972, p. 88.
7. Valerie Alia, *Names, Numbers, and Northern Policy: Inuit, Project Surname, and the Politics of Identity*, Halifax: Fernwood, 1994, pp. 30–31.
8. Deleuze and Guattari, *A Thousand Plateaus*, p. 500: "Never believe that a smooth space will suffice to save us."
9. Deleuze and Guattari, *A Thousand Plateaus*, p. 492.

10. Deleuze and Guattari, *A Thousand Plateaus*, p. 493.

11. Deleuze and Guattari, *A Thousand Plateaus*, p. 494. The use of this term "Eskimo" already signals acceptance of a depreciatory label used by outsiders, including anthropologists, and seems quite period-bound. The term's survival in *A Thousand Plateaus*, originally published in 1980, suggests that the authors were not aware that it went out of use in the mid-1970s and was replaced by Inuit. Edmund Carpenter, *Eskimo Realities*, New York: Holt, Rinehart and Winston, 1973, p. 192ff; cf. James Houston, *Confessions of an Igloo Dweller*, Toronto: M&S, 1995, p. 18. On the deployment of the term "ice space" see both *A Thousand Plateaus*, p. 574, n. 28 and p. 557, n. 56, and *Eskimo Realities*, p. 78.

12. Deleuze and Guattari, *A Thousand Plateaus*, p. 493.

13. Christopher L. Miller, "The Postidentitarian Predicament in the Footnotes of *A Thousand Plateaus*: Nomadology, Anthology, and Authority," in *Deleuze and Guattari: Critical Assessments*, vol. 3, ed. G. Genosko, London: Routledge, 2001, p. 1117.

14. Deleuze and Guattari, *A Thousand Plateaus*, p. 574, n. 28.

15. Carpenter, *Eskimo Realities*, p. 78; Deleuze and Guattari, *A Thousand Plateaus*, pp. 475–76.

16. Ernst Roch, ed., *Arts of the Eskimo: Prints*, Montréal: Signum Press, 1974, p. 20.

17. Department of Indian Affairs and Northern Development, *Identification and Registration of Indian and Inuit People*, Ottawa: DIAND, 1993, p. 24.

18. Richard Diubaldo, *The Government of Canada and the Inuit: 1900–1967*, Ottawa: Research Branch and Corporate Policy, Indian and Northern Affairs Canada, 1985, p. 111.

19. Deleuze and Guattari, *A Thousand Plateaus*, p. 477.

20. John MacDonald-Adam Bryx. Personal communication (July 17, 2003).

21. Alan Rudolph Marcus, *Relocating Eden: The Image and Politics of Inuit Exile in the Canadian Arctic*, Hanover and London: University Press of New England, 1995, p. 33.

22. Department of Indian Affairs and Northern Development, *Identification and Registration of Indian and Inuit People*, p. 23.

23. Alia, *Names, Numbers, and Northern Policy*, p. 14ff.

24. Deleuze and Guattari, *A Thousand Plateaus*, pp. 456–57.

25. Ludger Müller-Wille, *Gazetter of Inuit Place Names in Nunavik (Québec, Canada)*, Inukjuak, PQ: Avataq Cultural Institute, 1987; cf. Department of Natural Resources Canada, "Geographical Names of Canada." http://www.geonames.nrcan.gc.ca.

26. See James Williams, "Monitoring vs. Metaphysical Modeling: or, How to Predict the Future of the Postmodern Condition," *PLI* (October 1992): 55; and Michael Hardt, "The Global Society of Control," *Discourse* 20/3 (Fall 1998): 139–52.

27. R. A. Reiter, *The Fundamental Principles of Indian Law*, Edmonton: First Nations Resource Council, p. 14; and S. Imai, *The 1999 Annotated Indian Act and Aboriginal Constitutional Provisions*, Toronto: Carswell, p. 26.

28. See J. Poudrier, "Racial Categories and Health Risks: Epidemiological Surveillance among Canadian First Nations," in *Surveillance as Social Sorting*, ed. D. Lyon, London: Routledge, 2003, pp. 111–34.

29. Alia, *Names, Numbers, and Northern Policy*, p. 40.

30. Marcus, *Relocating Eden*, p. 32.
31. Guattari, "Semiological Subjection, Semiotic Enslavement," in *The Guattari Reader*, pp. 143–45.
32. Marcus, *Relocating Eden*, p. 33.
33. Department of Indian Affairs and Northern Development, *Identification and Registration of Indian and Inuit*, p. 23.
34. Marcus, *Relocating Eden*, p. 23.
35. Deleuze and Guattari, *A Thousand Plateaus*, p. 457.
36. R. Quinn Duffy, *The Road to Nunavut: The Progress of the Eastern Arctic Inuit since the Second World War*, Montreal-Kingston: McGill-Queen's University Press, 1988, p. 10.
37. Diubaldo, *The Government of Canada and the Inuit*, pp. 4 and 51.
38. Deleuze and Guattari, *A Thousand Plateaus*, p. 491.
39. Duffy, *The Road to Nunavut*, pp. 31–32.
40. David Damas, *Arctic Migrants/Arctic Villagers: The Transformation of Inuit Settlement in the Central Arctic*, Montreal and Kingston: McGill-Queen's University Press, 2002, p. 112.
41. Deleuze and Guattari, *A Thousand Plateaus*, p. 449.
42. Ibid., p. 453.
43. Alia, *Names, Numbers, and Northern Policy*, p. 102.
44. Ibid., pp. 102–6.
45. Jim Shirley-Adam Bryx. Personal communication (July 19, 2003).
46. Julie McCann, "Reclaiming Inuit Tags," *Canadian Geographic Magazine* (September/October 2003), p. 29.
47. Aaron Spitzer, "Getting the Names Right—Finally," *Nunatsiaq News* (October 2000). http://www.nunatsiaq.com
48. Re Tucktoo and Kitchooalik (Re: Deborah) (1972) 27 D.L.R. (3d) 225.
49. Deleuze and Guattari, *A Thousand Plateaus*, p. 40.
50. Zebedee Nungak, "E9–1956," Canadian Film Centre's Great Canadian Story Engine. http://www.storyengine.ca/serlet/ReadAStory?story=90. No date.
51. Rosalind Kidd, *The Way We Civilise*, St. Lucia, Qld: Queensland University Press, 2000, p. 309.
52. Marilyn Wood, "Nineteenth Century Bureaucratic Constructions of Indigenous Identities in New South Wales," in *Citizenship and Indigenous Australians: Changing Conceptions and Possibilities*, eds. N. Peterson and W. Sanders, Melbourne: Cambridge University Press, 1998, pp. 35–54.
53. Lauren Marsh and Steve Kinnane, "Ghost Files: The Missing Files of the Department of Indigenous Affairs Archives," *Studies in Western Australian History* 23 (2004): 125.
54. Tim Rowse, *White Flour, White Power: From Rations to Citizenship in Central Australia*, Melbourne: Cambridge University Press, 1998, p. 116; and idem, "Indigenous Citizenship and Self-Determination: The Problem of Shared Responsibilities," in *Citizenship and Indigenous Australians*, op. cit., p. 88.
55. John Murphy, *Imaging the Fifties: Private Sentiment and Political Culture in Menzies' Australia*, Sydney: University of New South Wales Press, 2000, p. 175.

56. Maggie Brady (ed.), *Giving Away the Grog*, Canberra: Commonwealth Dept. of Health and Ageing, 1995, pp. 54 and 63.

57. J. Milroy, "Introduction," *The Art of Sally Morgan*, Ringwood, Vic: Penguin, 1996, p. 28; and Sally Morgan and Jack McPhee, *Wanamurraganya: The Story of Jack McPhee*, Fremantle: Fremantle Arts Cooperative, 1989, pp. 16–17.

58. See "Dog Tags," in *Encyclopedia of Aboriginal Australia*, vol. 1, ed. David Horton, Canberra: Aboriginal Studies Press, AIATSIS, pp. 298–99. See also the statement of Ruby Langford, *Don't Take Your Love to Town*, Ringwood, Vic: Penguin, 1988, p. 48: "The Dog Licence was a product of the Aborigines' Protection Board. . . . The main function of the APB was to discriminate against Aborigines."

59. Murphy, *Imaging the Fifties*, p. 176.

60. Jakelin Troy, *King Plates: A History of Aboriginal Gorgets*, Canberra: Aboriginal Studies Press, 1993, p. 41.

61. See Judith Ryan, *Land Marks*, Melbourne: National Gallery of Victoria, 2006, p. 87.

62. Troy, *King Plates*, pp. 35–38.

63. Steve Butcher, "Firm Fined over Aboriginal Relics." www.theage.com.au/news/national/Firm-fined-over-Aboriginal-relics/2005/02/09/1107890272567.html.

64. Gorgets are not exclusively of Australian origin. They are artefacts of military governance from the eighteenth and nineteenth centuries, and both British and French colonizers of First Nations in pre-Canada used ornamental breastplates as signifiers of allegiance.

65. Stephen Muecke, "The Discourse of Nomadology: Phylums in Flux," in *Deleuze and Guattari: Critical Assessments of Leading Philosophers*, vol. 3, ed. G. Genosko, London: Routledge, 2001, pp. 1164–81. Elizabeth Grosz in *Chaos, Territory, Art: Deleuze and the Framing of the Earth,* New York: Columbia University Press, 2008, discusses two examples of western desert art at length, as cosmic and political forward-looking invocations of a future in which the earth will be returned to Aboriginal peoples; this will be accomplished by art's capacity to give autonomy to sensation as a resource for change: "The sensations unavailable now but to be unleashed in the future on a people ready to perceive and be affected by them" (p. 103).

66. See Laurie Barron, "The Indian Pass System in the Canadian West, 1882–1935," *Prairie Forum* 13/1 (1988): 25–41.

Chapter 3

Promises of the Post-Media Era

Jean-François Lyotard once reminded us that the prefix post-, for which he was well known from his path-breaking report *The Postmodern Condition*,[1] in suggesting both a "simple succession" and a "new direction," remained "perfectly modern."[2] In this light any turn to post-media must recognize that the break from the mass into a new condition carries forward a good deal of baggage: instead of surpassing the past, elements of it are repeated. The break is not really clean, and Lyotard has recourse to psychoanalysis to understand how his post- initiates an "initial forgetting" that the modern is working through.[3] We know that Guattari, who identified the model of the psychoanalytic unconscious as even more reductionistic than the figures of subjectivation generated on television, would develop schizoanalysis as a metamodel—a critique of models (norms, mediators, and patterns) and the "submission to modern systems of alienation and 'soft' exploitation."[4] He would countenance no easy recourse to orthodox versions of psychoanalysis. For Guattari, however, the shift from mass into post-media would not be sequential and definitive but coexistent, contestatory, and messy. Indeed, a hallmark of Guattari's thought is the refusal of phasal developmental schemas and an insistence on simultaneous elaboration: in short, a co-mingling polyphony without a centre. Polyphony among singularities and heterogeneity are key elements of Guattari's definition of processes of subjectivation, and the composition of the multitude and the production of the common owe a good deal to these inspirational ideas.[5] And Guattari vigorously protected his post- from association with postmodernism in order to avoid any suggestion that it might be apolitical and revolve around "the paradigm of every submission and compromise with the existing status quo."[6]

Writing in the late 1980s and early 1990s on the post-media hypothesis in a popular vein with a series of articles in *Le Monde* as well in the pages of the journal he co-founded with Deleuze, *Chimères*, Guattari speculated about entering into an era understood as post-mass in the sense that infotech interactivity would provide tools for resingularizing otherwise passive and alienated audiences.[7] Guattari's withering criticism of capitalist mass mediatic subjectivation as productive of a "somnolent" population is directed at a transformative process that turns "producer-consumer [prosumer] citizenry into serialized and desingularized, unoriginal zombies."[8]

The rise of minoritarian user groups that he witnessed on the French videotex system connected through the national telephone network, Minitel, with new modes of organization and the formation of new alliances around services inspired Guattari to tentatively theorize a proto-Internet as a site of desire driven by dissensus yet composing a collective diagram of commonalities. He was not so much concerned with the state telecommunications monopoly of France Télécom over Minitel, and the protectionism that defined this closed network. Rather, Guattari's focus was on machinic subjectivity production that would undoubtedly change with political and technological developments (selling off state assets like the telephone system and the emergence of a more open and flexible Internet), but which still gave rise to user-generated content and collective assemblages that promised a degree of self-management, even before the lifting of the typical molar blockages like the need to register and receive permission from the national telephone provider to offer a service.

Guattari sought enunciative singularity from his media, and if he could find it with a keyboard and screen, together with a few like-minded people, then this passion of a subject-group would suffice as an entry point into the post-mediatic age. He was well aware that technological evolution can both enhance and diminish processes of subjectivation. Nothing progressive is guaranteed in the assemblage of the human and technological. He often mentioned zapping—channel surfing—as an ambivalent example of a collective refrain of affluent sleep walkers, but also an instance of a more engaged audience, one with more choices (over content, programming, scheduling) to be sure.[9] Much of the material that Guattari discussed as post-media was not overtly technological and concerned how the question of subjectivation could be worked out against the tendency of capitalism to produce restricted versions of this process. In other words, Guattari sought out opportunities for "new emancipatory social practices and above all alternative assemblages of subjective production"[10] against capitalist tendencies to destroy collective values and recompose models of individualism and success. Overcoming fatalism and conservatism required the formulation and pursuit of "non-capitalist goals" that could not be hijacked by tired left-right political schisms.[11]

Reaching the post-media era is a programmatic goal of social ecology. Circa 1990, it looked like the potential media ecology would display a convergence of media—a networking, Guattari muses of computer, telematics, and television screens—with the important question being the capacity of creative users to utilize these systems in new ways due to a lowering of costs, widespread availability, and portability through miniaturization. Not at all referring to the NASDAQ, Guattari wondered: "The information and telematic revolutions are supporting new 'stock exchanges' of value and new collective debate, providing opportunities for the most individual, most singular and most dissensual enterprises."[12]

Guattari's post- marks out transitions: from consensual mass to a dissensual post-mass media. Both Guattari and Lyotard were critical of consensus as a master narrative of the project of modern emancipation, and the subsequent abandonment of universals (models, orthodoxies) and grand narratives in both of their philosophies opens the way for localized survivals of these concepts, as opposed to a complete surpassing of them. Guattari was especially sensitive to the ways in which dissensus could be simulated for short-sighted gains, yet in its most authentic forms was worth fighting for as the fundamental right to non-equivalent self-engenderings in relation to other singular alterities, whose proliferation and the manners in which they are assembled cannot be reduced to human individuals or persons, trapped in binary schisms, or devastated by the profit motive.

Guattari defined Integrated World Capitalism in terms of a description of global and post-industrial capitalism in which three evaluative terms are used: processes of machinic *production*; dominant economic-semiotic systems, considered in terms of the *market*; structures of social segmentation, considered in terms of the *state*. This mode of capitalistic valorization is described on the basis of the order of priority given to the three terms, in this case, production-market-state. The salient features are that production is more and more decentred from the factory and industrial labour and focused on signs, and subjectivity (hence, forms of immaterial labour: affective, cognitive), and that the capacity to integrate and exploit social diversity is unprecedented. Information and fluidity play key roles in this post-industrial capitalism that is marked threefold by modes of info-machinic production and a condition of permanent crisis; the market becomes transnational; and the state becomes minimal and speculative. I have argued elsewhere that Guattari anticipates by several decades the immaterial production hypothesis in posing the definition of a semiocapitalism (capital as fundamentally semiotic) in which the product is the process of subjectivation (involving affects, discourses, recombination of data) that created it.[13]

In concert with these developments, mass media encourages cynicism and the abdication of political and ethical responsibility (postmodern abandonism) and produces a subject reductionistically bound to equivalence and beholden to market fluxes. By contrast, a new participatory post-media held great potential, Guattari believed, that despite the work of the infantilizing effects of mass media that survive into the post-media era, as he experienced in the broadcasting of the first Gulf War, the mass mediatic "snare of Western subjectivity"[14] could be reappropriated and resingularized. Let's not forget that the urgency of shifting into a post-media era was underlined for Guattari during his viewing of the Gulf War on television. But it also concerned him greatly as he was worried about analphabeticization (the effects of post-literacy such as short attention spans and short-term memory and ephemerality) and the difficult to crack equivalence between media expression and the absence (masking and excluding) of singularity, a genuine incomparability so often subsumed by personalization services that accessorize preformed identities. Post-media signifies resistance to these factors and the active "aesthetic reappropriation of the production of images, and of audiovisual production"[15] and becoming heterogeneous of homogenetic subjectivations. For Guattari, resingularization was a precarious undertaking.

Given the saturation of Minitel in France, Internet use circa 1990 remained very low and was slow to develop, hypertext was brand new, and the World Wide Web would not emerge until the following year, followed by the browsers that defined the early web experience. Guattari's observations were understandably tentative because he did not live to see the promising new modalities of subjectivation in action available in the World Wide Web. He didn't really talk about the web, instead thinking in terms of planetary computerization. Still, he did mention the promises of "various 'hypertexts' " to open up new means of connectivity, but circa 1991 these were still the purview of specialist technicians and not yet available to the artists, teachers, and small subject-groups who could really utilize them. Guattari thought that hypertext might initiate a new form of writing more powerful than the Gutenberg revolution.[16]

In a post-mass media era the quality of interactions between users and creators shows potential to reinvent communication, redemocratize consumption, and enrich processes of subjectivation in the pursuit of self-reliance. The Guattarian subject is produced and punctuated by points of singularity and transformed by exploring the potential consistencies they bear in the process of inventing autonomy. Subjectivation is influenced by affects that stick to it and by refrains that count it out, both helping to build a territory in which it may existentially instantiate itself. Ecosophy contributes new incarnations inspired by artistic production. Famously, Guattari wrote that "one creates new modalities of subjectivity in the same way that an artist creates new forms from the palette."[17] When this palette is no longer paint but graphics programmes, when access to computer-aided drafting/design is widespread, and when the democratization of special effects software has occurred, Guattari hoped that a new social ecology among producers, consumers, students, and teachers would emerge. He believed that it was not new combinations along the existing axis of private-public that would bring about change, because "creation is wedged like a crowbar between public and private, neither of which assures its true freedom," rather, it would require novel configurations of production—what we see today in crowdsourcing and peer-to-peer networking.

Irreducible to a single common denominator, hence polyphonic, and indescribable in fixed genetic stages, subjectivity production is collective (and machinic) and self-posits through enunciative assemblages. Advances that provide new collaborative as opposed to proprietary platforms for assisting in the development of processes that are more complex, sustaining, and enriching would in turn help to push media evolution in a more promising direction. "We cannot expect positive repercussions from new technologies unless these technologies are adopted by way of individual and collective creative practices," Guattari maintained.[18]

Guattari's characteristically broad strokes were much in evidence when pointing a hopeful way forward. Guattari envisaged that limits on intellectual property would follow as more and more user communities got involved in infotechnology system design. Certainly, free and open-source software hackers have blazed important trails in inverting copyright with General Public Licenses.[19] In keeping with this theme, Guattari speculated about how research results should be shared, and "industrial secrets" must be limited.[20] The struggles over trademarking genetic data are a case in point. He also believed that national media ethics commissions and public re-education programmes would be founded to meet the challenges of corporate and state abuses of broadcast news media, especially in the light of the first Gulf War's circulation of a dominant mass mediatic homogenesis of subjectivation (the more one watches, the less one understands, and the more likely it is that one supports the action). These comments indicate that the transition from mass to post-media was stalling, and he called for "an entire public re-education program"[21] about how news is presented, about who owns the networks, and the ways news may be democratized. Guattari did not mention citizen journalism, nor did he experience the emergence of one of the key figures of our time, whistleblowing websites and blogs. But he did think in terms of the need for standing national public ethics commissions—not hastily assembled commissions and investigations—on media practices that had real teeth to bite into media abuses, like the tabloid scandals in the UK around so-called phone hacking that led to the Leveson Report in 2012.[22]

Guattari also sensed that media interconnectivity could have positive effects by developing new collective sensibilities. Guattari intuited that this would lead to minoritarian becomings linking local and regional upheavals to planetary problematics, suggesting the ways in which web activism would come to cross constituencies and organize on-and off-line actions. Post-media invokes a minor art precipitating non-countable, revolutionary becomings, freeing molecular components for new constellations—autonomous media like Insu'tv in Naples.

Guattari still believed in the future:

> The post-mediatic revolution to come will have to be guided to an unprecedented degree by those minority groups which are still the only ones to have realized the mortal risk for humanity of questions such as: the nuclear arms race; world famine; irreversible ecological degradation; mass-mediatic pollution of collective subjectivities.[23]

Guattari had already learned in the 1980s how the free radio movement in France made extensive use of Minitel services to constitute groups of supporters, and this cross-platform minoritarian resistance was one of his primary points of reference for post-media. This is perhaps why, as a supporter of free radios in France, he did not strongly criticize Minitel on the basis of its statist and centralized status. Indeed, he saw the potential of the user groups on Minitel as akin to the offline transdisciplinary groups he created and moved in. These minoritarian assemblages were the incubators for post-media subjectivations, as they plotted paths between the sirens of IWC and state co-optation. What really impressed him was the extent to which "the promoters of these devices [like Minitel] had not foreseen the 'indirect' uses which were to be made of them."[24]

Dents in Guattari's optimism were evident, and he wavered in his enthusiasm about post-media:

> One is forced to admit that there are very few objective indications of a shift away from oppressive mass-mediatic modernity toward some kind of more liberating post-media era in which subjective assemblages of self-reference might come into their own.[25]

Franco Berardi has helpfully suggested that the free radio experiments of the 1970s in Italy and during the 1980s in France in which both he and Guattari had been involved were "a general rehearsal"[26] for the subversive resingularizations and destructuring of mass media that the web helped to bring to fruition. As Guattari explained:

> But the point the organizers of the popular free radio stations particularly emphasize is that the totality of technical and human means available must permit the establishment of a veritable feedback system between the auditors and the broadcast team: whether through direct intervention by phone, through opening "studio doors," through interviews or programs based on listener-mades

> cassettes, etc. . . . We realize here that radio constitutes but one central element of a whole range of communication means.[27]

Guattari understood how Radio Alice kept sympathetic Bolognese informed about the riots in March 1977 by receiving reports by telephone and broadcasting them, but did not reduce this to a technical accomplishment. A free radio station is a node in a complex media ecology that is sustained by a micropolitics built upon experimentation that perfuses a social assemblage. Together Guattari and Berardi understood the power of the free radio movement as "the first experiment of deterritorialization of the telecommunications system"[28] and as a catalyst for social change beyond the technical level in critiques of restrictive legislation, intellectual property, autonomy from traditional organizations, from all levels of government, and so on. For Guattari "free radio is like a kind of match that you strike and then everything catches fire."[29]

The molecular revolution might not be televised, but it would be tweeted. Social media relayed reports on the protests in Tahrir Square in Cairo during January and February 2011 and had originally provided tools for the April 6 Movement. Wireless connectivity was attacked by the state, and the highly centralized and totalitarian Internet "kill-switch" was implemented. From a Guattarian perspective the parallels between free radio and social media are obvious at the technical level, and in both cases the violence of the state can be exercised to shut down but not silence post-mediatic tendencies towards resingularization. Two years later protests against the government continued in Egypt. The typical reading of the role of social media by the mass media today is that they continue to play roles in disseminating information about activities as they unfold. But this in itself betrays the forward-looking example of free radios. When social media are simply reinscribed as "instruments of information,"[30] they are remodelled as mass media, and the struggle for autonomy carried by multiple communications technologies, new social relations, and new sensibilities is diminished by the transmission function.

Only rarely would Guattari remark on the dangers of control, modulation, and surveillance within post-media; Big Brother was not the preordained outcome of new information technologies. He was certainly cognizant of these issues but did not fully connect them with the exploitation of user data that we see today with the corporate Internet and with threats to privacy (a notion that uncritically presupposes a preformed subject). He did not witness the Americanization of global Internet governance. He believed that singular productions of subjectivity that reappropriated media would be in some measure resistant to capitalistic exploitation, that is, not easily recuperable. His hopes for the passage into the post-media era were tentative, acknowledging risk, warning about the fallout from violent deterritorializations in the social field, and the ambivalent promises of new technologies bubbling up from the machinic phylum. Yet he mentioned that interactive, multimedia compact disks, cell phones, satellite television, television tuner cards for PCs, access to new databases—indeed, many then new "technological transformations"—could be used to enhance "personal programming."[31] But personal does not devolve into accessorization with gadgets because subjectivation is not a matter of personal choice but rather the interactions of pre-personal and collective entanglements, at different scales, and in terms of heterogeneous alterities.

In Guattari's explanation of free radio experiments, he experienced most intensely how the semiotic polyvocity of speech returned to prominence through a machinic orality entailed by the daily mental ecological need for poetry (both written and performed) that nurtures processes of subjectivation. On Radio Alice and Radio Tomate one could speak with one's mouth full; many people spoke at the same time, and this created new means of expression, and listening. This inspired Guattari to emphasize enunciative polyvocality. Free radio experimentation is indexed to the passage into the post-media era by means of heterogeneous machinic means like synthesized speech, promoting the creation of new and different enunciative assemblages, especially a focus on orality.

"The era of the digital keyboard will soon be over; it is through speech that dialogue with machines will be initiated."[32] Guattari was inspired by spoken word and sound performance, rap music, concrete poetry, and visits to the Polyphonix festivals (with friends Jean-Jacques Lebel and Sarenco). The text-heavy bulletin boards of the early web communities, as well as the low or no-graphics of teleputing like Guattari experienced, required more complex refrains built from musical aspects of speech. But neither like the pseudo-neutral voices of news readers nor the booming voices of super-ego leaders. Guattari imagined the future through the establishment of new conventions involving voice-machine enunciative assemblages, what we now call mobile communications with voice-command and recognition apps—though this is still an underdeveloped area.

But one of the most challenging dimensions of the post-media era is that critical attention will need to turn to machinic subjugation (an integrated piece "enslaved by") rather than social subjection (an exterior piece "subject to" a higher power).[33] A troubling consequence of the growing mutual imbrication of machines and processes of subjectivation are networked interactions that actually minimize and marginalize human processes of subjectivation; thus, a machinic enunciation may take place as a result of the displacement of anthropocentric perspective and with a sense that is strictly operational. I have elsewhere made the argument that the debit card and bank machine remain our best examples of this process,[34] and Maurizio Lazzarato has described how credit cards make their users ('dividuals) into tributaries of the credit-machine, authentication, and verification system.[35] One of Guattari's long-standing theoretical projects was the displacement of anthropocentrism in the direction of an autonomization of machinic enunciation, and through animal or vegetable becomings. In doing so he not only blurred the human-machine interface but also suggested the growing importance in the post-media era of machines that enunciate a-subjectively. However, his insights in this area were also in the service of a machinic animism, that is, the belief that not only living entities are autopoietic, but that the term encompasses non-living machines as well.[36]

In an interview with Guattari undertaken only two months before his death, he stated what is perhaps the most perilous feature of post-media life. Eschewing surveillance, and keeping his distance from the genealogical opposition between regimes—societies of discipline developed by Foucault and societies of control suggested by Deleuze—Guattari applied his principle of coexistence to both forms of "subjective integration" noting that control affirms a subjective modelization based on the actions and obedience of "a social robot," in other words, a strong machinic subjugation. He adds this remark: "There isn't even any need to keep the subject under surveillance or control."[37] Machinic enslavement to television was a real danger, and Guattari, in the depths of his own depression, could be found slumped in front of the tube. He understood the effects of serving as a tributary of the programme, inhabiting an existential territory defined by the speaker (i.e., the talking head), hypnotized by the blue glow and cut off from his friends: enslaved like a robot, merely a flickering intersection of a televisual microassemblage. But it wasn't only television that posed a danger; playing video games or getting hung up on comic books was just as likely to constitute a circuit for the exchange of instructions. Enslavement catapults the user to the status of an integrated, intrinsic, component part. Feeding data into Google's constant refinements of its page rank algorithms with every initiated search is a more contemporary way of framing machinic enslavement in the digiverse. But even here the robotic character of inputted choice is not really adequately expressed. The diminishment of subjectivation occurs within a field of so-called decisions about choices generated in advance on the basis of extrapolations from aggregated prior choices. The horizon is to apply past choices about the kind of objects selected and terms and images searched without any further searching in full anticipation of any future decisions. The uncanniness of approximate experiences of this sort on websites like Amazon through its "recommendations" is often humorous, but occasionally the results are eerily accurate when it comes to predicting, through automated analyses, personal preferences. This is a particularly fruitful direction for those interested in Guattari's post-media hypothesis.[38]

Infocapital's capacity to provide pseudo-singularization is constantly enhancing itself, and such a molar form of containment has inspired molecular constructions of resistance through the critical analysis of affective contagion, diagrams of distributed networks, and the Internet of things.[39] How does one hack a "social robot"? Recognizing the alterity of the non-human is a matter of some urgency for Guattari as the process of subjectivation is defined in relation to an alterity embedded in a network from which human subjecthood is not exempt.

Finally, cycling back to the insight that what is meant by post-media must coexist with mass media forms reminds us that even the capacity to think through changes in media studies, for instance, the transition from network television to the post-network era, can be separated neither from the kinds of subjectivation that viewer control, choice, and non-linear viewing provide, nor from the circulation of affects, intersecting communications, complex refrains, and ruptures of singularity (liberation) that help to complexify post-mediatic subjectivations.

NOTES

1. J.-F. Lyotard, *The Postmodern Condition*, trans. Geoff Bennington and Brian Massumi, Minneapolis: University of Minnesota Press, 1984.
2. J.-F. Lyotard, "Note on the Meaning of 'Post-,'" in *The Postmodern Explained*, trans. Julian Pefanis and Morgan Thomas, Minneapolis: University of Minnesota Press, p. 76.
3. Ibid., p. 80.
4. Félix Guattari, *Cartographies Schizoanalytiques*, Paris: Galilée, 1989, p. 65.
5. The Guattarian dimensions of the theorization of multitude—polyphony, singularity, subjectivation, and heterogeneity—are useful to recall in appreciating the reach of his concepts; Michael Hardt and Antonio Negri, *Multitude: War and Democracy in the Age of Empire*, New York: Penguin, 2004.
6. Ibid., p. 56.
7. The primary articles in this series are: "La révolution moléculaire," *Le Monde* 07/12/1990; "Pour une éthique des médias," *Le Monde* 06/11/1991 ["Toward an Ethics of the Media," trans. Janell Watson, *Polygraph* 14(2002): 17–22.]; "Ecologie et politique: Un nouvel axe progressiste." *Le Monde* 04/06/1992; and "Vers une ère post-média," *Chimères* 28 (printemps-été 1992). http://www.revue-chimeres.fr/drupal_chimeres/files/termin51.pdf ["Towards a Post-Media Era," trans. Alya Sebti and Clemens Apprich, *Mute* (1/02/2012). http://www.metamute.org/editorial/lab/towards-post-media-era].
8. "Un nouvel axe progressiste," *Le Monde* (04/06/1992).
9. "La révolution moléculaire," *Le Monde* (07/12/1990).
10. Guattari, *Cartographies Schizoanalytiques*, p. 55.

11. Félix Guattari, *The Three Ecologies*, trans. I. Pindar and P. Sutton, London: Athlone Press, 2000, p. 62.

12. Ibid., p. 65.

13. See Gary Genosko, *Critical Semiotics: Theory, From Information to Affect*, London: Bloomsbury, 2016, pp. 90–117.

14. Félix Guattari, "Did You See the War?" in *Soft Subversions*, trans. A. Loselle, New York: Semiotext(e), 1996, p. 133.

15. Ibid., p. 134.

16. "Towards an Ethics of the Media," p. 19.

17. Guattari, *Chaosmosis*, trans. P. Bains and J. Pefanis, Indianapolis: Indiana University Press, 1995, p. 7.

18. "Towards an Ethics of the Media," p. 19.

19. See Gabriella Coleman, *Coding Freedom: The Ethics and Aesthetics of Hacking*, Princeton, NJ: Princeton University Press, 2012, pp. 69–70.

20. "Towards an Ethics of the Media," p. 20.

21. Ibid., p. 20.

22. *An Inquiry into the Culture, Practices and Ethics of the Press* (2012). http://www.official-documents.gov.uk/document/hc1213/hc07/0779/0779.pdf.

23. *Cartographies Schizoanalytiques*, p. 61.

24. "Towards an Ethics of Media," p. 19.

25. Félix Guattari, "Regimes, Pathways, Subjects," in *The Guattari Reader*, ed. Gary Genosko, Oxford: Blackwell, 1996, p. 98.

26. Franco Berardi, *Félix Guattari: Thought, Friendship, and Visionary Cartography*, trans. C. Stivale and G. Mecchia, London: Palgrave Macmillan, 2008, p. 31.

27. Guattari, "Popular Free Radio," in *Soft Subversions*, trans. D. L. Sweet, pp. 74–75.

28. Berardi, *Félix Guattari*, p. 31.

29. Guattari, *Molecular Revolution in Brazil*, trans. K. Clapshow and B. Holmes, Los Angeles: Semiotext(e), 2008, p. 171.

30. Berardi, *Félix Guattari*, p. 31.

31. "Towards an Ethics of the Media," p. 18. Guattari devotes a few pages to the Interactive Compact Disks of the early 1990s that were non-networked proto-Play Stations for multimedia content (music, games, video). Although they lasted only a few years, for Guattari CDI (Compact Disk Interactive) presented the promise for a "new relation between the consumer and mass-mediatic object" ("La machine mass-médiatique navigue comme un bateau ivre," in Guattari, *Qu'est-ce que l'écosophie?* ed. S. Nadaud, Abbaye d'ardenne: IMEC and Paris: Lignes, 2013, pp. 441–42.

32. Guattari, *Chaosmosis*, p. 97.

33. Deleuze and Guattari, *A Thousand Plateaus*, pp. 456–57.

34. I first explored this in *Félix Guattari: A Critical Introduction*, London: Pluto, 2009, but I take up the matter in more detail in *Critical Semiotics*. A summary of this argument is included in Part IV.

35. Maurizio Lazzarato, *The Making of the Indebted Man*, trans. J. D. Jordan, Los Angeles: Semiotext(e), 2012, pp. 148–49.

36. Angela Melitopoulos and Maurizio Lazzarato, "Machinic Animism," *Deleuze Studies* 6/2 (2012): 243.

37. Félix Guattari, "The Vertigo of Immanence: Interview with John Johnston," trans. A. Goffey, in *The Guattari Effect*, p. 27.

38. See Neal Thomas' Guattarian reflections on Google algorithms on his web site http://hivemedia.ca.

39. See Tony D. Sampson on anti-feelings and love, *Virality: Contagion Theory in the Age of Networks*, Minneapolis: University of Minnesota Press, 2012.

Part II

PASSAGES OF DESIRE

INTRODUCTION

Guattari wrote short catalogue essays on a number of artists, including painter-poet-sculptor Jean-Jacques Lebel, painter George Condo, and painters Toshimitsu Imai and Yayoi Kusama, as well as longer essays on individual artists such as Balthus and Keiichi Tahara. He went beyond visual art to write substantive essays on the architecture of Shin Takamatsu, and the performances of Stanislaw Witkiewicz. His short reflection on David Wojnarowicz, however, belongs to the more casual, short form he sometimes adopted in response to requests to comment on work with which he was not already familiar. When writing about Lebel, for instance, Guattari's tone is familiar and laudatory, in keeping with their long personal association; in the case of Condo, he is responding to a packaged press release and plays the role of interpreting the critical panic unleashed by Condo's unclassifiable style and the buffoonery of his paintings, with their numerous references to canonical works. Guattari enlists one or two concepts with which to rethink the challenges posed by the works in question, referring to Lebel as a painter of transversality since he crosses so many practices in engaging multiple materials of expression. In both cases Guattari is focusing on the roles of creativity and differentiation in the actualization of virtual impulses, and the mutational role played by new technologies (video and photography),[1] and how he reflexively refused an easy recourse to the postmodern label. Instead, in his

Condo essay Guattari introduces the polyphony of stylistic periods, rather than attempting a period breakdown of creative process, and without reducing the citational extravagance to a postmodern "plastering of quotations."[2]

Guattari paid close attention to what he called the *personal* methods of the artists he admired, and Wojnarowicz's tape recordings and notebooks filled with dreams fascinated him; Guattari was also a collector of dreams, those from Kafka's letters and notebooks. The social-poetic-personal are intertwined in Wojnarowicz's production of paintings-writings, and these consist of existential transfers of social action and are reducible neither to an exclusive focus on political action on AIDs nor to the downtown New York art scene (sometimes East Village scene) of the late 1970s and early 1980s. Guattari did not want to trap Wojnarowicz in single categories such as AIDS activist, queer artist, but he did respect him for his courage and public engagements. Guattari's modest catalogue essay, invited by his friend and collaborator Marion Scemama, is important for scholars because it reflects a new reality in Guattari's writings and interviews about homosexuality as the 1980s came to a close. Much of what Guattari wrote about the links between desire and sexuality, and semiotic-sexual ruptures, and the subversive overflowing of homosexual desire,[3] dates from the 1970s, which cannot be mythologized simply as a pre-AIDS era.[4] His sense of concern about the pandemic not only grew through the 1980s, but by the year of his death in 1992, his public statements increased alarmingly to suggest an equivalence between finding a cure for AIDS and the future of humankind: "Biological sciences and medical technology will win the battle with this illness or, in the end, the human species will be eliminated."[5] Readers of Guattari know that he considered the 1980s to be period of greyness and political reaction, and he saw in the formidable mutations of subjectivation brought about by pandemics, computerization, global ecological events, and capitalism's breaking of the Berlin Wall, challenges to be addressed through a renewal of democracy, ethics, and collective intelligence. Indeed, he participated in discussions in the pages of *Gai Pied Hebdo*, whose role in promoting AIDS awareness was important before the magazine's demise in 1992, and spoke of the importance of recognizing a multiplicity of subjectivities within what is called oneself, that is, in a fragile existential territory occupied by converging becomings and a co-mingling of what might otherwise be considered as different phases of linear development.

Chapter 4, "In this Sleep: A Dream Pragmatics for David Wojnarowicz," is an expanded version of a French translation that appeared in Deleuze and Guattari's journal, *Chimères*.[6] It addresses the question of personal methods of aesthetic production and dream collection as a transversal practice, modelled on Guattari's own approach to Kafka, via Freudian dream interpretation.[7] This chapter presents a psychoanalytic Guattari, as he makes love to a certain Freud, for the sake of Wojnarowicz. Although such Guattarian concepts as transversality helped to put an end to lingering attachments to interpretation in the thinking of literature, what comes after interpretation puts an end neither to psychoanalytic approaches to art nor to dream interpretation. The mythic narratives of Freud survive not as primary reference points but, despite their limits, as inventive worlds of concept creation that Freudianism later petrified.[8]

Finally, chapter 4 brings to an uncertain closure Guattari's experience of a bohemian New York that he first encountered during the Semiotext(e) Schizo-culture conference in 1975, where French theory rubbed shoulders with subversive American fiction (William Burroughs, Kathy Acker, and Allen Ginsberg) and music (John Cage and Patti Smith). This is a trajectory mapped by Sylvère Lotringer for whom "schizo-culture equals New York."[9] The reference to Patti Smith in *A Thousand Plateaus* is attributed to this event and the myriad of meetings that took place. Lotringer would eventually converse at length with Wojnarowicz and his collaborators, following this line of flight deep into a radicle America.

Guattari and punk poetry: they still resonate in the writings of Franco Bifo Berardi when he turns to the lessons of the summer of hate. The slogan "no future" may have been articulated in London, but the exchange between the cities drove the violent global passage out of modernity of the late 1970s, and the end of heroes. David Bowie and The Stranglers knew this well enough, from "Heroes" to "No More Heroes," but this black hole effect was well understood by Richard Hell and the Vodoids in the form of belonging to a post-boomer *blank generation*. Guattari helped Berardi when he escaped from Italian injustice during the events of 1977, and Berardi began a long conversation and friendship with Guattari in exile in Paris, eventually becoming a refugee. Chapter 5 concerns Berardi's assessment of Guattari's thought that is built around the failure of desire in the ageing process and how depression weighs upon the activist ego. Berardi diagnoses Guattari's mental ecology in terms of a social and political deep freeze during the "winter years" of the 1980s when his friend became involved in hopeless Green political causes. This was far, very far, from the euphoria of production heralded in the pages of *Anti-Oedipus*.[10] It marked a kind of impotence whose potentiality was hard to grasp: can depression be happily transformative or at least *felix*?

In developing a theory of fascism, Guattari embedded in it black hole effects as an explanatory principle of how the energy of mass desire is channelled into self-destruction. The de-centring of this process (i.e., from around the gaze of the Führer)[11] clears the way for the emergence of a multiplicity of micro-fascist phenomena that resonate together. Resonance was a concept Guattari borrowed from René Thom and adapted to the new end of explaining small-scale—flexible, self-regulating, molecular—fascisms adapted to advanced forms of infocapital that help them seep into the pores of a society—the kind of society that elects Donald Trump as president. Trump had been on Guattari's radar for years, and he is deservedly bashed as a species of algae for his reckless property development schemes: "In the field of social ecology, men like Donald Trump are permitted to proliferate freely, like another species of algae, taking over entire districts of New York and Atlantic City; he 'redevelops' by raising rents, thereby driving out tens of thousands of poor families, most of whom are condemned to homelessness, becoming the equivalent of the dead fish of environmental ecology."[12] The resonances of Trumpian politics are explored in chapter 6, "Black Holes of Drugs and Politics," through the proliferation of the Sad Frog Meme, a potent and contested symbol of the alt-right, and the involutive, inspiraling forces of post-truth, alternative facts, hate, racism, and sexism in the choked mental ecology of America today.[13]

NOTES

1. Félix Guattari, "Jean-Jacques Lebel: Painter of Transversality," trans. M. McMahon, *GLOBE* 8 (no date): http://www.artdes.monash.edu.au/non-cms/globe/issue8/jjltxt.html.
2. Félix Guattari, "Introduction," *George Condo*, Paris: Daniel Templon, 1990, p. 12.
3. Paul Eliot devotes a few pages to Guattari's Wojnarowicz essay in his book *Guattari Reframed*, London: I.B. Tauris, 2012, pp. 112–14.
4. An example of Guattari's construction of homosexual becoming from the mid-1970s is "Une sexualisation en rupture," entretien avec Guattari et C. Deschamps, *La quinzaine littéraire* 215 (1975): 14–15.
5. Félix Guattari, "Remaking Social Practices," in *The Guattari Reader*, ed. G. Genosko, Oxford: Blackwell, 1996, p. 268.
6. Gary Genosko, "Félix Guattari et David Wojnarowicz: Essai de schizo-analyse," trans. Anne Querrien, *Chimères* 88 (2016): 187–96.
7. Félix Guattari, *Soixante-cinq Rêves de Franz Kafka*, Paris: Lignes, 2007.
8. On this point see Simon O'Sullivan, *On the Production of Subjectivity*, London: Palgrave Macmillan, 2012, p. 106.
9. "Sylvère Lotringer: Interview with D. Grau," *Purple Magazine* 26 (2016). http://purple.fr/magazine/fw-2016-issue-26/sylvere-lotringer/. And, Deleuze and Guattari, *A Thousand Plateaus*, p. 19.
10. This chapter was originally published as "Happy Depression: Franco Berardi and the Unpaid Bills of Desire," in *Contemporary Italian Philosophy*, ed. A. Calcagno, New York: SUNY Press, 2015, pp. 199–215. It appears here in a new form adapted for reading alongside chapter 6 with the overlapping themes of defeat, addiction, and narcissism.
11. Félix Guattari, *Lines of Flight: For Another World of Possibilities*, trans. A. Goffey, London: Bloomsbury, 2016, p. 89.

12. Guattari, *The Three Ecologies*, p. 43.

13. Chapter 6 contains parts of a previously published essay "Daddy's Little Helper: Félix Guattari and Gamma OH," *Parallax* [Special issue on Resonances in Deleuze and Guattari] 18/1 (2012): 47–61, and the section on micro-fascism is an unpublished presentation, "The Proliferation of Micropolitical Fascisms," from the Spectres of Fascism Free School at Simon Fraser University in March 2017. I am grateful to Samir Gandesha for his kind invitation to participate in this event.

Chapter 4

In This Sleep: A Dream Pragmatics for David Wojnarowicz

> We are not far from Freud, but the Freud of the good years, the mad years of The Interpretation of Dreams and Jokes and Their Relation to the Unconscious.
>
> —Guattari[1]

At the invitation of photographer Marion Scemama, Félix Guattari provided an essay titled simply "Notes" for a xeroxed catalogue of David Wojnarowicz's show *In the Shadow of Forward Motion* at P.P.O.W. gallery in New York in 1989. Scemama had been a patient of Guattari in Paris, and her partner at the time, filmmaker François Pain, was an old friend of Félix.[2] Despite Guattari's long-standing interest in contemporary art, he wasn't familiar with Wojnarowicz's work and his experience of it was based on the materials that Scemama provided to him: a French transcription and translation of the artist's oral explanation of his work delivered to her by cassette tape, and a prepared slide show. Sylvère Lotringer translated Guattari's text into English for the catalogue. In an interview with Lotringer, Scemama remarks that she thought Guattari's essay "was a little superficial," and she described the conditions of its production, which were largely of her own making, as "restrictive"[3] given the paucity of materials; yet for Wojnarowicz it was important to be recognized by a major intellectual, some of whose work in translation was in circulation given the alternative scene Semiotext(e) assisted in creating for the reception of so-called French theory beyond the academy, beginning in the mid-1970s in a very different bohemian, "schizo-cultural" New York.

The first task of this chapter is to acknowledge Guattari's statement in support of Wojnarowicz's personal courage in the face of an HIV+ diagnosis, and his political acumen in openly challenging censorship and reactionary interference in the arts grants process; including his presence on the streets with

ACT-UP, and in the courts successfully fighting copyright infringement of his work by the American Family Association, and supporting Karen Finley after she was defunded by the National Endowment for the Arts. My focus is on the observation, by Guattari, concerning the artist's forging of a highly singular cartography based significantly on dreams. What might a schizoanalytic approach to Wojnarowicz's dreams look like? My work here is, then, largely prepatory and based on working through Guattari's directions for a *dream pragmatics*.

What conditions need to be in place for such an approach? Wojnarowicz's diaries are filled with dreams. *In the Shadow of the American Dream: The Diaries of David Wojnarowicz* contains many accounts and occasional reflections on them. He notes in the spring of 1979 that "dreams in the last month [May] have been like slides clacking into an old viewer snap snap snap—scenes/characters/associations/life—rhythms reasons forms all change fast."[4] The machinic rhythms of slide trays and carousel slide projectors that he invoked provide suggestive examples of the importance Wojnarowicz accorded to machines, and Guattari quotes him on various machines at length in his short essay, emphasizing how dream contents as well as fantasies are connected with defunct machines that now litter the landscape that they helped to colonize (especially steam engines) and are sometimes elevated to pagan god status (computer microchips, a view similarly held by Guattari).[5] Wojnarowicz's personal method of dream recording, using tape recorders and note books, impacted both his writing and visual art, and these, in turn, fed his continual self-reinvention; as an anti-postmodern, Wojnarowicz is authentically ideological and in an openly pitched struggle with reactionary forces using the imaginary tools of his own creation to lend support to his militancy aimed at changing the social field of how mass public health challenges like the AIDs crisis were cruelly mismanaged in the US. Guattari's admiration for Wojnarowicz surpasses the somewhat non-fashionable examples often cited by him in the realm of painting, and his encounter with East Village Art was revelatory; additionally, Guattari doesn't trap Wojnarowicz in an echo chamber of self-reinvention but embeds this aesthetically mediated process in public militancy against the stigmatization of gay culture and HIV+ men and women, both gay and straight. When considering Wojnarowicz there is ample room for renewing the question of an autonomous aesthetics—immanent to the artist's personal life, milieu, and numerous collaborations, yet autonomous (in privileged isolation) from institutions whose confines are refused and exited from, as Stephen Zepke has argued more generally.[6] The aesthetical dimension is, however, inseparable in Wojnarowicz's case from the socio-sexual sites of autonomy in the abandoned warehouses and piers along the industrial shipping line of a stretch of the Hudson River that he began haunting in the late 1970s and into early 1980s: the "sexual underground," as he called it. Dreams were his literary machines; but the piers were his energy source:

> I have all these journals from day in and day out, all the warehouse activities, things I witnessed of men, piles of men everywhere, fucking in these different rooms, qualities of light and sound, all my own experiences. When I wrote them I was so excited to write them, to document them. I thought they were the most amazing things I had ever seen.[7]

Guattari mentions only in passing the graffiti and stencil tags, murals painted and drawn by Wojnarowicz and other artists in the piers, without specifying the multiple roles of these places, especially serving as cruising grounds for public sex, and as a multimedia canvas for Wojnarowicz, and for many other large-scale, unsigned "vagrant frescoes."[8] Some of these frescoes were not static but tended to come to life when framed by the bodies of men. The piers first provided him with a respite from the streets, and his descriptions of the sound qualities, the darkness, the wind, the slow disintegration of the standing structures, and at times the solitude are remarkable; his seed bombing even created "industrial meadows" within the abandoned structures, and it was the anonymity of this and other gestures, largely non-recuperable by the art market, that he favoured: "You couldn't sign a blade of grass that says Wojnarowicz."[9] In an effort to create an alternative exhibition scene, Wojnarowicz did advertise the Ward Line Pier Project in 1983. Together with Mike Bidlo, he invited artists to collaborate on site in a non-curated, non-gallery environment, animated by an anti-*art dealer* sentiment, and explore the life of this autonomous zone.[10]

Writing and aesthetic production function for Wojnarowicz in relation to desire; indeed, this is the role Guattari assigned to homosexuality as a new link of semioticization across which energy passes into journal writing and other aesthetic machines, including the recording of dreams and street art.[11] Machines of anonymous sex and art criss-cross and animate one another. Wojnarowicz himself introduced breaks into such flows by reflecting on his activities at the piers and his journal writing: "I remember when I first started becoming more and more aware of AIDS. And here I am sitting with all these journals, looking at them in total disgust."[12] This reflection on "irresponsibility," that culminated in his tearing up of some of his own works, became a flow: "And now, years later, I shifted again and want these things. They are wonderful; they should be celebrated; we need to be surrounded by sexy images—it's not all death."[13]

My schizoanalytic approach to Wojnarowicz's dreams is also informed by Guattari's essay "Sixty-Nine Dreams of Franz Kafka," in which he outlines his method of collecting and analysing dreams from Kafka's notebooks, letters, and novels, mixing periods together in the process. I will also "collect" Wojnarowicz's dreams from a number of his writings as well as his visual sleep works, hence diverse semiotic optional matters, without numbering them but providing a threefold assemblage with a view to extracting salient dynamics from them; further, I move towards articulating a principle of selection and finding a point of entry into one dream that reflects the critical ambitions of Guattari's own self-analysis of his dream of a lost automobile. Establishing a corpus across periods and years may frustrate the biographically minded, but the movement of exploration passes through sorting and shifts from the collection to one of its resonant features. Readers should both respect Wojnarowicz's biographer Cynthia Carr who remarks on the artist's play with "datelines,"[14] and note Guattari's selection of a single dream that "like a hologram, comprises numerous long-standing over determinations that I have found at all the important junctions of my life."[15] A single dream loaded with a life lived fully.

KAFKA'S DREAMS

First, then, a return to Kafka. For Guattari, Kafka's recording of his dreams "certainly constituted for him more than a source of inspiration: a tool for writing and a method for the elaboration of his literary objectives."[16] As a richly mythological literary writing-thinking, Freudian interpretation gets on the royal road to the unconscious yet runs into a dream's navel, which Freud described as "a passage . . . which has to be left obscure; this is because we become aware during the work of interpretation that at that point there is a tangle of dream-thoughts which cannot be unravelled."[17] But is this where Freudian dream interpretation stops? Guattari thinks so: "At the point where Freudian interpretation stops—before what Freud called the *ombilic du rêve*, everything begins for Kafka."[18] Is this hard contrast a reductionistic view of dream interpretation and the Freudian fungal metaphor? The tangle of dream thoughts is the manure upon which a dream fruits, "like a mushroom out of its mycelium." Freud specifies that the navel is the "unplumbable"[19] which ends the prospect of interpretative trail blazing along the hyphae. No, it is not a reduction, but Guattari's alternative model of an immanently machinic unconscious finely attuned to micro-productions of all sorts, and not stuck on a buried knot.[20]

Kafka's extraction and multiplication of singularities begins "without structural overcoding of any kind,"[21] Guattari claims. Freud's recourse to the fungal branching characteristics of the meshwork to which the navel connects cannot play much of a role in the enrichment of a mutant subjectivity. Kafka's dream pragmatics point neither to an unknown nor all-too-well-known set of coordinates, but function intersubjectively to elicit the dreams of his fiancé that he considers to be dreamed "collectively" for the couple. Beyond this specialist role, Guattari observes three major dream-contents in Kafka's texts: (i) fluxes of letters, (ii) writing machines, and (iii) packs of young girls. Guattari also cites numerous examples (teeth, dogs, prostitutes, blind girls) of the "transference of the singularity of dreams to the writings (and the inverse)"[22] back and forth, then, between dreams and imaginary universes. For Guattari, however, every point of singularity needs to be analysed or "treated" by means of three "techniques" without hardening into a static symbolics: (i) minor events triggering major catastrophes, (ii) neutralization of events, and (iii) re-assertion of an incident's motor force in the literary process.[23] These treatments expose the role of dreams in the literary processes of subjectivation that Kafka unleashes.

A dream pragmatics refers directly to the approach of schizoanalysis and the rejection of "pre-formed subjective structures towards assemblages of enunciation able to forge new coordinates for reading and to 'bring into existence' new representations and propositions."[24] The interpretation of these assemblages involves taking into account contextually embedded referents that can have pragmatic effects within the confines of institutions as well as in the broader social and political fields, and to consider how they influence both semiotic and material dimensions of the production of subjectivity. The schizoanalyst will then select from the assemblages and lay out those that will play the role of analysers of the unconscious; the protocols for the selection and interaction of analysers will break from preformed coordinates and "given" forms of legitimation and normalization. Instead, such analyser assemblages will be subject to the feedback on and from the analytic situation, and concatenate according to whether this is negative (calling for recalibration) or positive (generating pragmatic effects and affects).

Schizoanalysis is a metamodelization process that critically concerns itself with mapping trans-assemblage relations between the four domains of the unconscious: Flows-Phyla-Territories-Universes. The assemblage relations are neither reducible to a linguistified unconscious nor beholden to preset complexes, yet there is an ontological "topography" of sorts at stake, and a loosely structured inter-dynamism between the "registers." For Guattari, this doesn't mean that in an assemblage one never encounters fixed and invariant complexes. Guattari clarifies that mapping junctures and coordinates among assemblages is not reducible to "fixed constraints." If the components of an assemblage lose some consistency, this needn't be blamed on clinging to a lost object and a series of inhibitions. Expectations of "long marked out pathways" give way to what Guattari calls "pragmatic transformations" that allow for idiosyncrasies that reorganize the assemblages in ways that do not collapse or contract around specific objects. The example used by Guattari is a singer's loss of two octaves in her range following the death of her mother. The obvious death and loss connection is too object-focused and restrictive, argues Guattari, and not enough attuned to positive transformations: "An a-signifying index—the restriction of vocal performance—marks the stopping of something, without, as the context reveals, preventing something else from occurring."[25]

IN THIS SLEEP

I am working across three texts, *In the Shadow of the American Dream*, *Close to the Knives*, and *Memories That Smell Like Gasoline*, in search of transferences of singularity between the dreams and the writings—memoirs, diaries, memories, commentaries. But there is more. In *Memories*, there are line drawings with narrative captions of undated dreams,[26] drawings and paintings of dream contents (*Dream Drawing*, 1987), and simple discursive entry points of the dream texts themselves, announced by phrases: "in this sleep," "in this dream," "this kid walks into my sleep," and simply "dream" and "sleep." These mark thresholds where the author changes registers, and his recording practices are not only contextualized, but his literary process is underlined. *Close to the Knives* contains multiple modalities—personal journals with dream fragments and difficult awakenings, transcripts of tape-recorded interviews, excerpts from letters, art gallery talks, ACT-UP research notes. Dreams are also illustrated; they are painted, for instance, in the "from sleep" paintings of the late 1980s (*Some Things from Sleep: For Jane and Charley,* 1986; *Something from Sleep II,* 1987–1988). We are not limited to single semiotic substances, as in the Kafka example. For Guattari, Wojnarowicz's "'method' consists in using his fantasies and above all his dreams, which he tape-records or writes down systematically, in order to forge himself a language and a cartography that literally enable him to permanently reconstruct his own existence. This gives his oeuvre an extraordinary vigor."[27] The vigor consists of a heterogenesis of affects. During his brief phase as a no-wave musician with 3 Teens Kill 4, Wojnarowicz provided tape-recorded found sounds. He never gave up his tape recorder. Subjectifying singularizations are not isolated on the imaginary plane but connect to historical events—the heyday of the piers for cruising, the early years of the 1980s when AIDS as a diagnostic label was first applied, the incredible energy of graffiti and street art, performance art, and small press publishing. Wojnarowicz's dream and other intimate disclosures, however, carry powerful affects that stick to readers/viewers and collapse the distance between them. For Guattari, "affect is the process of existential appropriation by the continuous creation of heterogeneous durations of being."[28] affects promote becomings and work on their own. "The image," wrote Guattari of

Wojnarowicz, "is not only meant to exhibit passively significant forms, but to trigger an existential movement, if not of revolt, at least of existential creativity."[29] Guattari is more than willing to accept Wojnarowicz as a political artist whose singularity galvanizes viewers into taking action on key social issues and to question their own responses to both the everyday existential praxes and aesthetic investigations of gay erotic life: "Something emerges from Wojnarowicz's chaos which places before us our responsibility for taking a stand in the course of the world's movement."[30] Guattari was well aware of the spirit of renunciation that held sway in many circles in his reflections on the "winter years" of the 1980s and looked optimistically to Wojnarowicz's personal and political statements, especially the explicit integration into his work of the course of own illness and how he responded to it, to struggle against the cold. Wojnarowicz's meditations on desire and death and the complexities of living with an HIV positive diagnosis conjoin with Guattari's sense of how artists can take hold of a-signifying ruptures and transform their work in the process, constituting collective assemblages that have the power to communicate further influences in subjectivation in an expanding field.[31] Wojnarowicz put this differently in terms of how bringing the private into the public domain exploded the artificially maintained illusion of a restrictive consensus reinforced by particular institutions—the state, church, medical establishment, mass media, and self-appointed upholders of morals (named by Wojnarowicz "one tribe nation") and how micro-artistic gestures put into circulation tools for dismantling these equipments of power. Where Wojnarowicz saw one tribe, Guattari saw a general function "implanted within the modes of semiotization, subjectivation and praxis of human groups."[32]

The initial step in a dream pragmatics is defining dream contents:

i A preponderance of creatures in confined spaces:

- an enormous machinic spider with the body of a gas tank, clicking with its eight legs in the confined space of a small room in which the artist sleeps;[33]
- two sexy thugs with the faces of prisoners hold a glass box containing a "pygmy rattler" without a rattle, which once removed bites an unfrightened Wojnarowicz on the nose;[34]
- nighttime in Times Square from his hustling days, but not as a youth, as he's a bit older; there's a cardboard box and two little birds jumping around it; he puts them into the box and gives them a drink with an eyedropper when they open their beaks;[35]
- something flew into his mouth and he fished it out, discovering it was an unconscious mermaid three-quarters of an inch long; after drying her off, and in trying to move her, she is accidentally torn in half; horror gives way to embarrassment.[36]

In addition to the menagerie, of real and imagined creatures, there is an ambiguous dynamism of containment and release, care and damage. Wojnarowicz loved animals as a child and stole reptiles from pet shops regularly through his teens, integrated a complex animal symbolism in his visual art—indominable beetles and ants, taxidermied buffaloes, and industrious monkeys; and he kept his own terrarium with a pet scorpion, gathered animal skeletons, dressed up cockroaches as rabbits, and so on. Animals survive in the empty containers of civilization, not only in the boxes and rooms of his dreams but in the ruined machines littered across the machinic phylum. Do not confuse Wojnarowicz's fascination with and even great concern for animals with the care-taking image of putting a creature into a confined space, or the risks of releasing it from one. Rather, the predefined space is a mould into which a living creature is made to fit, and persist for a time. Wojnarowicz places the image of an eagle inside the excrement ball rolled by dung beetles (*Dung Beetles II*, 1986). An elephant being driven by a man standing on top of it with a short control pole floats in a bubble in the painting/collage *Something from Sleep II*, 1988–1989.

ii Strange suburban territories as settings for troubled communication:

- crawling across manicured lawns and into the cracks of houses in order to awaken the sleepers and tell them about his life as a child hustler and the dangers of one john in particular—whom he would have strangled if his hands would have fit around his neck;[37]
- moving through a neighbourhood of white houses in a suburban town looking for a bar; instead he finds Syd, a lawyer from his Times Square hustling days, who hands Wojnarowicz some letters he wrote to him; he then encounters Syd's wife, who is reading one of the letters, which he tears out of her hands, but she finds another, and he makes excuses; Syd is on the phone with her, but she hangs up and speaks as if nothing has happened;[38]
- another rambling interior of a suburban home, this time his brother, Steve, tells him his son is here; not realizing he had a son, Wojnarowicz sees this eleven year old and feels incredibly happy, but he doesn't know his name, so avoids him. Steve whispers the boy's name in his ear but he can't quite hear—Hun or Huné? He chooses the latter as it sounds gentler, so approaches the child and he looks at Wojnarowicz and says he has some drawings he wants him to see.[39]

Here are the suburbs of New Jersey from his childhood, with multiple appearances of his brother Steve, intersecting with characters from his life as a homeless youth hustling in Times Square, a recurring setting in his diaries. The interiors and exteriors have to be navigated and are treacherous. Misrecognition abounds. But the "neatly clipped lawn," a recurring trope in *Close to the Knives*, inspires horror at the uncontested violence that takes place there within the undisturbed boundaries of private property.[40] The unknown son's name of Hun or Huné not only introduces a rich site of exploration, to which I will return in the conclusion, but is one of two parapraxes in the dream. The recording media—handwritten letters, telephones, faulty memory, garbled speech—allow misrecognition to sometimes work and at other times falter. Problems of inscription populate Wojnarowicz's dreams; for instance, he gets a bad tattoo on his chest, not sure why, although it seems to be of his works (burning building stencil), but he realizes how much it would cost to get it removed.[41]

iii Desire after an HIV positive diagnosis:

- explains to a sibling that he has ARC (artefact of the early years of AIDS research that showing symptoms excluded one from health care funding) and breaks down into violently sobbing;[42]
- illustrated dream scene with text—one beating up a young attractive man whom he wanted to kiss but who wanted a fight instead; suddenly discovers he possesses boxing skills;[43]
- a further illustration with a description of a naked man covered in lesions bursts into his home and throws him on the bed, exclaiming you would have thought I was sexy before I got sick; the naked man is pushed away;[44]
- a flirty guy from ACT-UP starts kissing him and he's mad about this guy but Wojnarowicz is ARC and it prevents him from feeling attractive; the two suddenly end up in a construction site on an escalator that breaks up, the guy is going one way and Wojnarowicz another; the latter falls trying to reach him but is caught with a cable that is in a knot; but will this cause the escalators to stop working? How can Wojnarowicz tell him he's positive? Suddenly the man is his boyfriend Tom Rauffenbart.[45]

After the spring of 1988, Wojnarowicz's journal writings turned from the issue of his own rage at the dying of his friends, lovers, and collaborators to his own diagnosis, and he accelerated his public activism through works such as *ITSOFOMO* (with Ben Neill, 1989) and *Fear of Disclosure* (1990). The transition from a culture of death to desire in people living with AIDS is accompanied not by an acceleration of dreams with these contents but by a paucity of them. When his dreams dry up and he can no longer remember them, Wojnarowicz expresses his thanks when the emptiness is briefly and meagrely populated.[46] This disconnection damages his writing machine.

It may be recalled that dreams of death are railroaded by Freud onto the tracks of childhood death-wishes within Oedipal mythic-desire.[47] The dream cited earlier of the pygmy rattler is introduced as "Dream. Night before Peter died." Former lover and mentor photographer Peter Hujar passed away in the fall of 1987, and his demise is chronicled scrupulously, and his body photographed after death by Wojnarowicz.

Guattari asks us to search for the co-transferential passages of singularity between the dreams and writings, which I locate by means of containment and uncontainment, of care as capture and release as fatal escape, exemplified by animals, but also by restrictive architectures, yet regaining openness through decomposition, like the pterodactyl on the walls and windows of a room in the abandoned piers, and the stegosauruses of his dream drawings and paintings with his name written above their spikes.

GUATTARI'S SELF-ANALYSIS

In addition to the reference point of Kafka, it is useful to consult Guattari's self-analysis of his dream of the lost car and of a woman identified as A.D. discussed in the essay "The Refrains of Being and Sense." Here is a "machinics of the surface of the text" that leans forward into the future, and it is semiotic heterogeneity that interests Guattari, more than a deep look into the latent contents of primary processes and their repression. This dream of an absent machine (lost automobile) which he unsuccessfully seeks around a rectangular square has its share of "background worlds" almost twenty years apart (two different makes of auto, two different partners, two different collaborators, lingering jealousy for one's spouse projected onto his friend's spouse) to draw upon based on Guattari's personal history, but the interpretation plays mostly on a slip of the tongue (lapsus) that confuses curatorial collaborator Yasha David for Gilles Deleuze, even while correcting himself in the dream itself, and the swarming of initials (including BMW and spouse A.D. and later lover [Ad]elaide, another A.d.) as an abstract machine. Everyday psychopathologies like parapraxes, jokes, double entendres are privileged by Guattari but are not burdened with the role of compromise; instead, they connect with lines of subjectivation he classifies according to the domains of his meta-model and the associations attached to them:

> Existential territories: diagram of a square in a market town, associated with similar places where he lived throughout his life, and also where he vacationed;

> Incorporeal universes: coarté affects are affective intensities belonging to non-discursive universes, as opposed to the signified utterances that have discursive coordinates (space-time and energy exo-references); jealousy of the sexual freedom of female partners in particular;
>
> Machinic phyla: lost car is a desiring-machine connected to his acquisition of a driver's license at a late age, as well as an earlier event wherein he proposes to drive Deleuze home and after spending some time searching for his car beneath the Centre Pompidou, realizes he walked there in the first place;
>
> Fluxes: one- and two-way traffic flows along street in the aforementioned diagram that are associated with troubling directions within his metamodel (exclusions of direct transit between phyla and territories and fluxes and universes), its asymmetry and detours suggesting interior vacuoles.

Moreover, Guattari deploys several features—how he selected these among the many other tensors is not explained—of the relations between and within domains:

> Inter-domain synapses between F/P [structural] and T/U [systemic]: psychopathologies not indexed to hidden reductionistic causes such as complexes but bearing semiotic and/or material potentialities that these multiply, articulate, and thus constitute and in a reversible process influence assemblages of enunciation;
>
> Black hole: an effectively charged nothingness resonating across territories, featuring an object that is "lost," an abyss, an obscure "cave";
>
> Harmonic constellations refer to the relations among nuclei within incorporeal universes; deterritorialized abbreviations and reterritorialized speech sounds: A.D.—Adelaide; Mexican state of Michoacan-Micheline Kao.

The key to the dream is the advice his father gave him, on his deathbed, about getting his driver's license, and even passed him a small amount of cash to pay for it. The machinic linkage between the loss of the car, the use of the car to gain independence but the libidial problems it created (a divorce due to newfound freedom, using the vehicle to jealously track down a liberated partner, delivering himself to sites where his inhibitions about violence and homosexuality found expression) and anxiousness about dying, that is both "essential and derisory" as the father's gesture of giving 50-francs to him as if it was still worth something.[48] The misplaced car serves as Guattari's technical desiring machine, which enters into an assemblage that positions it alongside fear of death; he claims that the lapsus is a protective device that positively rerouted him into more neutral zones of friendship, with Yasha and Gilles, where such emotions would be out of place.

EXTRACTING GUATTARIAN CARTOGRAPHIC COORDINATES

Guattari's self-analysis of his dream of the lost automobile indicates the role of the fourfold cartography of the unconscious in the analysis of dream materials, and I will attempt later to situate my observations earlier about multiple dreams among the quadrants. This applied meta-modelling constitutes an effort to arrive at some preliminary conclusions about how to distribute Wojnarowicz's dream texts.

I would situate the background worlds that most vividly appear in specific dreams but also across the categories:

:existential territories relating to his youth and teenage years;

:harmonic constellations of homophonic universes that erupt around communication breakdowns and bear upon friends, collaborators and lovers from across his life worlds and which begin with Hu-, namely, [Peter] Hujar, [Herbert] Huncke, [Jesse] Hultberg;

:fluxes of sexual desiring machines and a post-positive erotics of the gay male body, negotiations of anonymous sexual encounters and the ethics of disclosure;

:phyla of animals and their behaviours both in confinement and released from it, through broader processes of domestication, extinction, co-evolution.

Guattari sees parapraxes like Huné—a misrecording of the Parisian bookstore La Hune in Saint-Germain where Wojnarowicz liked to go during his visits with his sister who lived in the city—in the dream of the unknown son as connective, blazing new trails for enunciative assemblages, rather than in the Freudian analysis of slips, especially involving foreign words, of unconscious determinations conceptualized as inadequately repressed impulses. Yet it may be retained from Freud that the connection of unconscious thoughts with external associations that activate them could be productive if it were not for the commitment required to a stultifying metapyschology. Indeed, I would suggest that a schizoanalysis of a single dream could revolve around the unknown son's name, recorded in 1979, opening onto Wojnarowicz's visits to Paris over some ten years (1978–1988), his sense of betrayal during the birth of his sister Pat's child there, relationship with his lover Jean-Pierre Delage, and ultimately his decision to get tested for HIV—after all, another Hu(man)—after returning to New York from his final trip to Paris in 1988. The selection of "h" engages a multiple muteness: in the dream, it is a choice of "gentleness" of a letter in French that is silent, as the artist was accustomed to the hard "h" of American English and turned away from its harshness, selecting Huné. It is worthwhile underlining the semiotics of silence in the multimodal artistic lexicon of AIDS activism in the years after the dream in question was dated in the pink triangle posters of ACT-UP and the film of Rosa von Praunheim, in which Wojnarowicz would appear, decrying the "silence" of the Reagan administration in the midst of a public health crisis, and extolling the maturation of an ethics and erotics of "safe sex" *before the letter*. An entire cultural politics was mobilized behind the delivery of messages that had remained *unheard*. Indeed, Wojnarowicz declared on a number of occasions that meeting this silence with a radical gesture, not words, was appropriate: "What I would really love, the moment I die in the hospital, is for somebody to take my body, get in a car, go to Washington, break through the front gate of the White House, just throw my body onto the steps."[49]

The question for dream pragmatics as far as "hu-" words and silences are concerned is how they advance from the status of "residues" from dreaming and waking life and gain some a-signifying independence, crystallizing new universes of reference and thus enacting their mutational roles.[50]

What also makes this thread viable is that it also reveals a principle that Guattari alights on, namely, an attempt to self-correct or self-reference in a dream itself, in addition to a reflexive grasp of meta-modelling as favouring some movements between domains over others that are restricted, so that associative relations would not be entirely free in the cartography; the principle is that each domain retains a degree of autonomy, consisting of unique entities that nevertheless "write themselves"[51] through one another, but there is no way to establish direct passage between territories and phyla and fluxes and universes, without first passing through tensors between territories and universes and fluxes and phyla. While the fluxes of cruising could access directly the territories, they would need to be passed along to the constellated universes of intensive reference, which means they could be reduced neither to biography nor to specific locations pure and simple (piers, the Tuileries), but to the writing process and indirectly cited texts. Indeed, the secondary slip of the pen in the dream of the unknown son concerns Attila the Hun and Wojnarowicz's recollection that he was reading about him in a history book by a certain "Tares[?]," introducing the term for weeds in the biblical parable (in Matthew) of the wheat, referring to the stigmatized, "evil" ones who sowed weeds among the crops (it is from this harshness that he turned away). It is by undertaking the process of categorization, sifting through the collection, following the reflexive application of principles, that a selection of an analyser can be made that is adequate to the task of undertaking a dream pragmatics with a lively and labile translatability.

Guattari's remark to the effect that he views dreams as holograms places schizoanalytic dream pragmatics on the machinic phylum in a fraught techno-cultural object which functions by recharging the non-separability of inside and outside, part and whole (the whole coexisting with every part, and as another part). Guattari uses the hologram as a tool for transversal exploration across spaces and times, making translocal and temporal translations possible that exceed the constraints of the ontological quadrant.

NOTES

1. Guattari, *Schizoanalytic Cartographies*, p. 223.
2. Cynthia Carr, *Fire in the Belly: The Life and Times of David Wojnarowicz*, New York: Bloomsbury, 2012, pp. 412–13. And I am grateful to Marion Scemama for her helpful clarifications about Guattari's short text.
3. Sylvere Lotringer, "Interview with Marion Scemama," in *David Wojnarowicz: A Definitive History of Five or Six Years on the Lower East Side*, New York/Los Angeles: Semiotext(e) and The MIT Press, 2006, p. 131.
4. David Wojnarowicz, *In the Shadow of the American Dream: The Diaries of David Wojnarowicz*, ed. Amy Scholder, New York: Grove, 1999, p. 107.
5. Félix Guattari, "David Wojnarowicz." http://www.editions-laurence-viallet.com/cahier/david-wojnarowicz/ (1989); and "David Wojnarowicz, in the Shadow of Forward Motion," *Rethinking Marxism* 3/1 (Spring 1990): 75–84.
6. Stephen Zepke, "From Aesthetic Autonomy to Autonomist Aesthetics: Art and Life in Guattari," in *The Guattari Effect*, eds. E. Alliez and A. Goffey, London: Continuum, 2011, p. 215.
7. Lotringer, "Interview with David Wojnarowicz," p. 194.
8. David Wojnarowicz, *Close to the Knives: A Memoir of Disintegration*, New York: Vintage, 1991, p. 22.
9. Barry Blinderman, "A Compression of Time: An Interview with David Wojnarowicz," in *Tongues of Flame*, New York: Distributed Art/University Galleries of Illinois State University, 1990, p. 56.
10. Carr, *Fire in the Belly*, pp. 224–26.
11. Félix Guattari,"A Liberation of Desire: Interview with Félix Guattari by George Stambolian," in *The Guattari Reader*, p. 209.
12. Lotringer, "Interview with Wojnarowicz," p. 194.
13. Ibid.
14. Carr, *Fire in the Belly*, p. 5.
15. Guattari, *Schizoanalytic Cartographies*, p. 191.
16. Guattari, *Soixante-Cinq Rêves de Franz Kafka et Autres Textes*, p. 11.

17. Sigmund Freud, *The Interpretation of Dreams*, trans. James Strachey, Standard Edition vol. 4, London: The Hogarth Press, 2001, p. 325.
18. Guattari, *Soixante-Cinq*, pp. 12–13.
19. Freud, *The Interpretation of Dreams,* SE 4, p. 111, n. 1.
20. Jean-Claude Polack, "Analysis, Between Psycho and Schizo," *The Guattari Effect*, p. 65.
21. Guattari, *Soixante-Cinq*, p. 13.
22. Ibid., p. 19.
23. Ibid., pp. 24–26.
24. Guattari, *Schizoanalytic Cartographies*, p. 17.
25. Guattari, *Schizoanalytic Cartographies*, p. 25.
26. Wojnarowicz, *Memories That Smell Like Gasoline*, San Francisco: Artspace, 1992, p. 41.
27. Guattari, "David Wojnarowicz," p. 76.
28. Guattari, *Schizoanalytic Cartographies*, p. 204.
29. Guattari, "David Wojnarowicz," p. 77.
30. Ibid.
31. Félix Guattari, "On Contemporary Art: Interview with Oliver Zahm," *Guattari Effect*, pp. 48–49.
32. Guattari, *Lines of Flight*, p. 11.
33. Wojnarowicz, *Knives*, p. 24.
34. Ibid., p. 99.
35. Wojnarowicz, *American Dream*, pp. 222–23.
36. Wojnarowicz, *Knives*, pp. 256–57.
37. Wojnarowicz, *Knives,* p. 81.
38. Wojnarowicz, *American Dream*, pp. 104–5.
39. Wojnarowicz, *American Dream*, p. 108.
40. Wojnarowicz, *Knives*, p. 151.
41. Wojnarowicz, *American Dream*, p. 195.
42. Wojnarowicz, *American Dream*, p. 213.
43. Wojnarowicz, *Memories That Smell Like Gasoline*, p. 41.
44. Ibid., p. 45.
45. Wojnarowicz, *American Dream*, pp. 216–17.
46. Wojnarowicz, *Knives*, p. 257.
47. Freud, *Interpretation of Dreams*, pp. 248–68.
48. Guattari, *Schizoanalytic Cartographies*, p. 202.
49. Lotringer, "Interview with Wojnarowicz," p. 175.
50. Guattari, *Schizoanalytic Cartographies*, pp. 161–62.
51. Ibid., p. 59.

Chapter 5

The Unpaid Bills of Desire

> Depression. We don't find such a word in Guattari's texts: it is left in the margins, as if it were an incompatible topic for the creationist energy that animated his work, his research and his existence.
>
> —Franco Bifo Berardi[1]

My goal is to grasp how a depression can be happy: not, of course, simply by exposing cleverly mounted constitutive definitions, but, rather, through the multiple tensions that the construction "happy depression" releases across the realms of thought, friendship, and desire. I will first turn by way of an introductory contextualization to Antonio Negri, Sigmund Freud, and then Guattari's own perspective on his influential book, written with Gilles Deleuze, *Anti-Oedipus* before looking more closely at how Franco Bifo Berardi figures the oscillations of hope in a paradoxical depression. Berardi's insight into the fragile status of desire in and beyond the period of *Anti-Oedipus* forms the backdrop for this chapter. Berardi read *Anti-Oedipus* while in prison in 1976 on a false charge. It was Guattari who assisted both him and Negri when they fled Italy for France. But let's be clear that the fragility of desire is much more than these sorry episodes, which led to raids on Guattari's apartment and clinic, as well as Deleuze's shift from desire to perception and the theory of the haecceity in his philosophical biography. Reflecting on his friend Félix, Berardi maintains that depression played a significant role in relation to Guattari's later life—the 1980s were his last full decade before his untimely death in 1992—but is also isolated as the unaccounted for element, that is, the cruelty, in desiring-production, and in revolutionary desire itself, beginning historically and most explicitly with the example of Lenin but generalizable to militancy and the depressed male activist in late modernity. This is a rather sprawling claim, I admit. To be more precise, it all comes down to the 1970s.

In addition to depression, Berardi diagnoses panic syndromes, excesses of expression, and schizophrenia, among others, as typical of labour today. He deploys depression and other conditions in the service of a philosophical critique of what he calls *semiocapitalism*. Further, in his recent writing he constructively offers new models of healing in a framework where poetry merges with therapy, and activism is an ill to be managed by quasi-analytic practices of "post-autonomy." Thus, excavating how Berardi reframes autonomist politics as a therapy, while borrowing heavily from Guattari's schizoanalysis, will assist in assessing the prospects of this course of treatment. The portrait of Berardi that I wish to paint is of a philosopher of depression: certainly not a clinician, but perhaps a militant engaged in a long recovery. What is it, then, to be happily depressed?

WE, THE DEFEATED

Unlike others who claim the essays in Guattari's book *The Winter Years/Les Années d'Hiver 1980–1985*[2] display a brave refusal to "modify his previous positions in order to adapt them to the tastes of the day,"[3] Berardi recognizes a kind of defeat lurking under the cover of grey northern European skies. In this regard he is not far from Negri who wrote to Guattari of defeat, but mostly of its "ontological significance" (the significance of its intensity and the new confrontations it opens) within the context of revolutionary struggles during a decade where the "victory of capitalism" was not in doubt.[4] Indeed, Negri's wintry mid-1980s collaboration with Guattari in *New Spaces of Liberty/Les nouveaux espaces de liberté*[5] elicited remarks like those of Alice Jardine who found it "terribly depressing."[6] But Negri himself is not depressed about this defeat, and he is a resource for Berardian paradoxical buoyancy. Yes, we have been defeated, but we remain optimistic! How can this be? What is its basis?

The foundation of Negri and Guattari's optimism about the prospects for a renewed communism, despite their vocabulary of defeat, was based on the processes of subjectivation that may together in an assemblage of singularities constitute something new in the face of the defeats of action. The desire for revolution is irreversible and is bound to the global triumph of capitalism: "Look, mister, you've got the power. You've got everything you want. But we're still here. We're here as contradiction. Every move you make reproduces contradictions."[7] The foundation of optimism is complexity: multiplications of points of confrontation, transversal lines of openness across cultural innovations, the intellectualization of labour (not, of course, as such), and emerging dissident singularities in the forms of desire engendering new subjectivations.

Negri is a theorist of new forms of the dispersed subjectivity of labor beyond the mass industrial worker. He is counted among the leaders of the Italian extra-parliamentary leftist groups Potere Operaio (Workers's Power) and Autonomia (Autonomy). Guattari defended his friend, then professor at University of Padua, in a series of appeals after Negri was named in an arrest warrant as a terrorist, pointing out that he and his fellow Italian intellectuals had nothing to do with the armed violence of the Red Brigades, among other extremist groups. Guattari helped Negri while in Paris, until his arrest in 1979, as did Deleuze. Negri was held in prison for four years during which time Guattari visited regularly and began collaboration on the aforementioned book. Negri won his freedom in 1983 by means of winning a parliamentary seat and receiving immunity, which was shortly thereafter revoked. Again, he fled to Paris with Guattari's help. Two years later in 1985 their collaboration on the reinvention of communism was completed. Both thinkers worked through their debts to Leninism and refocused theoretical attention on the political problem of subjectivity as labour was in the process of becoming more immaterial; that is, its products were less and less like traditional material goods and more and more productive of exciting relationships (like virtual "friends" and "favorite" tweets), compelling images, and attractive subjectivities.

The historical foundation of defeat as Thatcher, Reagan, and Mulroney among other neo-conservatives rose to power is not in doubt. Deleuze's short but stirring statements such as "This Book Is Literal Proof of Innocence" address the "Negri Affair" in terms of its democratic deficits: logical inconsistency of the charges, the violations of a "basic legal identity,"[8] and ludicrous manufacture of a "false thinker";[9] the abuse of evidence by an insistent and paranoid deployment of disjunction and exclusion as inclusion of contradictories; and culpability of the press in Europe which enshrine little more than falsehoods in their pages. Further, Deleuze insisted on Negri's innocence through the evidence of what he presents in his books. The public and political character of these reflections on philosophy by Deleuze and Guattari, buoyed by a genuine concern with democratic institutions like the courts and the press, joined a widespread struggle for democracy against its abuse by Italian lawmakers. Defeat is not only personal, but generational; it also refers to the state of the extra-parliamentary left and political disarray from the long Years of Lead in Italy (roughly from the 1960s to the mid-1980s). In Negri's case, it did not mean that his productivity ceased: his brain could not be stopped by a prison sentence! Berardi begins his book about Guattari by recalling his own use of the lessons of schizoanalysis in order to escape from military service and how, later, he received a copy of *Anti-Oedipus* during his own incarceration; he explains that Félix helped him re-establish his life after mobilizing European intellectuals against Italian political repression, which set the stage for Berardi's release.[10]

At the same time as Guattari was helping his friends escape the miscarriages of Italian justice, he was collaborating with philosopher Eric Alliez and putting into place a novel theory of capitalism adapted to the times: a minimal model of global and post-industrial capitalism in which three constant evaluative terms are used: processes of machinic production; dominant economic-semiotic systems, considered in terms of the market; and structures of social segmentation, considered in terms of the state.[11] This mode of capitalistic valorization is described on the basis of the order of priority given to the three terms, in this case, production-market-state. The key features are that production is decentred and focused on signs, and subjectivity, and that the capacity to integrate and exploit social diversity is unprecedented. Information and fluidity play key roles in production. This nascent theory of globalization, a semiotic variant on post-Fordism, developed collaboratively in the early "winter years" spelled out the terms of defeat: this stage of post-industrial capitalism is marked threefold by modes of info-machinic production that binds immaterial labour to high technology in a condition of permanent change; the market becomes transnational, and standards become unglued as financialization becomes a norm; and the state becomes minimal and speculative:

> Integrated World Capitalism . . . [is] based upon semiotic means of evaluation and valorization of capital which are completely new and have an increased capacity for the machinic integration of all human activities and faculties.[12]

Human semiosis itself ("general intellect") is directly and immediately productive of value, coagulating in semiotic objects (i.e., in the online activities of visitors to social media websites which, in turn, extract and exploit user data). This is an emphasis that puts less weight on, and hybridizes, the materialities of the worker and the products of labour. Guattari wrote:

> Post-industrial capitalism . . . tends increasingly to decenter its sites of power, moving away from structures producing goods and services towards structures producing signs, syntax and . . . subjectivity.[13]

As a precursor to semiocapitalism in which capitalist production has become semiotic and "seizes individuals from the inside,"[14] subsumption (capital looks inside and expands intensively) becomes real and not only formal (capital looks outside and incorporates non-capitalistic processes).

For Berardi, Guattari's depression cannot be reduced to "the winter years"—"it's not the winter's fault."[15] The discoveries about capitalist evolution and mutation during the 1980s are not to blame. What—or whom—is the issue?

ENJOY YOUR SELF-LOATHING

Freud's analysis of melancholia as the migration of disappointment into self-torment—"which is without doubt enjoyable" (as much as sadism is satisfying)[16]—in which the ego looks upon itself as an object to be tortured for moral failings leads to a remarkable image: "Melancholia behaves like an open wound."[17] This wound attracts and converts cathectic intensities and uses them to pulverize the ego. Communicating about this crushed state, the melancholic in turn tortures, thinks Freud, those around him, but especially a love object whose loss—real or threatened—precipitated the regression of libido in the first place. The potential for viciousness that ambivalence in love harbours once directed inward is put on display.

Although melancholia, as a severe form of depression, can, according to Freud, end in suicide, this is not an inevitable outcome. As the analogy with mourning suggests, the melancholic may also heal slowly, like a mourner. While it is undoubtedly the case that a defeated line of flight might curl into a line of death, "the passion of abolition,"[18] an activist's depression may result from failure to create the conditions for lasting change, and this line of defeat might crash and turn on itself. What Berardi means by depression is anti-production: the suspension of meaningful connections with others, with causes, or with connective syntheses in general. The body-without-organs appropriates desiring-production and, like Freud's device of the open wound, converts connections (and) into disjunctions (either/or). Suffering and self-enjoyment belong together on the body-without-organs as recording inasmuch as energy devoted to production is transformed into consumption (pleasure). The intensive, auto-erotic pleasure enjoyed by a subject-in-formation along the markings (gradients, vectors) of the body-without-organs is almost unbearable.[19] Yet it is not only identified—"that's what it was"—but, "it's me." The subject in question is residual, Deleuze and Guattari insist; it is neither the centre nor the source; its identity is not fixed because it takes shape, and is reshaped, through and by means of the intensive states through which it passes. However, efforts at hoarding passages by transforming them into fixed attributes arrest the process by centring it. These passages are given a name—my failures, my suspicions—and incorporated, acquired, to be chewed over. This presupposition of a fixed subject is rejected by Deleuze and Guattari in favour of regaining a schizophrenia materially in touch with desiring production and the real, and thus liberated from the shackles of the ego, the Freudian complexes, and from distantiating desire-as-lack (missing objects, theory of needs, the impossible real), and the disempowering effects for subjectivation of structural-linguistic psychoanalysis. The Guattarian subject is located at the intersection of machine and structure beyond the individual and human collectivity in an order of scientific and technological advances of growing importance for contemporary life. Depression does not enter the picture. This is the bill that went unpaid in the theory of desire. Of course, no one is claiming that Guattari fails to mention melancholia in his writings. A mere mention doesn't amount to much.

FELIX AND FÉLIX

Berardi begins his meditation on "The Happy Depression" playing on the Latin *felix* as in happy or lucky, in his book about his friend, with a twofold insight: what Guattari designated cryptically as "the winter years" were in fact years in which Guattari struggled with depression. "Winter" is a rubric, for Berardi, under which Guattari filed depression: "Depression presents us with the bill. The Subject can't refuse to pay the bill. . . . Depression is the bill."[20] The publication of *The Winter Years* did not pay the bill of depression. The bill remained unpaid. Guattari did not tell the story of his depression, but Berardi would like to tell his version of it, based on biographical circumstances and philosophical exclusions, the latter predating the period in question and indexed to the philosophy of desire that informed the landmark book, *Anti-Oedipus*.

This book was an awkward assemblage as Guattari's journal entries indicate for the period of October 1972. The book's success underlined Guattari's outsider status among philosophers and created an unshakeable second fiddle syndrome: "It's so hard being strapped onto Gilles!"[21] Guattari knew that mediatic fallout and reputational massaging in a highly narcissistic milieu were not real desiring-machines but contraptions, but they stuck to him nonetheless, spinning in the background. Of course, Guattari could be lucid about Deleuze's own predicament, commenting with levity: "I would never go and talk at a university in France (and they don't invite me). But Deleuze, for example, is planted, tied like a goat to the university."[22]

Yet there remain other clues. At an especially Oedipal witching hour in Guattari's journal that appears in *The Anti-Oedipus Papers*, he wrestles with a litany of psychoanalytic complaints. On a night, then, in September, 1971 in Cour-Cheverny, the molecules flow and reveal that there is something else in the mix. Guattari notes:

> Isn't it precisely what happened the other night, and what is the point of this dream, when, taking advantage of the confusing effect of the Gamma OH, I told Arlette [Donati] about my desire to put an end to this oppressive conjugality?[23]

Guattari's head gets "foggy" on the brink of the oedipal precipice. Yet he is roused enough to deal with the effects of depression, a sleep disorder, anxiety, antisocial feelings, and couples issues. Rewinding a little earlier in August at

Dhuizon in the same year, Guattari writes: "Gamma OH last night. Arlette woke me up and I talked to her under the—relative—effects of the 'drug.' We have to change things. Regain some independence."[24] A questioning tone: what is Gamma OH? Are its effects relative as in mild? Is this stretch of what might be called *controlled self-medication* an admission of depression—without recourse strictly speaking to the clinical entity ("disorder") that goes under this name in contemporary diagnostics.

Berardi insists: "The methodology of *Anti-Oedipus* is not easy to reconcile with the possibility if delving into depression. . . . *Anti-Oedipus* does not know depression; it continuously overcomes, leaping with psychedelic energy over any slowing down and any darkness."[25] *Anti-Oedipus* would represent a cleavage between Guattari's theoretical work and his personal life. This distance is already alluded to by Guattari, and deepened by the conjugal issues. Today, Gamma OH is a controlled substance in most countries around the world; it is known as GHB or diversions from Xyrem, a drug for treating narcolepsy. Guattari's remark about Gamma OH's "confusing effects" likely refers to a known side effect of induced sleep—grogginess upon waking. This corresponds to the classical "post-high slowness"[26] valorized elsewhere. It is impossible to tell whether Guattari's insomnia was a cause or effect of the Gamma OH, either of which is entirely possible. Would Guattari have otherwise spoken to Arlette about their situation and his desire for them to figure out what to do about how they were no longer working together? Many of us know the contours of such conversations, with or without any medication.

In an interview, Berardi has remarked: "In depression, there is a cognitive, philosophical and political content that, I feel, was not fully developed by Guattari."[27] While Berardi clarifies that he is referring to a deep "personal depression" into which Guattari fell in the 1980s and that his friend's commitment to Green politics was simply a way of holding on during a rough period, the diagnosis of depression also refers to earlier periods, as well as to his final years. Guattari was a trained "mixer of substances" in Berardi's estimation, drawing upon young Félix's failed attempt to study pharmacy—perhaps we should say semiochemistry—at university, and the depression that periodically gripped him throughout his life put Guattari's desire at odds with the real: "When you realize that your desire no longer has any place in the real. This is the deep core of depression. If you insist in not wanting to see this fact, you end up continuing to use tools that prevent you from acting."[28]

UNHAPPY DEPRESSION: FRAGILE AND SEXY

Desiring energy gets trapped in couples issues, and Berardi meditates both on Guattari's last partner, the much younger Joséphine whose presence divided his friends—"this depression, we called it Joséphine"—and the myriad of pills on display on Guattari's desk. Berardi writes: "One day I went to see Félix. He looked more mysterious than usual, he smiled sadly and told me, pointing at the medicine bottles on his desk: you see, I prescribed all these medications for myself just to become stupid."[29] This is the same thing Guattari used to say about watching television. And Berardi, among others, has said of watching Joséphine. The year was 1986.

François Dosse's section devoted to "Joséphine" in his *Intersecting Lives* displays a curious tension. The relationship between the lovers and then newlyweds is described as "disastrous."[30] Whether there is any other kind of experience of coupledom in Guattari's vocabulary is not a moot point. The figure of Joséphine that emerges is cut from a known tapestry: beautiful junkie, doorkeeper of the expensive flat on rue Saint-Saveur from which Félix's children were barred and friends discouraged from entering; gold-digger. Berardi remembers her at the time of a visit to Bologna with Félix as "fragile and unstable, sexy in her spiky heels and black-and-while polka-dot skirt."[31] Dosse gives us his best Platonizing rendition of the situation—a cave upon whose walls are cast the shadows of a neo-mort, namely, Joséphine. These are truly Guattari's personal "winter years." His friend, artist Jean-Jacques Lebel, reported that "he [Félix] used [her] to destroy himself."[32] Yet by the time this section of Dosse's account ends, a redemption of sorts is achieved courtesy of Félix's daughter Emmanuelle. Guattari's lengthy, later depressive period, about which Berardi wrote, is the condition of the possibility of a genuine connection between father and daughter, not in the flat, but at La Borde.[33]

This connection was made possible by the depression, but it also needed a number of supports: television and prescription drugs and, earlier, Gamma OH (a mere "health supplement" at that time and not the date rape drug it would become). Television emerges as a protagonist in its own right in Dosse's account, just as powerful as any drug, as it drags Guattari along in the wake of its transductive detritus. Guattari is no video Buddha before the screen; he is an idiot, a catatonic. Dosse shows him to be hunkered down before the screen night and day, "gaping" as the box aggressively addresses its solitary viewer. It, too, cast its own shadows and influences subjectivation, establishing a well-defined territory with distinct milieu components. Emmanuelle comes to his rescue by noting that intellectually "he never stopped, even while he was in front of the television."[34] The blue hole of subjectivation—television—typically exerts a strong fascination by neutralizing becoming and blocking minoritarian proliferations. By listening to his daughter, it would seem that Guattari was an exception. He would not be defeated by television.

THE POTENTIAL OF DEPRESSION

The few fragments quoted earlier from *The Anti-Oedipus Papers* tell us that Berardi's insight that Guattari didn't tell the story of his depression—"he chose not to tell it"—is essentially sound. The depression in question is not reducible to its actual biographical details. Berardi is interested in the "cognitive potential" of depression, something much broader than Guattari's personal circumstances, and more than finding the missing pieces of *Anti-Oedipus*; he is also pursuing a different line than Negri with regard to "the winter years":

> The dissolution of shared experience is the entopy we have lived starting from a certain moment in time—we could say from the very beginning, but more intensely, painfully, rapidly, catastrophically during the 1980s. The Winter Years.[35]

Negri clings to the power of contradiction, whereas Berardi observes: "the contradiction dissolves."

Berardi defines depression as a problem connected with making sense, with meaning giving acts. The creation of sense invests in desire. And it is desire that rapidly dissipates when depression strikes: "Depression is the fallout of the megalomania in the construction of sense."[36] On the cliff-edge before the abyss of depression, enunciation fails to rise to the challenge of new questions. Berardi hints at the decompression of protention, which figured largely in the phenomenological tradition: depression meets new questions with recourse to regrets and self-reproaches about older questions, and in the process the fullness of the future deflates.[37] This hardening of the present and creation of an imaginary past is what Deleuze found in examining the links between alcoholism and depression in the novels of Fitzgerald and Lowry.[38] Depression is not stigmatized. There is a time for it, writes Berardi, when desiring energy is dispersed so that it cannot be concretized in concepts, which project sense onto a shared world: "The concepts didn't grasp reality any more." Shared experience breaks down at certain periods, and the projective concepts are no longer grasped in their world-forming potential, but instead lay on barren ground, an existential territory that has itself been depleted—"become poorer, more rarefied, and artificial."[39] Neither the existential territory nor the desiring community can support shared thought and action, whether these are in bed, on the barricades, in surprise encounters, among friends. For Berardi the fallout is that the desiring community no longer proliferates, and duty replaces desire, as provisionality fades away.

IMPOTENT GREENS

Berardi gives further texture to "the winter years" by linking Guattari's commitment to Green politics during this period to his depression. Depression has, then, another name. Having jettisoned militancy after the failure of the Italian movement of 1977 that involved counter-cultural formations outside the traditional workers' parties agitating against big unionism, state socialism, and ownership of the media,[40] Berardi would find himself on the receiving end of Guattari's friendly barbs—"jokingly but not really"[41]—about the need for getting involved in party politics. For his part, Guattari ran unsuccessfully for office under the Green banner in the Paris regional elections in 1992. He took out memberships in both factions of a split French Green Party and tried to build transversal bridges between the two and underline the necessity of dissensus for a new politics within a renewed public intellectual sphere. Berardi was not convinced that he should take this route, neither among Greens nor by seeking any public office: "For me, militant will and ideological action had become impotent."[42] Humouring Guattari, he attended meetings of the Greens and found them "senseless." This brand of politics was reducible to "pure resistance" and, thus, lacked hope because it aligned itself with ideas that had no purchase on reality. Hence, the impotence of Green politics is an enjoyable symptom of a depressive state:

> Félix knew this, I am sure, but he never said this much, not even to himself, and this is why he went to all these meetings with people who didn't appeal to him, talking about things that distracted him and making lists of deadlines and appointments.
>
> And then he would run off, adjusting his glasses to consult his overflowing daily planner. And here again is the root of depression, in this impotence of political will that we haven't had the courage to admit.[43]

Guattari developed a theory of ecosophy that aimed at regenerating depleted existential territories and making them newly inhabitable, able to sustain the creation of collective assemblages of enunciation based on eco-political and aesthetic principles that promote resingularizing subjectivations. For Berardi and others, Guattari did his best, maybe despite himself in some respects, to throw up blockages and detours in his own intimate life-world. The promise of Green politics was in Guattari's estimation an antidote to the neo-liberal myths of the 1980s and a critique of capitalist market logics following their entry into the post-revolutionary Eastern bloc. However, he was well aware of the pitfalls:

> If the ecological movement in France today, which appears to have so much promise, fails to engage with this problem of recomposing militant situations (in an entirely new sense, that is to say, of collective assemblages of subjectivation) then it will certainly lose the capital of confidence invested in it, and the

> technical and associative aspects of ecology will be recuperated by the traditional parties, State power, and eco-business."[44]

Berardi neither pinpoints the "political origin" of Guattari's depression in the Greens nor forgets Joséphine. He writes: "I just want to say that depression is born out of the dispersion of the community's immediacy. Autonomous and desiring politics was a proliferating community. When the proliferating power is lost, the social becomes the place of depression."[45] The quality of the experiences and experiments in collective enunciation such as the pirate radio station Radio Alice and in the journal *A/Traverso* were models against which Berardi assesses the dispersal of sense—it becomes impossible to find and to create. This is desire's destiny: to slacken against the youthful models that give the false impression of unending production. Again, the precipice of depression is the insight that there is no future. Protention flops. Simultaneously we get the summer of hate and the crash of the movement of workers' autonomy. The future of no future had arrived.

Picking up the relation between depression and suicide discussed earlier, Berardi maintains, following Julia Kristeva, that depressive affect is "flimsy" protective support against suicidal feelings that are stripped of anguish by a pulverized symbolic. Still, waking up to a senseless universe "comes closest to truth," Berardi asserts.[46] Depression can speak this truth and in this way gain insight into an otherwise inaccessible or deeply masked phenomenon: "Depression sees what the public discourse hides. Depression is the best condition from which to access the void that is the ultimate truth."[47] However, depressive affect reduces or destroys the meaningfulness of any action, catching in its wide berth of libidinal paralysis the ability to act on this truth and make it sharable (and this is a major struggle that the image of Guattari, slumped before the television, evokes, and that he works through by writing about it in his final published attempts to explain different varieties of affect at play in his predicament). Still, Berardi retains depression as a route into radical ontological understanding, similar to Negri's grasp of defeat, but linked to a number of mystical traditions, which I won't pursue here. Instead, I want to draw attention to how he recodes depression in the concept of chaos in Guattari and Deleuze's last writings, inflecting it in the same manner as fog and miasma but also as colours, lights, emotions.[48] Chaos is ally and enemy; so, too, is depression. If one merges with chaos through refraining, what escape route is open to depression?

DEPRESSIVE TECHNOLOGIES

Berardi has argued that one of the defining pathogenic characteristics of the digital nervous system under neo-liberalism is that the chemically maintained techno-euphoria produced an abundance of psychopathologies among which, in its heyday, CrackBerry (BlackBerry's nickname earned in 2006 but in circulation informally before then) addiction may be added as a key example. What he considers to be devastating for the mental and physical ecologies of individuals and for social relations, enterprise intellectuals began to investigate and exploit techno-obsessive-compulsive disorders, keeping them separate from economic crisis and productivity issues, but close to discipline and even the "counter-surveillance" of employers by employees.

Periodic outages in the internal data traffic management system of BlackBerry's maker Research in Motion (RIM) since 2007 reveal, as McLuhan once observed, a breakdown to be the breakthrough of an otherwise-hidden service environment. Typical press reports in North America about the disruptions walk a tightrope between habit and relief: there are executives who look at their BlackBerries every minute *even when they are not working*, and those who experience outages as the alleviation of a distressing obsessional syndrome. Outages overexpose RIM's messaging system, and the degree of double dependency plays into fears of lawsuits and loss of market share as consumers flee to the products of competitors.

The corporate valorization of an addiction as a form of discipline, and the depressive syndrome that forms around it, means that it cannot be overcome without financial consequences for the owners of the technology and its users (in other words, it is hopefully incurable), and that it may yield an escape route from this bind of an entirely different order: users who redirect their skills and remobilize their intense attachments, parameterizing their attachment, towards the creation of other worlds beyond the pathologies of capitalist discipline. These are the truly happy addicts who have turned the corner of innovation towards autonomy.

Berardi's insight that techno-addictions are made operational in the high-tech sector, whose depressive spirals are then temporarily managed by big pharma's euphoria-inducers and neuromobilizers (contrast the modern chemical battery with Guattari's flirtation with the alegal social enhancer Gamma OH), is not an end in itself but a clue to how depression might become happy. Depression spikes in direct proportion, borrowing from Alain Ehrenberg, as entrepreurism and competition come to dominate working life and become social norms.[49] Berardian post-autonomy in its simplest form involves regaining relaxation and collective processes not indexed to constant output and an economic yardstick. It is mounted as an exit sign from "corporate life . . . the antechamber of depression."[50]

CONCLUSION

Semiocapitalism describes a process of real subsumption of society by capital that is intensive and renders production progressively immaterial and makes subjectivity directly productive of value. Following Guattari's insights into the economic semiotization that marks advanced types of capitalism in the network society, Berardi pinpoints the interdependence of depression and other psychopathologies under semiocapital. Berardi finds promise in the abject conditions of networked life and labour by appealing to exceptional examples like Julian Assange and WikiLeaks and the hacker cadres of Anonymous who challenge corporate and governmental ownership of information by returning it to common and free networks for new critical uses in the name of connected intelligence. What is valorized here is not digital activism or citizen journalism. The militant psyche, modelled on Guattari and Lenin, is fragile: "Male narcissism was confronted with the infinite power of capital and emerged from it frustrated, humiliated, and depressed."[51] Bouts of depression correspond to the Bolshevik turn, the Second International, and the spring of 1917: "Leninism's intellectual decisions were so powerful because they papered over depression with an obsessive male voluntarism."[52] Berardi observed a similar syndrome with regard to Guattari's participation in both factions of the split French Green Party and the period of *The Three Ecologies*, which dates from the late 1980s. It was Guattari, however, who argued that the collective voluntarism of Leninism that precipitated the revolutionary "Leninist cut" in history failed to account for the role subjectivation played, the molecular perturbations of personality conflicts and semantic bickering, and for the signifying effects of revolutionary discourse, in the fantasmatic construction of the collective will in proletarian class consciousness, and the megalomania of Bolshevism. The radical cut changed subjectivities and rewrote signifieds, thus entering into and changing history. Once these were forgotten, the revolution could be diverted by Stalin.[53] Berardi inserts into this analysis an original parameter, Lenin's depressive bouts, and derives a Guattarian moral from them: all activists must take this into account and heed this warning—settle the bills of desire.

Today, we see the value of this, with hindsight, in the example of hacktivist Aaron Swartz, whose "depression" (although this is subject to debate)[54] turned to suicide. Swartz is perhaps best known from his 2008 "Guerilla Open Access Manifesto" in which he agitated for open access to academic publications against a climate of "private theft of public culture" by major publishing interests (specifically naming Reed Elsevier) and targeting JSTOR. His overly aggressive prosecution by the US attorney for Massachusetts, and the so-called neutral stance taken by MIT on whose campus he was apprehended, against the background of JSTOR's dropping of the case, contributed to the mounting pressures Swartz faced. Depression was not absent from Swartz's vocabulary. Perhaps it was not spoken enough. He found it impossible to be happily depressed.

Like Guattari, Berardi links depression to repetition: the hardening of and obsession with an existential refrain.[55] When everything is hung on one refrain—the militant's cause and outcome of an action—movement becomes difficult and meaning evaporates. But depression can be addressed through creative and controlled deterritorializations, a calculated chaoticization. Healing is a labour of resingularization and not a re-normalization. But this kind of healing is also interminable: desire endlessly rebooting itself. Depression has a happy outcome when desire can be refocalized and new existential refrains can be played. It is only when growth can be abandoned, and pleasure disentangled from possession, that a truly "happy adaptation" can be said to be under way in the direction of novel forms of autonomy.[56]

NOTES

1. Franco Bifo Berardi, *Soul at Work: From Alienation to Autonomy*, trans. F. Cadel and G. Mecchia, Los Angeles: Semiotext(e), 2009, p. 128.
2. Félix Guattari, *Les Années d'Hiver 1980–1985*, Paris: Les Prairies Ordinaires, 2009. New edition of the 1986 original.
3. Roger Gentis and Jean Chesnaux, "Félix, Our Friend," in *Deleuze and Guattari: Critical Assessments*, vol. 2, ed. G. Genosko, London: Taylor & Francis, 2001, p. 544.
4. Antonio Negri, "Letter to Félix on 'Social Practice,'" *Deleuze and Guattari: Critical Assessments*, vol. 2, ed. G. Genosko, London: Taylor & Francis, 2001, p. 554.
5. Félix Guattari and Antonio Negri, *New Spaces of Liberty/Les nouveaux espaces de liberté*, Paris: Dominique Bedou, 1985. Partial translation as *Communists Like Us*, trans. M. Ryan, New York: Semiotext(e), 1990.
6. Alice Jardine and Brian Massumi, "Interview with Toni Negri," in *Deleuze and Guattari: Critical Assessments*, vol. 2, ed. G. Genosko, London: Taylor & Francis, 2001, p. 564.
7. Ibid., p. 567.
8. Gilles Deleuze, "Open Letter to Negri's Judges," in *Two Regimes of Madness*, trans. A. Hodges and M. Taormina, Los Angeles: Semiotext(e), 2006, p. 170.
9. Gilles Deleuze, "This Book Is Literal Proof of Innocence," *Two Regimes of Madness*, Los Angeles: Semiotext(e), 2006, p. 173.
10. Franco Bifo Berardi, *Félix Guattari: Thought, Friendship and Visionary Cartography*, trans. G. Mecchia and C. Stivale, London: Palgrave Macmillan, 2008, pp. 4–5. Guattari's key statements appeared under the title "La Rencontre de Bologne de Septembre 1977," in *La révolution moléculaire*, Paris: Union générale éditions10/18, 1980, pp. 153–77.
11. Félix Guattari and Eric Alliez, "Capitalistic Systems, Stuctutures and Processes," in *The Guattari Reader*, ed. G. Genosko, Oxford: Blackwell, 1996), pp. 244–46.
12. Ibid., p. 244.
13. Guattari, *The Three Ecologies*, p. 47.
14. Félix Guattari, "Capital as the Integral of Power Formation," in *Soft Subversions*, trans. C. Wolfe and S. Cohen, New York: Semiotext(e), 1996, p. 220.
15. Berardi, *Félix Guattari*, p. 9.

16. Sigmund Freud (1957/2001), "Mourning and Melancholia," trans. James Strachey, *The Standard Edition*, vol. XIV (1914–16), London: Hogarth/Vintage, p. 251.
17. Ibid., p. 253.
18. Deleuze and Guattari, *A Thousand Plateaus*, p. 229; see also A. Woodward, "Deleuze and Suicide," *Deleuzian Encounters*, eds. A. Hickey-Moody and P. Malins, London: Palgrave Macmillan, 2007, pp. 62–75.
19. Gilles Deleuze and Félix Guattari, *Anti-Oedipus*, trans. R. Hurley, M. Seem, and H. R. Lane, New York: The Viking Press, 1977, pp. 19–20.
20. Berardi, *Félix Guattari*, p. 9.
21. Félix Guattari, *The Anti-Oedipus Papers*, trans. K. Gotman, Los Angeles: Semiotext(e), 2006, p. 404.
22. Félix Guattari and Suely Rolnik, *Molecular Revolution in Brazil*, trans. K. Clapshow and B. Holmes, Los Angeles: Semiotext(e), 2008, p. 442.
23. Guattari, *Anti-Oedipus Papers*, p. 326.
24. Ibid., p. 308.
25. Berardi, *Félix Guattari*, p. 11.
26. Deleuze and Guattari, *A Thousand Plateaus*, p. 282.
27. Ibid., p. 158.
28. Ibid., pp. 160–61.
29. Ibid., p. 10.
30. François Dosse, *Intersecting Lives*, trans. D. Glassman, New York: Columbia University Press, 2010, p. 425.
31. Berardi, *Félix Guattari*, p. 10.
32. Dosse, *Intersecting Lives*, p. 426.
33. See also Emmanuelle Guattari's reflection on growing up at La Borde with her father, *La petite Borde*, Paris: Mercure de France, 2012.
34. Ibid., p. 427.
35. Berardi, *Félix Guattari*, p. 11.
36. Ibid., p. 10.
37. On this point see Herbert Spiegelberg on Ludwig Binswanger, *Phenomenology in Psychology and Psychiatry*, Evanston, IL: Northwestern University Press, 1972, p. 227.
38. Gilles Deleuze, *The Logic of Sense*, trans. M. Lester, New York: Columbia University Press, 1990, p. 158.
39. Berardi, *Félix Guattari*, p. 11.
40. Franco Berardi, *After the Future*, Baltimore: AK Press, 2011, p. 48.
41. Berardi, *Félix Guattari,* p. 13.
42. Ibid.
43. Ibid.
44. Guattari, *Chaosmosis*, p. 125.
45. Berardi, *Félix Guattari,* p. 13.
46. Berardi, *After the Future*, p. 64.
47. Ibid., p. 65.
48. Berardi, *After the Future*, p. 160.
49. Berardi, *After the Future*, p. 65.

50. Ehrenberg quoted by Berardi, ibid., p. 67.

51. Ibid., p. 37.

52. Ibid., p. 38.

53. Félix Guattari, *Psychoanalysis and Transversality*, trans. A. Hodges, Los Angeles: Semiotext(e), 2015, p. 247ff.

54. Peter Singer and Agata Sagan, "The Death of Aaron Swartz," *The New York Review of Books* (January 18, 2013). Accessed on July 21, 2014. http://www.nybooks.com/blogs/nyrblog/2013/jan/18/death-aaron-swartz/

55. Berardi, *Soul at Work*, p. 216.

56. Berardi, "How to Heal a Depression," p. 3. http://www.16beavergroup.org/bifo/bifo-how-to-heal-a-depression.pdf.

Chapter 6

Black Holes of Drugs and Politics

> Drugs. Ditto. Stupid drugs, machinic drugs. . . .
>
> —Guattari[1]

Gamma OH is the first subject of this investigation. We made the acquaintance of this substance in the previous chapter. In order to understand Guattari's use of it, we will need to understand what sort of substance it is and where it stands semiochemically. But evidence is scant. How, then, does one best mount a series of contexts in which the relation of Félix-Gamma OH may be critically understood? Of equal importance is the link between Gamma OH and the couple, which tends to be identified with the women in his life—for example, Arlette and Joséphine, among others. But the journal entries from *The Anti-Oedipus Papers* ask us something else. Another couple in question was Félix and Gilles, not a conjugal couple, but a couple consisting of, to borrow Deleuze's words, mutual "mediators" engaged in a cross-creation through falsification.[2] The couple cannot be restricted to the conjugal pair, or the heterosexual couple, married or otherwise. Status before the law is not the issue. Guattari insists that the conjugal couple is not engaged in mutual mediation but, rather, in " 'low-heat' self-destruction through the other one's fire."[3] This makes the conjugal couple the "elementary social structure in a capitalist regime" that bestows a fraudulent identity and legitimacy, but remains beholden to the oedipal triangle that overcodes and alienates desire. For Guattari, "the couple's intimacy oozes death like jealous honey."[4]

What about a third party, that is, a child? For Guattari "the perversion of the couple finds its completion only in the interdiction of the third party."[5]

His daughter and son provide, respectively, too much oedipal desire for Félix to bear. Yet a conjugal de-coupling reveals something else at play that the son can confirm. In order to get at the relation of Félix and Gamma OH one needs to go through Bruno. I will conclude on this passage.

In the meantime, my broader focus will be on Guattari's position on drugs and their social significance, as well as how drug-taking fits into his theorization of subjectivity. Drugs posed intractable problems for Guattari, although his productive use of Gamma OH in the construction of his own subjectivity should not be taken as evidence of an attitude of casual experimentation with illicit drugs and alcohol. Extrapolating from astrophysics, Guattari reassigned the concept of black hole to social and psychical referents as a gap that contains "hyper-concentrations of energy,"[6] attracting sign-particles, passions, affects, redundancies, and representations. It can trap these components, therefore inhibiting subjectivation, or release newly charged particles that are liberatory for desire in any number of ways.

Many drugs, both legal and otherwise, would seem to count as substances that increase powers of action, and while Guattari supported decriminalization of all illicit drugs, especially marijuana in the light of France's draconian search and seizure legislation against which he signed, along with Deleuze and many others, "L'Appel du 18 joint,"[7] he also debunked the Beat mythologization of drug culture. Drug addiction is for him a black hole of signifying disempowerment, echoes of which are heard in the far reaches of one's universes of reference, fatally attracting numerous components of subjectivation. Robert Castel has put it this way: drug addiction organizes one's entire existence around a dominant biographical line that grabs and holds a number of redundancies in a set pattern.[8] This is what Guattari calls the "echoes of the black hole" that form around some drug-taking and introduce strong reverberations (i.e., all the components get hitched to the black hole and support it exclusively, despite the fact that it rests on nothing). Yet at the same time black holes emit very special Guattarian particles, part-signs, that defy the semiological strata and are creative, loosening, and unblocking (even if sometimes they unblock reactionary and racist tendencies). "Drugs do not guarantee immanence": this statement in *A Thousand Plateaus* clarifies that the authors were not seduced by stoner talk about the specific perceptions that substances grant their users.[9] In other words, the study of Gamma OH establishes one among many features of a pharmaco-ontology that Guattari developed in his work that stretches from licit to illicit, controlled use to addiction. I begin with a description of his sense of the forces that drug users confront. It is worthwhile noting at this juncture that Gamma OH, in its contemporary form as the club drug GHB, is addictive unlike many other such drugs. Therefore, the recourse to Guattari's addiction discourse is not without an anchor in the semiochemistry in question, although his personal use of Gamma OH is not easily linked to addiction.

The second focal point of this chapter is politics, specifically the proliferation of micropolitical fascisms around the American presidency of Donald Trump.

Guattari thought it was a good idea to discuss the topic of fascism freely while it was still possible to do so. This ominous remark opened an intervention he made in 1973 on the occasion of an Italian conference on "Psychoanalysis and Politics." It is worth noting that this talk eventually got translated into English under the title "Everybody Wants to Be a Fascist," while the more pedestrian title "The Micro-Politics of Fascism" is also in use by other translators.[10] It is the former provocative title that quickens the pulse because it seems to implicate us all in an attraction that on the face of it we purport to resist. The key question for Guattari is, then, the relationship between desire and fascism. Let me put it somewhat simply, but nonetheless poignantly: fascism is immanent to desiring-production: fascism "seems to come from the outside, but it finds its energy right at the heart of everyone's desire."[11] Fascism is everywhere, and to desire is to activate it in some measure at different scales within a microphysics of power relations. Fascism is not merely a historical phenomenon (with German, Italian, and Spanish varieties) that has passed away and will never happen again; it is not outside, that is, retrievable and renewable like a complete artefact, in that respect. Guattari would outline three approaches to fascist movements in order to develop his own theory of micropolitical fascisms relevant to his and our contemporary contexts. His approach is neither historical nor sociological; indeed, it is not a political theory that defines fascism "macropolitically" in relation to the totalitarian state, which with it shares certain features. Guattari believed it was necessary to conduct a micropolitical examination of the molecules of fascism because it has survived its historical mutations and adapted itself to contemporary institutions, knowingly or unknowingly clinging to subcultural and political expression: "It passes through the tightest mesh; it is in constant evolution."[12] Guattari's approach renders moot the question whether fascism can rise again, and dispels the naïvité of those who are astonished that their beloved democratic institutions could ever support it, in any form.

BLACK HOLES OF SUBJECTIVATION

Most readers of Guattari may be familiar with his two primary examples of redundancy—faciality and refrains. Corresponding to these dominant redundancies are resonances that have various effects depending on the type of existential consistency in which they are found (signifying resonances are paired with redundancies of machinic interaction in Guattari's analysis of coordinates of efficiency): they have weak effects in highly stratified, overcoded, and hierarchized molar consistencies; and strong effects in rhizomaticized, more malleable, molecular milieux; or display capitalist abstractions (capital "P" Power) of abstract consistency with more machinic interactions of abstract machines and part-signs. Redundancies of resonance are linked to signification—rigid and literal translations, for example, in the molar; or diverse semantic fields in the molecular; and constellations of part-signs in the abstract. "Capitalistic faciality proceeds by redundancies of resonance and by binary reduction," Guattari maintains.[13] These are the least machinic redundancies since they "work to subjugate desire." Likewise, "a face is always associated with a refrain; a significative redundancy with a face, with the tone of a voice."[14] For Guattari, redundancies play leading roles in the formation and interaction of the components of semioticization, subjectivation, and consciousness.

Modelling his theory on triangular forms, Guattari adapts the classic triangle of meaning. From left to right across the base one moves from *signifier* to *matter* along the nominalist designation, either approaching or withdrawing from it; on top of which is the *soul or interpretant or mental reference* (approaching or withdrawing from the divine signification) in order to show how the individuated subject is an artefact of semiological subjection. The angle of significance opens on the left side of the triangle (marking individuation) stretching rightward onto a space of representation across the triangle. Semiological formulae are imposed upon individuated subjects, and Guattari derives seven of these from semiotic functions and stacks them in a triangular form converting semiological into subjective redundancies in three types: those based on the three angles of the triangle (symbol/referent/reference = asignifying/morphemes/icons) and on the sides (designation/representation/signification) and on the centre (subjective). He then recodes these semiological redundancies in nosological terms in order to describe seven reterritorializations of consciousness. From left to right beginning across the base:

REFERENCE

Iconic/Hysteric

Signification/Interpretation—Subjective/Anxiety—Representation/Paranoia

Asignifying/Obsessional—Designation/Phobic—Morphemes of the Referent/Schizoid

SYMBOL REFERENT

Although he borrows much of his conceptual language regarding resonance from René Thom, as Watson has pointed out,[15] there are limits clearly set out by Guattari. For Thom, resonance involves a kind of objectively verifiable mutual influence, as in his example of the tuning forks. It is instructive to fill in the ellipses in Watson's quote:

> Consider two identical tuning-forks D and D', and suppose that D is vibrating. If we bring D close to D', then D' starts to vibrate by resonance with D. Part of

> the kinetic energy of D is thus transferred to the tuning fork D', which vibrates synchronically with D. Fundamentally, that is the schema typical of all resonance: at the start we are given two completely independent dynamical systems S and S' which both present stable dynamic regimes R and R'. The two systems are brought closer together so that they can interact freely. In general the composite system thus obtained becomes unstable, for instead of having the simple topological product S x S' of the two systems, with the product regime R x R', in general, there will be degeneration towards a common, more stable regime, the regime of resonance. Each of the systems S and S' loses its individuality and there will only be a mixed system which, in practice, is indecomposable.[16]

The outline of influence on Guattari is clear enough: there are a transfer of energy (and a presupposition of common vibratory modes), a degeneration of individualities, and a common regime. However, for Guattari, resonance also involves interference. Thom also wanted to describe the "feeling of meaning" between the individuated subject and the soul in terms of different degrees of resonance—in terms of the relative stability of mental representation—" 'acute resonance' between the concepts evoked by words and real properties of objects in the external world."[17] Guattari rejected this reductive, conformist approach that "smooths over semiotic rough patches [mouline les aspérités sémiotiques]" for the sake of his diagrammatic, dynamic, transformational, transversal schizoanalytic cartography which "facilitates the extraction of proliferating singularities and the blossoming of minor languages." In short, Guattari rejected outright Thom's recourse to mediating, invariant representations of agreement for a theory in which meaning is neither central nor beholden to such "sharp resonance": thus, when Thom asks "can we not agree that the factors of phenomenological invariance, which create in the observer the feeling of meaning, come from real properties of the objects of the external world and the objective presence of formal entities linked to those objects, which we call 'bearers of meaning'?"[18] Guattari cannot agree. Why? The problem with Thom's version of the semiological assemblage is that it doesn't permit a critical interrogation of the limits of "feeling" (both conformist and radical) and how representation hides dominant codes of social and semiological subjection at the heart of resonance. Thom admits variations on resonance effects—blurred in the case of weak, unstable, and fluctuating effects on the independence of the systems at stake; and sharp, where a stable interaction not only strongly effects the independence of the systems but also permits a noiseless superimposition of the features of one upon the other.[19]

Within the redundancies of consciousness, resonance produces a black hole effect that does two things: it recentres and disempowers the semiological redundancies and empties them of content, but at the same time machinically super-empowers them by granting them autonomy. The redundancies of resonance become more and more deterritorialized, less and less efficient, but extremely powerful. At the same time, the redundancies of consciousness ensure that subjectivity loses all of its coordinates, so that it turns in on itself. This is the black hole of subjectivity that exists at the centre of the semiological triangle. Resonance in addition is transferred to one or more of the redundancies of consciousness where it sets up a bastion from which it controls the others; these are named by Guattari following typical clinical syndromes, one of which exercises special influence. The important point is that the black hole has both disempowering and superpowerful effects; its energy may release particles that escape from all systems of redundancies. It is both involutive and potentially creative. Thus, Guattari adapts Thom's terminology but in the process retains, in addition to the degenerative dimension of resonance (disempowerment) in the triggering of a black hole of subjectivity, the hypothetical "quanta of possibility" carried by the matters of expression (a-signifying part-signs) emitted from it.

If we pick up Thom's statement about resonance here, the regime of resonance is consonant with a centred system.[20] Such a signifying regime is defined by redundancy of the "pure formal" type—a facialized signifier. It is one among several such regimes, and its privilege is called into question. Guattari borrows indecomposability to express the absolutely indestructible character of the abstract machines (matter-function pilots) and the inability to break them down and sort them into semiological distinctions. Ultimately, what is most basic for Guattari is the mixity of sign systems—semiotic hybridity—abandoning signifying representations for parts without wholes.

One of Guattari's most compelling deployments of the black hole effect is in his description of the kind of subjectivation arising from the use of hard drugs. In the phrase "echoes of the black hole" he captures a general phenomenon of collapse that gets caught up with a range of different "drugs"—whether these are a favourite rock band, recourse to mind-altering behaviours, building, maintenance and practice of a territory, or a ritual.[21] These attachments "provide a sensation of belonging to something, of being somewhere, along with the sensation of forgetting oneself."[22] One of Guattari's most amusing examples is a kind of machinic doping that concocts new subjectivations—like hitting a bucket of golf balls alongside other enthusiasts in the early morning at an urban driving range. Black holes generate echoes and in the case of hard drug consumption do so in a micro-fascist way. Guattari writes:

> These black holes swarm and proliferate across the social field. The question is whether subjectivity is going to echo them in a way that an individual's entire life, all one's modes of semiotization, depend upon a central point of anguish and guilt. I propose this image of a black hole in order to illustrate the

> phenomenon of the complete inhibition of semiotic components of an individual or group which finds itself cut off from any possibility of an exterior life. By the expression "echo of a black hole" I aim to establish resonances among several systems of blockages (i.e, you have a stomach cramp and you can no longer think about it; you "embody" it; you invest an erogenous zone on your pain; you persecute your partner, your children, and all these domains begin to resonate). (Trans. adjusted).[23]

Systems of blockages begin to resonate together—vibrate synchronically—under the influence of one or more black holes. While on the one hand the components of consciousness, reterritorialized in nosographic redundancies, create the subjective black hole by presenting subjectivity with the nothingness of the empty resonances that sets it spinning; on the other hand, the black holes manipulate these nuclei of nothingness from consciousness and semiosis by forcing them to a limit from which they cannot escape (but this limit is porous enough to permit the sign-particles to pass through). These strange a-signifying particles carry "charges of nothingness" but depending on how consciousness has arrayed the semiotic components of signifying disempowerment over the black hole, subjectivity merely affirms their impotency by echoing them, or gives them free reign. Super-empowered, deterritorializing sign-particles are born in a place of grief and distress.[24]

Few escape from this resonating black hole of hard drug use, Guattari claims, even those who either theatricalize their addictions, like rock star junkies, or those who emulate or seek advice from them; "happy addicts" are rare, compared with the "happy depressives" that Berardi diagnosed in the previous chapter. Collective drugs like fascism are difficult to shake. Guattari was not very sympathetic to hard drugs, referring to them as fundamentally microfascist and precipitating "molecular assemblages of desire that crystallize subjectivity in a vortex of abrogation."[25] While Guattari is interested in the chemical properties of drugs, specifically in the production of machinic buzzes, that is, endorphins and how they may be generated by activities as diverse as jogging or the existential abyss of Kafka's solitude as it is revealed in reading his diaries, he also dwells on the sociosemiotic dimension of the complex drug-taking assemblage and how it produces a certain kind of individuated subjectivity, namely, one of "solitude without recourse" (exacerbated by hard drugs) or the more hopeful route of soft drug use that entails the "complete inability to accept any form of solitude, and a constant call to all kind of dependency, all the 'hang-ups' (sports, television, conjugality, work, place in the hierarchy, etc.)."[26] Guattari believed that soft drugs are vehicles of social critique and held some potential for self-reinvention because they occupied a "lesser" place in collective assemblages. Soft drugs possess some measure of diagrammatic, transformative energy; Guattari wrote: "I know certain intellectuals who smoke a lot of marijuana, and this stimulates them in their work. Conversely, this is not true of other drugs where there is a rapid degradation of the mental faculties (cocaine, for example)."[27] However, his use of the related concepts of echo and resonance reveals the degree of entrapment by hard drug use and how this captures and engulfs all parts of life.

THE MANY NAMES OF GAMMA OH

The centring of the black hole of subjectivity over drug use with the qualitative differences between the effects of hard and soft drugs, not necessarily rehearsing the distinction between illegal and legal drugs, but emphasizing the quite different elements of exploitation and persecution pertaining to each, brought Guattari to the position that some creative components may be emitted and used to loosen the "hang-ups" mentioned earlier. One of these hang-ups was married or partnered life, a key reference for Guattari in working through the potential of soft drug use, including his own use of Gamma OH. But as I cautioned earlier, the couple is not the only context of reference and Gamma OH was not illegal at the time of his writing in 1971. There are a number of contributing resonances to the pull inward, and fly outward, from Guattari's subjective black holes.

Is Gamma OH—gamma hydroxybutyrate—a drug? The discovery of Gamma OH—a French trade name—in the early 1960s is credited to the French biologist and cybernetician Henri Laborit. In his Laboratoire d'Eutonologie in the Boucicaut hospital, Laborit added an OH (hydroxyl) molecule to the carbon of butyric acid (decreasing oxidation) in an effort to develop an anaesthetic, not unlike the use of ketamine or "special k" in emergency wards today. Gamma OH was used in childbirth as a substitute for nitrous oxide.[28] Since it is a naturally occurring neurotransmitter, it was not for much of its early life a regulated substance, even in modified form. Many of the positive qualities of Gamma OH are attributed to Laborit's proselytizing efforts and have persisted within the cultural profile of the substance that has attracted interest from a series of subcultures over the decades. Its reputation is multiplex—sleep enhancer, anti-anxiety disinhibitor or sociabilizer (euphoric properties), aphrodisiac, antidepressant, and so on, and it eases withdrawal symptoms. The list is long and tenuous. One wonders whether this is in part attributable to Laborit's countercultural credentials as professor-theorist of interdisciplinarity at Vincennes[29] or the remarkable attributes of the molecule itself as non-toxic. The "drug's" availability as a nutritional supplement in health and sex shops made it attractive for recreational uses within, first in the 1970s, countercultural circles in its capacity to strip away social inhibitions; second in the 1980s, the body-building community because of its characteristics of reducing appetite and encouraging the release of growth hormones; third, in the 1990s, within the gay and rave club cultures due to its mood-enhancing and alleged aphrodisiacal properties, heightening clitoral and penis sensitivity; most recently in the zero zero decade, it has gained notoriety as an acquaintance rape drug because of its capacity to induce sleep and leave ambiguous trace levels in its victims. The current cultural profile of Gamma OH is embedded in its lists of stoner and sexist names—Liquid E, G, Easy Lay, and so on, and studies of its illicit and recreational applications reveal a good deal of contradictory data, although few dispute the severe side effects that may occur when it is either willingly or surreptitiously mixed with alcohol, cocaine, and ecstasy, and some confusion persists about its chemical identity (i.e., it is unlike "E" or MDMA yet often takes its name in whole or in part).[30] During the period of Guattari's controlled experiments with Gamma OH, the substance was unregulated, which he flags by putting the word in quotes effecting a "rhetorical displacement" as one sees with similar references to tobacco and alcohol.[31]

The black hole connected with conjugality is echoed by the Gamma OH; yet, in this resonance there is something positive, not merely anti- as in antidepressive. Rather, with Deleuze, Guattari wrote: "It may be necessary for the release of innovative processes that they first fall into a catastrophic black hole: stases of inhibition are associated with the release of crossroads behavior. On the other hand, when black holes resonate together or inhibitions conjugate and echo each other, instead of an opening onto consistency, we see a closure of the assemblage."[32] Guattari experimented with a "molecule" in order to find an opening and elude the echo chamber of couplehood, even though he selected a substance with an uncertain potential to convert stasis into release. The conjugal couple was intersected by colliding echoes of the collaboratory work of Félix-Gilles.

Berardi fondly remembers his friend Félix as the one who "brought the molecules" to his collaborations. But how does one reconcile this with the difficulty of "choos[ing] the right molecule"? After all, even "drug" users do not exactly choose under the effects of the black hole's echoes. Yet this is the predicament that Guattari found himself in and tried to work through by experimenting with a molecule with enough diagrammatic force to serve as a component of passage, to form bonds, and excited by the black hole's own active energy, escape from it. Even if Bifo's account of Guattari's life in the 1980s and early 1990s suggests that his escape was not fully accomplished, that he could not beat his depression, there remains a constancy to the convergence of self-medication and an involutive conjugality.

Why are echoes of a black hole of subjectivity so dangerous? Echoes are reflective resonance phenomena that provide alibis for the false separation of all the components they hang on a single involutive process. The delayed reflection of an echo creates the illusion of separation from its source. Moreover, as an echo, path may move around more and more of the affected components and their inter-componential relations may evoke the same denial, thereby expanding the stifling draw of the black hole. Guattari investigated the properties of Gamma OH as a diffuser rather than as a canceller of echolalic capture. The choice of a "natural" antidepressant seems sufficiently benign, given the substance in question flew under the radar of control, yet the hippy disinhibitor has its own inhibiting dimensions, which Guattari recognized in the intimate yet strictly exceptional synonymity of closure and creation, that is, when a mild buzz gets good results; Laborit's own description of preliminary studies in the early 1960s using Gamma OH in psychiatry evokes a countercultural assemblage in the "pleasant hypnotics" the drug produces. The pernicious version of this soft machine has been widely discussed—a drug "grants" something to its user that would otherwise remain inaccessible and that inhibitions of one sort or another would otherwise suppress. Laborit's strategy from the outset was not to inhibit but to select orientation, to enhance sociality and conviviality, rather than blunt emotions or reduce interests.

For Guattari the bastions along the echo path are problematically productive, and that taking Gamma OH is not an obviously effective way of surviving a relationship, but a means nonetheless unfortunately resonant with depression. And one of the most difficult things for depression is to connect with a liberatory machine. One black hole may find and connect with another, both of which resonate with conjugality: a break-up and rebound: "Naively, I had thought I was done forever with this kind of conjugality!" Guattari wrote of his break-up with Donati, "But I got right back into it, and this time by my own doing. . . . I immediately dove right back into the bitter joys of jealous madness with it domestic vertigo and conjugal possession."[33]

Guattari attempted to model the double-bind of the couple in expansive terms of 2+n persons that leads to the pair's dissolution, and in oedipal terms as 3–n in which jealousy of the imaginary homosexual body of the lover, reflected narcissistically, fabricates a family drama.

The couple is a recurrent theme that reaches past the heterosexual pair into the world of the homosociality of collaboration, another coupling that Guattari consistently interrupted via many women in a series of conjugal enunciations. Deleuze, for his part, in regaining the mythology of desert islands placed the couple at the origin, but not at the new beginning, in this way ensured that the "more essential" second origin could not be reduced to such a clichéd form.[34]

Reading Guattari's brief journal entries conjures a reference to Walter Benjamin that is perhaps inescapable. Amid the buoyant literary highs and freedoms from desire, tricks of speech, colour, space, and time, a knot forms during Benjamin's experiments with various drugs: it is the loosening knot of a junkie couple (with a preference for opium), his cousin Egon and his wife Gertrude. Hashish heightens the sensual relations Benjamin had with her but devolved into a depression that was intimately bound up with this passion. Egon's jealousy flairs and Gert dances before Benjamin—"What odalisques can do for pashas when they dance before them, Gert did for me. But suddenly there broke from her lips a torrent of abuse . . . hours later [after] attempts at consolation . . . I could not longer be saved."[35] Benjamin reminds us that a couple is never simply two persons, but is mediated by a number of others and things and spaces. This is a hallmark of institutional analysis, and it directs us into the institution of the couple par excellence, marriage, and all forms of partnership.

BROKEN LINES OF DESIRE

Throughout his writings, Guattari mentions in passing in a number of places the issues raised by couples; for him the couple is on par with the family as a site that warrants critical scrutiny, but it is a concern that crosses multiple domains from the "dual" analytic situation and the transference, which he sought to transversalize, to his awkward memories of his jealousy of Arlette Donati with whom he lived in the 1960–1970s as he recounts in his own dream analysis, discussed in chapter 4. Guattari also found some impetus for new collective assemblages of enunciation in minoritarian homosexual desire: "Once there's heterosexuality, in fact, once there's marriage, there's no more desire, no more sexuality. In all my twenty-five years of work in the field I've never seen a heterosexual married couple that functioned along the lines of desire."[36] Yet homosexual conjugality was a typical form of semiosocial subjugation and an Oedipal trap for desire. Adolescents are subjugated by normativity like heterosexual sexuality, and the revolutionary becomings that puberty bring are quickly tied up by social controls and internalized fantasies about normal adulthood and "joining the usual circuit," with an opposite sex partner in tow. In a more promising light Deleuze imagined "nuptials without couples or conjugality skirting a ponderous, transcendent heteronormative conjugality."[37]

Experimentally self-medicating with Gamma OH is an echo of the subjective black hole formed over the conjugal couple Félix-Arlette, but vibrates with the collaboration of Félix-Gilles. Highly diffuse echoes of this black hole overlap as Guattari struggled during the period of the writing of *Anti-Oedipus* with the demands of recurring bouts of depression, his separation with Arlette, and demands of the solitude of writing, which took him out of the group creation with which he was most comfortable. He complains about being chained to his journal. He struggles with the manuscript of *Psychanalyse and transversalité*, which also appeared in 1972. He can't see himself in the polished pages of *Anti-Oedipus*—"it's so hard, being strapped onto Gilles!"[38] The powerful image of the strap-on will reappear in the chapter on the collaboration of Félix and Gilles in the following section.

Bruno opens up another route into the Félix-Gamma OH ligature. Trained as a biochemist and employed in Laborit's lab for some ten years from 1981 to 1992, Félix's son views Gamma OH as a hospital drug—administered only in a hospital—invented for use in anaesthesiology. Gamma OH may be counted among a range of "[dis]inhibitors of inhibitions" like antidepressant Minaprine that did have psychiatric applications, and Laborit visited La Borde through the assistance of Jean-Pierre Muyard, a psychiatrist working at La Borde and described as a "professional networker" by Dosse, to conduct a clinical trial.[39] The results of this trial appeared in Laborit's journal *Agressologie* in 1972, roughly corresponding to the period of Guattari's mentions of Gamma OH in his journal in the summer and fall of 1971.[40] The Laborit-Guattari meeting was the occasion for Félix's experimentation with Gamma OH, but also proved felicitous when Bruno was much later looking for a lab position to fulfil his residency requirements.

Whether Gamma OH was successfully deployed as a diffuser of resonance heightened by different kinds of couplings is perhaps less the issue than what the interpretation of the episodes tells us about the complexity of resonant phenomena where colliding echoes—some more relevant, others more tangential and false—have multiple effects ranging from confusion (masking echoes) to coherence (finding a stable resonance frequency). The regimes of colliding echoes and overlapping frequencies move energy around but remain trapped by disempowering influences and ambiguous becomings-other.

Gamma OH and GHB, two different functional names for the same substance, open onto widely divergent cultural lives between anaesthesiology to pill-popping in club land,[41] from childbirth to drink spiking and acquaintance rape, from bodybuilding to very occasional, experimental self-medication.

BLACK HOLES OF POLITICS: RESONANCES OF MICROFASCISM

Guattari's first approach to fascism is to develop a threefold typology of how its forms are typically analysed. He starts with a sociological category, based on analytical-formalist distinctions that identify species of fascism (national historical types); finds common traits among them; and then describes small differences between them. Differences are minimized the more commonness is elevated, and differences are magnified the more they help to isolate layers and kinds. He finds little of interest in this approach.

The second approach he notes is neo-Marxist thought grounded in a synthetic-dualist paradigm. The approach here is to appreciate how to both acknowledge the revolutionary desire of the masses and recognize the mediations from Marxism's theoretical vocabulary imposed upon them, indeed, "massifying" mass-desire: "restored to standardized formulations whose necessity is deemed to be justified in the name of the cohesion of the working class and party unity."[42] Overcoming the distinction between theoretical description and revolutionary praxis yields only the dualist trap of the code-wielding political caste and the obedient mass followers, which is played out reductively and its impotence multiplied along a series of "schematic oppositions" (i.e., city/country; good and bad camps) and a unique third object (the power of the State) that gives meaning to them. He wishes to outflank such dualisms and their distancing mechanisms.

Thirdly, Guattari mounts what he calls an analytic-political approach that he makes his own. He does not abandon the question of what kind of state is built under fascism, but he reserves this investigation for elsewhere in *A Thousand Plateaus*, to which I will return momentarily. In the meantime, the third approach launches a series of provisos: "A micropolitics of desire would no longer present itself as representing the masses and as interpreting their struggles."[43] At the same time he doesn't entirely reject the need for a political analysis of party lines and actions, and underlines the importance of diversifying and pluralizing any already-formed and centralizable wholes into social groupings beyond the working class and its set task of dissolving the contradiction its embodies, refusing to yoke it to dominant expressions of its character, whatever these might be, that allow it to carry out unique tasks according to stated objectives of its party in relation to the mediations of the transcendent object of the state. No more Leninist exhortations straight out of the "April Theses" of spring 1917 to make the masses see the true form of revolutionary government and to interpret their practical needs in this light.[44] Instead, a conception of desire without an object, without a centre either in a person or in a body, constituted as ideally pre-unified. Desire is multiple and different; it consists of singular intensities that combine with one another in incompatible ways, rather than in terms of identities that may be totalized by a party apparatus, that is, "by the totalitarian machine of a representative party."[45] Lenin, it may be said, tried to tap into the molecular revolutionary forces that expressed themselves in a unique moment of hope, and for this he was considered to have gone mad. This is the Lenin Slavoj Zizek admires and wants to regain; yet as I just pointed out, the contrary tendencies at play in the "April Theses" are just as strongly expressed through specific representations and interpretations, that is, direction and explanation of the non-spontaneous awakening of desire of a mass of proletarians as it is coaxed into existence and led to make the right choices by the mobilized party.

Nevertheless, Guattari claims mediators must be bypassed in the relationship between social objectives and praxis. Desire tends to wander and to get off topic and away from ready-made encodings. A micropolitical analysis of desire doesn't represent what is already formed but contributes to the formation and thus is "immediately political." What does Guattari mean when he claims that "when saying is doing" micropolitics is immediately political? No more specialists either of saying or of doing. Collective assemblages (rather than individual idiolects) within the mass find their own means of expression, perhaps combining fragments of archaic discourses, recontextualized images, slang, and recycled codes. A rehearsal of the correct slogans is not required. It is theoretically messy to give permission to the masses to speak. There are no guarantees. The crystallization of situational collective desires in utterances, and other semiotic materials always struggle with the influence of dominant overcodings and are directly linked into machinic processes of all kinds, like mangling auto-correct functions, that underline the distorting a-signifying elements of contemporary communication. Theorists of digital disobedience, especially distributed denial of service attacks, note that the a-signifying dimension of disabling and "disrupting" servers is closely tied to the imperative to communicate in contemporary capitalism, and with the focus on circulation over meaning, breaking the "reproducible signal value" of messages, that texting and social media have perfected, acquires a powerful effect of redirecting attention away from the usual suspects of the sending and receiving estates in the name of new stakeholders.[46]

There are all kinds of fascisms: "A micropolitics of desire means that henceforth we will refuse to allow any fascist formula to slip by, on whatever scale it may manifest itself, including within the scale of the family or even within our own personal economy."[47] Fascism is irreducible to historical phenomena like National Socialism. Its study is not the purview of professional historians. No one should bury it in historical periodicity and feel relief that it is over; the good guys having triumphed in the end in the beautiful confluence of the Red Army and Allied forces at the River Elbe, and meeting of the heads of state at Yalta. There wasn't only one Nazi Party: Guattari wants to avoid simplifications that make us blind to how the elements of certain historical forms of fascism continue to exist. Fascism leaps transhistorically between generations and adapts itself to new conditions along the way: "What set fascism in motion yesterday continues to proliferate in other forms, within the complex of contemporary social space."[48] Fascisms proliferate and never stop adapting.

Updating Guattari, the icons of Hitlerism may be combined with Donald Trump's name by those, for or against him, who have no need of any firm ideas about Nazism. To see a graffito like swastika-r.u.m.p. as a micro-crystallization of fascism adapted to our contemporary political landscape requires a reflection on the digital source materials for semiotic production. Indeed, a good place to begin is Dale Beran's attempt to formulate an interpretation of Trump's appeal through the mutations of 4chan—the "opprobrious" image board and sprawling forums/chat site launched in 2003 and known for its incivility and creativity as incubator of Anonymous, trolling, rickrolling, memes, and just doing it for the lulz.[49] The Guattarian theory of desire both de-centres the individual person as source and the object as lack instead positing an assemblage of mutable heterogeneous components as a process that is auto-organizing but also influenced by dominant historical trends, such as the mutual imbrications of humans and machines in the time of immaterial labour and production. But Guattari is a kind of Arendt in full reverse. If humans are cogs, and they are machinically enslaved, there is potential there, because they no longer have the kinds of social identities that are easily alienated. On 4chan, anonymity is the goal but not always the rule, but based on a local ethic, individuation is strongly denied to persons and persona, until games of status erupt and off-line events intervene to manufacture celebrity. These are still largely anathema. The fusion of the post and the subjectless subject or Anon. releases intense flashes of desiring production, which can only be described as a "cesspool." For Beran, Trump is the alpha and beta, the fantasy of winning and the despair of losing, both at once rolled into the loser who won. He builds an analogy based on Charles Bukowski's novel *Factotum* in which two underpaid warehouse workers devise a scheme to accept money from their coworkers to bet on horse races but all the horses selected never win, because the bets are never placed. In the words of Manny and Henry:

> "Hank, we take their bets."
> "Those guys don't have any money—all they have is the coffee and chewing gum money their wives give them and we don't have time to mess around with the two dollar windows."
> "We don't bet their money, we keep their money."
> "Suppose they win?"
> "They won't win. They always pick the wrong horse. They have a way of always picking the wrong horse."
> "Suppose they bet on our horse?"
> "Then we know we've got the wrong horse."[50]

This is the pathetic reality of the Trumpians, according to Beran: "Younger Trump supporters know they are handing their money to someone who will never place their bets—only his own—because, after all, it's plain as day there was never any other option." Further, Beran concludes: "Support for Trump is an acknowledgement that the promise is empty." Trump's bizarre behaviour leads Beran to state "Trump is 4chan . . . a labyrinth with no centre" of swastikas, sexist jokes, and posturing. There is nothing really discordant about how this works. This is the Guattarian theory of machines (some highly abstract, others highly technical) that constantly seek out dis/connections (breaks and flows and residualities) with other machines for which they are flows. It's not exactly a Goldberg machine, but a 4chan contraption in which anonymous processes of subjectivation subsist in the bowels of unfettered digital desire: where semiological powerlessness meets machinic superpower, with strange results. The more the machine goes off the rails, the better it works, the more collectively enunciative 4chan becomes as its denizens take new formations, much to their own surprise: unstructured, ad hoc, short-lived assemblages, some of which are offline! The foundation of Trumpian politics might very well be the cesspool in which micro-fascist forces connive and collide. The cesspool is not empty. It attracts and holds the attention spans and affects of many. Guattari called this a black-hole effect: a phenomenon of subjective collapse that is attached to empty promises, and spectacularized policy, like televised executive orders that are reproduced widely in the post-mediasphere. The memefication (Sad Frog Meme) of Trump as Pepe the Frog, the spectre of this prank invoked by Hillary Clinton as a white supremacist figure, and unleashed into the wild by alt-right appropriators and anti-defamation league critics alike, demonstrated the semiotic potentiality of comic strip characters to interact with wildly diverse components from across the political spectrum.[51] The black hole both swallows up empty promises and groundless pronouncements, racist and paranoid POTUS tweets, the laments of the frog's creator Matt Furie, and spits out newly charged semiotic components that liberate the desire immanent to the political landscape and make it resonate across the alt-right mediascape.

Intense attachment fosters belonging and forgetting, and echoes them in public reproductions of the signifiers of rampant misogyny and raging xenophobia. As Bruce Bennett put it, Trump's body is a "semiotic salad"[52] that fails to cohere; and this is part of the appeal as every effort to discredit him at once builds his legitimacy among astonished believers and detractors. Mass processes of subjectivation are given but one option to align with the resonances of undelivered wagers and belligerently confirm their impotence. This is how Deleuze and Guattari define microfascism: it occupies micro-black holes and resonates among them acting on the masses through millions of catastrophes.[53] Black holes are not exactly empty, and this is where Guattari helps us to refine Beran's insight; they absorb the energy of empty promises, the unplaced bets, as it were, and trap subjectivity in their resonances across the social field, interacting with a range of political beliefs: 1950s nostalgists; emptiness is good for business yahoos; and maybe, for the millennials, a vote for emptiness is a "defiant expression of despair," as Beran describes them. It even suggests the revenge of Oedipus: help me again Mommy and Daddy I can't make it without you!

The analysis of desire's microfascism sounds a bit science-fictional, Guattari admits, but he is not deterred, because fascism is for him a dangerous, cancerous molecular phenomenon: "What makes fascism dangerous is its molecular or micropolitical power, for it is a mass movement: a cancerous body rather than a totalitarian organism."[54] It is not a question of going small for the sake of minutae, or for that of a Pascalian view of how different things would have been if Cleopatra's nose had been a bit longer.[55] Adopting the language of mutation, proliferation, and molecularity allows Guattari to think through the capacity of fascism to spread throughout the social body. And eventually try to overwhelm it, or "win" it electorally. This "potentially" gives to desire a fascist inclination since desire is not undifferentiated and instinctual, but results from highly complex and supple micro-formations and refined interactions (like so-called the Great Meme War of 2015–2016), the kind we see on Internet Relay Chat on 4chan but just as well on Breitbart News.

For Deleuze and Guattari in *A Thousand Plateaus*, what makes fascism so frighteningly catastrophic for capitalism is that, unlike totalitarianism, especially of the Stalinist type, it liberated the desire of the masses for their own deaths, in spite of themselves. They were neither tricked nor desirous of their own masochistic repression. They were not driven internally to suicide by a death drive. Rather, fascism constructs a totalitarian State that is suicidal. National Socialism was focused on destruction, of everyone, including all Germans, as a project that would resonate throughout Europe and beyond. Suicide of the state and the end of its own people would be a "crowning glory."[56] When there were no means to subdue mass desire to fulfill its own destruction (Guattari calls it a "deadly form of libidinal metabolism"), no deals can be brokered. The only option was an alliance for the US and UK with Stalinism, because its brand of terror was acceptable, a more stable and efficient system for controlling mass turbulence (by the working class, colonials, and minorities), and it too was threatened by National Socialism. For Guattari, "the last World War will thus have been the opportunity to select the most efficient totalitarian machines, those best adapted to the period."[57] Yet microfascisms have managed to seep into capitalism as Stalinism failed to molecularize its economy and labour force. Capitalism searches for new models of totalitarianism inside itself, and finds all kinds of "new forms of molecular fascism."[58] These find an environment conducive to infestation in infocapitalism's forms of affective and communicational labour that are directly productive of value.

New microfascisms find fertile ground in the fast-circulating redundancies of Internet memes and other post-media artefacts like the use of echo quotations as antisemitic signifiers. Extremely involutive black holes draw processes of subjectivation into themselves as their power increases with every iteration of them. Caught up in the pleasures of empty promises, Pepe memes, 4chan rants and actions, combover and spray tan jokes, comedic mimesis and alt-right semiotics, and staging policy by spectacle, with so many supercharges of nothingness to go around, desire cannot extract itself from the echo chamber of emptiness that modulates its existence, making it lose its bearings, finding solace in distress, that travels surprisingly well along the bubbling resonances of social media. For Guattari, "fascism, like desire, is scattered everywhere, in separate bits and pieces, within the whole social realm; it crystallizes in one place or another, depending on the relationships of force."[59] The Trump presidency is a kind of black hole into which the swirling phenomenon of emptiness is drawn, simultaneously providing an attachment that allows belonging and forgetting to coexist, as it emits forged lines of alterity: alternative facts, courtesy of Kellyanne Conway (counselor to President Trump), and bottomless post-truths that deflect and distract sober investigation and resist analysis.

Guattari reminds us that it is incumbent upon theorists of microfascism to search in the most "'incomprehensible' revolutionary transformations"[60] for investments of desire. In the transition from classical types of fascism to molecularized microfascisms, desire is at once liberated and subjected to repressive attributions tailored to new modes of production. This is why the Trump and 4chan hypothesis is so compelling as it directs us to epic fails, perhaps beginning with the inauguration: the more it breaks down, the better it works, which is the credo of Deleuze and Guattari with regard not only to capitalism, but to America as well.

NOTES

1. Guattari, *Anti-Oedipus Papers*, p. 91.
2. Gilles Deleuze, *Negotiations 1972–1990*, trans. M. Joughin, New York: Columbia University Press, 1995, p. 126.
3. Guattari, *Anti-Oedipus Papers*, p. 318.
4. Guattari, *Anti-Oedipus Papers*, p. 326.
5. Ibid.
6. Janell Watson, "Black Hole," in *The Deleuze and Guattari Dictionary*, eds. E. B. Young, G. Genosko, and J. Watson, London: Bloomsbury, 2013, p. 49.
7. Jean-Jacques Abrahams et al., "L'Appel du 18 joint," *Libération* (juin 18, 1976).
8. Robert Castel, *Les sorties de la toxicomanie*, Fribourg, Suisse: Editions Universitaires, 1998, pp. 26–27.
9. Deleuze and Guattari, *A Thousand Plateaus*, p. 286.

10. Félix Guattari, "Everybody Wants to Be a Fascist," in *Chaosophy*, ed. S. Lotringer, New York: Semiotexte, 1995, pp. 225–50; "The Micro-Politics of Fascism," in *Molecular Revolution: Psychiatry and Politics*, trans. R. Sheed, Harmondsworth: Penguin/Peregrine, 1984, pp. 217–32.

11. Félix Guattari, "Everybody Wants to Be a Fascist," p. 245.

12. Ibid., p. 244.

13. Félix Guattari, *The Machinic Unconscious*, trans. T. Adkins, Los Angeles: Semiotext(e), 2011, p. 101.

14. Ibid., p. 109.

15. Janell Watson, *Guattari's Diagrammatic Thought*, London: Continuum, 2009, p. 84.

16. René Thom, *Mathematical Models of Morphogenesis*, trans. W. M. Brookes and D. Rand, Chichester: Ellis Horwood, 1983, p. 170; quoted partially in Watson, *Guattari's Diagrammatic Thought*, p. 194, n. 23.

17. Guattari, *Machinic Unconscious*, p. 209; and Thom, *Mathematical Models of Morphogenesis*, p. 169.

18. Thom, *Mathematical Models*, p. 169.

19. Ibid., p. 171.

20. Deleuze and Guattari, *A Thousand Plateaus*, pp. 111 and 115 (i.e., centred on the linguistic sign).

21. Félix Guattari, "Socially Significant Drugs," in *High Culture: Reflections on Addiction and Modernity*, eds. Anna Alexander and Mark S. Roberts, Albany: SUNY Press, 2003, p. 200.

22. Félix Guattari, *Soft Subversions*, trans. C. Wiener, New York: Semiotexte, 1996, p. 101.

23. Guattari, "Socially Significant Drugs," p. 201.

24. Félix Guattari, *La revolution moléculaire*, Fontenay-sous-Bois: Encres/Editions Recherches, 1977, p. 331.

25. Guattari, "Socially Significant Drugs," p. 203.

26. Ibid., p. 202.

27. Ibid., p. 206.

28. See M. E. Tunstall, "Gamma OH in Anaesthesia for Caesarean Section," *Proceedings of the Royal Society of Medicine* 61 (August 1968): 827–30.

29. See Jean-Michel Djian, *Vincennes: une aventure de la pensée critique*, Paris: Flammarion, 2009.

30. Gregory P. Wedin, Carl S. Hornfeldt, and Lisa M. Ylitalo, "The Clinical Development of Gamma-Hydroxybutyrate (GHB)," *Current Drug Safety* I (2006): 99–106; and Henri Laborit, "Sodium 4-Hydroxybutyrate," *International Journal of Neuropharmacology* 3/4 (September 1964): 433–49; and WHO, "Pre-review of Gamma Hydroxybutyrate (GHB)," 34th ECDD. (2006). http://www.who.int/entity/medicines/areas/quality_safety/5GHBPreReview.pdf.

31. Jacques Derrida, "The Rhetoric of Drugs," in *Points: Interviews 1974–1994*, trans. P. Kamuf et al., Stanford, CA: Stanford University Press, 1995, p. 232.

32. Deleuze and Guattari, *A Thousand Plateaus*, p. 334.

33. Guattari, *Anti-Oedipus Papers*, pp. 331–32.

34. Gilles Deleuze, "Desert Islands," in *Desert Islands and Other Texts 1953–1974*, trans. M. Taormina, Los Angeles: Semiotext(e), 2004, pp. 13–14.
35. Walter Benjamin, *On Hashish*, trans. H. Eiland, Cambridge, MA: The Belknap Press, 2006, p. 64.
36. Genosko, *The Guattari Reader*, p. 213.
37. Deleuze and Parnet, *Dialogues II*, trans. H. Tomlinson and B. Habberjam, New York: Columbia University Press, 2002, p. 8.
38. Guattari, *Anti-Oedipus Papers*, p. 404.
39. Dosse, *Intersecting Lives*, p. 172.
40. Unpublished e-mail correspondence with Bruno Guattari (February–March 2011); Laborit and Fabrice Rouleau, (n.d.) "Sur la minaprine Agr 1240 (Cantor)." http://semantiquegenerale.free.fr/Articles/minaprine.htm. Accessed March 2017.
41. See Gena Covell Britt and Elinore F. McCance-Katz, "A Brief Overview of the Clinical Pharmacology of 'Club Drugs,'" *Substance Use & Misuse* 40 (2005): 1189–201.
42. "Everybody Wants to Be a Fascist," in *Chaosophy*, p. 29.
43. Ibid., p. 230.
44. Lenin in Slavoj Zizek, *Revolution at the Gates: Zizek on Lenin: The 1917 Writings*, London: Verso, 2002, p. 58.
45. "Everybody Wants to Be a Fascist," p. 231.
46. Molly Sauter, *The Coming Swarm: DDOS Actions, Hacktivism, and Civil Disobedience on the Internet*, New York: Bloomsbury, 2014, pp. 28–31.
47. "Everybody Wants to Be a Fascist," p. 239.
48. Ibid., p. 236.
49. Dale Beran, "4chan: The Skeleton Key to the Rise of Trump," themedium.com (February 14, 2017): np. https://medium.com/@DaleBeran/4chan-the-skeleton-key-to-the-rise-of-trump-624e7cb798cb#.g6bubp3lq and see Gabriella Coleman, *Hacker, Hoaxer, Whistleblower, Spy: The Many Faces of Anonymous*, New York: Verso, 2014, p. 41.
50. Charles Bukowski, *Factotum*, New York: Ecco, 2002, pp. 106–7.
51. See Elizabeth Chan, "Donald Trump, Pepe the Frog, and White Supremacists: An Explainer" (September 12, 2016): https://www.hillaryclinton.com/feed/donald-trump-pepe-the-frog-and-white-supremacists-an-explainer/ and n.a., "Nazi Pepe Controversy," (2016). http://knowyourmeme.com/memes/events/nazi-pepe-controversy.
52. Bruce Bennett, "Blog: Trump's Body," *The Sociological Review* (November 18, 2016). https://www.thesociologicalreview.com/blog/trump-s-body.html
53. Deleuze and Guattari, *A Thousand Plateaus*, p. 214.
54. Deleuze and Guattari, *A Thousand Plateaus*, p. 215.
55. "Everybody Wants to Be a Fascist," p. 237.
56. Deleuze and Guattari, *A Thousand Plateaus*, p. 231.
57. "Everybody Wants to Be a Fascist," p. 242.
58. Ibid., p. 244.
59. Ibid., p. 245.
60. Ibid., p. 248.

Part III

CRISS-CROSSING PATHS

INTRODUCTION

I began the "Introduction" to my three-volume edited set of critical literature on Deleuze and Guattari with a reflection on the relationship between the authors under scrutiny.[1] The emphasis was on *and*: *between* and *beyond* the proper names. "Between-the-two" and not: a conversation, a union, a juxtaposition; but, an affirmation, always out of step, stumbling in a crowded field of "more-than-twos." Deleuze observed that Félix was never one to worry about unity; after all, his name had a schizo quality to it, Pierre to family and Félix in professional life, as did his preoccupation, militancy, and psychoanalysis. The problem I wanted to get at was a tendency in the critical literature to erase Guattari, and to place all of the emphasis, especially in the co-authored books, on the lead author, Deleuze, who stood for both. This is a sociological tendency about the assignation of primary credit. And a bad scholarly habit. Not everyone agreed, of course, and some showed impatience with author-crowd idea, not to mention the claim that Guattari could be subdued and captured by brackets, erasure, blockage. Guattari was aware of the omission of his name from discussion of jointly authored books as an example of "political malice." For Guattari, Deleuze became a "common noun," and a brand of thought that could define a century, according to Foucauldian hyperbole, but only after his name was conveniently erased. Such an assemblage as "Deleuze-thought" might very well have nothing to do with either of them. Thus, *Deleuze and*

Guattari: Critical Assessments is a snapshot of where I was at the end of the 1990s, and my close-up was volume two devoted to Guattari, the first collection of critical studies devoted to his life and work.

The chapters in Part III use comics and graphic novels as guy-ropes of sorts. These are perhaps even minor literatures in their own right, displaying intensive lines of escape.[2] Chapter 7 "Guattareuze & Co." orients itself through reference to the brilliantly cruel comic of French illustrator Gérard Lauzier that parodies "Deleuze-thought" through the horrible figure of Gilles Guatareuze.[3] This chapter settles down at the end through a more relaxing and gentle reference, courtesy of Charles Stivale, another graphic novel, *Salut Deleuze!* Eventually, in chapter 9, "Epilepsy, Speed and Affect," which presents a study of Guattari and Paul Virilio's interest in epilepsy, the graphic novel by David B, *Epileptic*, plays a guiding role.[4]

Chapter 8 "Do It! Negri and the Yippies" resulted from a collaboration with Dr. Roberta Buiani on a postdoctoral project to bring into English translation Antonio Negri's "Introduction" to the Italian translation of Jerry Rubin's book *Growing (Up) at Thirty-Seven*.[5] Accompanying Buiani's translation, we argued that the parallels Negri drew between American Yippies and Italian anti-authoritarian youth subcultural formations constituted an important and promising rapprochement between what has been erroneously thought to be a divide between different strains of workerism—one devoted to a more centrist and official party and another attached to ephemeral cultural creativity, often associated with Bifo Berardi such as Radio Alice and *A/Traverso*, by the youth underground. This chapter follows up on the study of the relationship between Berardi and Guattari in "The Unpaid Bills of Desire."

The final chapter of this part is a short homage to Guattarian anthropologist Barbara Glowczewski.[6] It is augmented to include further remarks on Guattarian method and the political commitments entailed by schizoanalysis, of the kind that didn't make it into my dictionary definitions.[7]

NOTES

1. Gary Genosko, "Introduction," in *Deleuze and Guattari: Critical Assessments of Leading Philosophers*, volume 1, ed. G. Genosko, London: Routledge, 2001, pp. 1–13.

2. See Erin La Cour, "Comics as Minor Literature," *Image & Narrative* 17/4 (2016): 79–90.

3. "Guattareuze & Co." in *The Cambridge Companion to Deleuze*, eds. D. W. Smith and H. Somers-Hall, Cambridge and New York: Cambridge University Press, 2012, pp. 151–69. This revised version links with the following chapter on Negri, the chapter on Berardi, and opens onto the return to graphic novels in chapter 9, on Virilio and Guattari.

4. The chapter follows the Spanish translation, "Vacío de afecto: el sujeto epileptic," in *Actualidad del sujeto: Conceptualizaciones, genealogies y practicas*, eds. A. S. Lopera, F. D. H. Riveros, M. Z. Pardo, and Z. P. Gomez, Bogotá: Editorial Universidad del Rosario, 2010, pp. 283–300.

5. The translation by Roberta Buiani, "Little Brother Breaks the Fifth Commandment" (trans. of Antonio Negri's Introduction to Jerry Rubin's *Growing Up at Thirty-Seven*), appeared with a jointly written essay, "Negri and the Yippies"), in *Cultural Studies* 26/6 (2012): 934–55. A shorter version of the essay appears here.

6. Originally appearing as "Micropolitics of Hope—Response to Barbara Glowczewski," *Spheres* 2 [Ecologies of Change] (2015): http://spheres-journal.org/micropolitics-of-hope/.

7. Gary Genosko, See "Schizoanalysis," in *The Deleuze and Guattari Dictionary*, ed. by Eugene Young, with G. Genosko and J. Watson, London and New York: Continuum, 2013, pp. 271–73.

Chapter 7

Guattareuze & Co.

A COMIC COMPOSITE

It is perhaps a testimony to their influence and notoriety that Deleuze and Guattari can be located at a number of stations along the continuum between parody and homage. I want to briefly consider three seemingly distant stations, each with its own humorous elements, but deployed to different ends. These prefatory considerations will open onto questions and demonstrations of how to characterize Deleuze and Guattari's collaborations, that is, how they, and others, posed and answered such questions, and what these tell us about their joint work. The emphasis in this contribution is less on the content of the books they wrote together than on characterizations of their process and how these have been deployed and redeployed to different ends.

The late French cartoonist and illustrator Gérard Lauzier (1930–2008) was known, among other things, for his parodies of intellectuals and the Left, including Deleuze and Guattari. Lauzier collapsed Deleuze and Guattari into a third figure of "Gilles Guatareuze" (one "t" only), described tentatively by François Dosse in the rather neutral term "coalescence."[1] Dosse provides some dialogue from a single panel—the final one—of Lauzier's illustrations of "Enfin le cri," and, quotes François Fourquet somewhat tangentially, in order to explain how an already-fragile Guattari was deeply wounded by such cruel commentary:

> Mad drama. 5 policemen wounded at Saint-Tropez. Gilles Guatareuze called the police to have his mistress interned. The least surprising wasn't seeing the famous theoretician of antipsychiatry running after the police chief of Saint-Tropez pleading, "You aren't going to put her at La Borde or with the nice people, right! They could screw up and let her escape! They could screw up and let her escape! No, no a serious place, right? A padded cell and everything."[2]

Dosse has not actually seen these illustrations. But the cartoon panel continues in this way: "Otherwise the next time she may tear me to bits." Over the course of a few lurid colour pages, the fear experienced by Guatareuze of Solange, his hysterical mistress, whose desire is rendered explicit as she bites and scratches him after he tries to convince her that she is an imposter who has replaced his true lover (the name "Solange" parodies both the sheperdess-saint and the region where La Borde is located). Guatareuze is pompous, fat, grey-haired, and bespectacled; his arrogance is palpable; he is manipulative, complaining that his desire has become a gulag, that he has been reduced to a slave. His face reddens in exasperation at his hitherto oblivious lover before she finally attacks. The final panel is a news report, from which the preceding quote is taken. The comic strip works a number of acute angles of highly vicious parody, mocking Guatareuze as "the Lenin of the libido" and of trees as having "tellurian erections" but concludes with Guatareuze's betrayal of his own principles (even if, strictly speaking, those of anti-psychiatry were decidedly not Guattari's own since he considered it too easily recuperated by reformist concessions and its maintenance of familialism). The label of anti-psychiatrist remains attached to Guattari, at least in the imagination of French cartoonists. Lauzier is not alone in this. Guattari was much more of an anti-anti-psychiatrist or a Lacanian of a dangerous pedigree. For Guattari, "deviant psychiatrist" R. D. Laing eschewed the discovery of "sexual machinism" for the safety of familialism, personology, humanism, and unfortunately preferred counter-cultural utopianism for the domain of concrete struggle by mental health workers and psychiatric inmates.[3] In Guattari's estimation, experiments in psychiatric alternatives, especially the variety of communitarian projects, typically lacked support from the political Left, from state health bureaucrats, from the unions of psychiatric nurses, and were subject to a widespread "anti-mad" racism.[4]

There is another "Guatareuze" in circulation, but this time it is neither in France nor a parody. Rather, it is an homage, and a heroic one at that. As Nick Thoburn observes the Bolognese pirate radio station: "Radio Alice . . . used the composite 'Guattareuze' [double 't'] to characterize their practice."[5] In a section concerning the characteristics of a "minor music" in the Collectif *A/traverso* textual collage *Radio alice radio libre*, the formulation is attributed: "as Guattareuze would say."[6] Homage to Guattari, who sought to transfer some of the energy (with a strong coefficient of deterritoralization, flush with politics, and collectively assembled enunciations) that the free radio station catalysed; and also to the creative deviation of minoritarian becoming that Guattari developed with Deleuze, but stretching beyond literature. While Berardi did not coin the word "Guattareuze," he recalls that it dates from the *A/Traverso* magazine of September 1977. Its origin remains embedded in a collective enunciation.

AN UNCOMMON COUPLING

Moving, then, from the caustic through the valorizing to the awkward assemblage, Guattari's journal entries for the period of October 1972 are a rich source of reflections on the implications of the process of writing *Anti-Oedipus*. Here we find Guattari's outsider status—"a common psychoanalyst and an author"—on full display to the extent that his manner of working puts him at odds with the "systematic academic" approach mastered by Deleuze in the field of philosophy. Guattari asserts: "I don't really recognize myself in the A.O. [*Anti-Oedipus*]. I need to stop running behind the image of Gilles and the polishedness, the perfection that he brought to the most unlikely book. Dare to be an asshole. It's so hard being strapped onto Gilles! Be stupid in my own away."[7] Guattari isolates a residue of the process of writing with Deleuze: strapped onto Deleuze in a way that forms a contraption within a stereotypical hierarchy of the extra-academic (muddy and banal) and academic (pristine and polished) relationship. How many Deleuzians have claimed that the difficult final chapter of *What Is Philosophy?* must have been written by Guattari because it is the least clear! The contraption was a consequence of the popular success of *Anti-Oedipus*; it is a contraption rather than a desiring-machine because it is a tool-like projection imposed upon Guattari by the fallout of the book; it gets between him and his own practices, for instance, leading to a false distribution of mastery, to a second-rate identity, thus interrupting by deactivating desire, also distorting his relationship with Deleuze. Guattari strapped onto Deleuze makes up a rattletrap. As Guattari once said in a joint interview: "We couldn't just hook a Freudian engine up to the Marxist-Leninist train."[8] Not any old assemblage suffices to rescue desiring-production from the perils of its separation from the economy.

WHAT ME WORRY?

It may be true that "Genosko has done the most to restore Guattari to his rightful place as equal collaborator" in his work with Deleuze, as Julian Bourg so generously put it,[9] but it is a task that requires constant attention and reinforcement. As Berardi suggests, what is called "DG thought" is a semio-compound of Guattarian molecular perturbations and Deleuzean ontology of events.[10] However, there is, he insists, a Deleuze without Guattari and a Guattari without Deleuze. But when they worked together, they set in motion a "rhizomatic machine" to whose functioning Guattari's contributions cannot be underestimated and, therefore, to treat this machine as a whole determined by Deleuze alone (and with Guattari strapped on) is not only to distort it but to suppress the collective assemblage of its functioning. Any denial of the two who are several who are also a crowd, the admission that begins *A Thousand Plateaus*, diminishes the assemblage's creativity and arrests the transversal movements of its components of passage. The insertion of a hierarchy into the rhizomatic machine in the form of an authorial contraption like the academic/militant re-identifies who is doing most of the writing. Deleuze has observed that he and Félix did not write a book in which one played the madman and the other the analyst; rather, "we did write a book [*Anti-Oedipus*] in which you no longer know who is speaking."[11] The goal was to avoid traditional dualities and not to have recourse to stereotypical hierarchies like the lead author and assistant; any effort to slip a totality into a book of flows runs it aground on one bank. The "flow-book" calls into question co-authorship in its traditional sense. On one hand, a book's body is caged by signifiers, criticism, containment, and the authorial desire to teach a lesson: root-book. On the other hand, a rhizome-book lives in its passages with an outside, although when it is plugged into an outside it doesn't always meet with electric machines that help liberate its potentials, but runs smack into the broken circuits, the analysts, and anybody who doesn't respect its autonomy. The electric book can be a corporate device (Kindle, iPad) diabolically smoothly striated. No place for an immanentist critic. The critic is an operator whose task is to transmit from the book its enfolded potentials or impulses of virtuality that are not exhausted in and by selective actualizations. A tall order: how to maintain the emergent novelty of each critical engagement? Much the same challenge finds authors during interviews. Such a critic qua catalyst must walk the wibberly-wobberley line (or witch's flight) not of the book as such but rightly of the book's field of potential. And an author joins this flow.

It is useful to refer to specific academic straps-ons. The use of parentheses is commonplace. Take, for instance, Patricia Clough's quoting of *What Is Philosophy?* a book apparently by "Deleuze (and Guattari)."[12] Such is a simple qualification of Guattari's authority. And, of course, one winces at Slavoj Zizek's somewhat clichéd attempts to separate the "Deleuze proper" from the "guattarized" books.[13] Clearly, I have not done enough over time to discourage these practices. But some solace can be taken that acknowledgements of the problem are more and more often published, like Nicolas Bourriaud: "Guattari may still seem significantly under-estimated to us, and he is often reduced to the role of Deleuze's foil, yet it does today seem easier to acknowledge his specific contribution to the co-authored writings."[14] Easier, but no less treacherous.

Deleuze is perhaps one of the most insightful decoders of Guattari as an author and as a collaborator. Considering Guattari as a group schizo-subject consisting of an anti-self, Deleuze figures his friend as a "catatonic stone" (when Félix is without his glasses) who also "lights up and seethes with multiple lives the moment he looks, acts, laughs, thinks or attacks."[15] Pierre and Félix (Pierre-Félix Guattari): militant and psychoanalyst. It is useful to look at the figures to which Deleuze has recourse when describing how he worked with Guattari, for they are remarkably consonant with his characterization of Félix. Deleuze responds to Japanese translator and former student Kuniichi Uno to this effect: Deleuze is the unmoving hill, with some internal movements, talking little; and Félix is the rolling sea, "sparkling with light." Deleuze then finds a sporting figure, which is rare in his writing (the exception is tennis), that suits them: "Together, Félix and I would have made a good sumo wrestler."[16] While enigmatic, the principles Deleuze evokes with this figure are based on size and strength—the wrestler's body type—and lightning quick reflexes and power exercised within a confined space of the circular ring. Traditionally, the sumo wrestler belongs to a stable and lives collectively—hence, he is a group subject. Deleuze continues with a number of contrasts: Félix tinkers with diagrams; while he prefers articulated concepts; their written letters to one another, composed for *Anti-Oedipus*, were "disorderly" and the manner in which each handled them put their rhythms of work at odds with one another; Félix had "brainstorms," and Gilles was a "lightning rod." What Deleuze emphasizes is the "accumulation of bifurcations" in a rhizomatic proliferation. To which he adds, during the process of writing *A Thousand Plateaus*, "resonances" established between disciplines in which they worked; and mutually fructuous "guesses" about where they would go next. Deleuze even writes about being "under Félix's spell" and in this state perceiving new worlds. Deleuze's careful and imaginative figurations of his relationship with Guattari are consistently laudatory and insightful, yet also seem to be resisting pressure—not from the cliché of Guattari's erasure and the rise of the first author, full credit system—but from the normative force of a pairing, sliding irrevocably into the couple, which stills process and stalls proliferation. The couple has a bad name in Deleuze and Guattari's thought. To be coupled by others (doubled) is a difficult fate, but to find oneself acting like a couple (i.e., finishing each other's sentences and dressing alike) is even worse. Coupling can be like a drug, Guattari thought, that people take in order to protect themselves from greater dangers. Pairing-off is an event of adolescence: flows of desire are channelled in stereo.

Deleuze's brief remarks in "For Félix" are reserved for his friend's creations, noting at the outset the "discovery and joy" of their collaborations, but the wish "not to talk about the books [they] wrote together" after Félix's passing.[17] Relief: not to yet again explain their collaboration, but to focus on the singular creations of Félix. Not to profess their mutual love, or find witness-readers to it. But identify and problematize a symptomatic response to joint publications read without love: referring to *Anti-Oedipus*, Deleuze once commented that "I've wondered whether one general reason for some of the hostility toward the book is simply the fact that there are two writers, because people want you to disagree about things, and take different positions. So they try to disentangle inseparable elements and identify who did what."[18] A partnership with problems is good for the business of criticism. Bickering satisfies the critics. Bile pollutes love.

MACHINIC NUPTIALS

In *Anti-Oedipus* machines couple according to the productive, connective synthesis: and . . . and then. . . . Constant coupling is the productive force of this synthesis that connects flows and partial objects, "continually producing production."[19] When this rule is bent and broken, a contraption results, and the process stalls; but this is not an element of anti-production. It is the influencing machine of couplehood that persecutes partnerships (but without Victor Tausk's reduction of machines to genitalia). A coupled contraption doesn't simply break down; rather, a couple oozes self-destruction. Intimacy is toxic: "The fraud of the person rests on that of the couple and that of the couple rests on the oedipal triad."[20]

There is a continuum between machinic coupling and a married heteronormative couple. Deleuze and Guattari create figures of their collaboration that deflect all efforts to push them towards the conjugal pole, whether it is by means of the critical need for knowing who wrote what (disentangle), or the creation of cartoon monsters (entangle). They resist this overcoding which infects the representation of all partnerships under capitalism. When Deleuze and Guattari retort, they do so in the name of machinic couplings and assemblages; for Deleuze, the priority is given to nuptials rather than couples, exchanges, binaries. Many critics find this strategy disorienting and resort to interpolating themselves as the third party who completes the couple by expressing the truth of the relation, which is generally at the expense of Guattari and, secondarily, and often unintended, both authors. The question of how to distribute the weight of authorial input and authority correctly still bewitches readers of Deleuze and Guattari.

Any deviation from the intermezzo in favour of an average, or one or the other of authors, is a betrayal of the logic of the *and*. In this sense, then, Dosse's effort around how to explain the workings of the "duo"[21] is not designed to sweep both away "reciprocally implicated and transformed in a transversal cross-cutting."[22] Sweeping away the question of *who wrote what* (still, Dosse wants to attribute biographically specific concepts to Guattari like the ritornello because he was a pianist) and restoring Guattari's so-called competence through his "palpable mark" are laudable goals. But *both and* are never really swept up and away in this approach. The conjunction of the duo remains too exclusive, and departures are forfeited. According to the logic of the ampersand, then, the emphasis is placed on the *and* between Deleuze and Guattari. By the time we reach *A Thousand Plateaus*, the language of synthesis has been displaced by linguistics in which a redundancy of ampersands and . . . and . . . and [*et*] gets the upper hand on *est* ("is") to introduce continuous variation into language.[23] "And"—an "atypical expression"—works as a tensor: "It causes language to tend toward the limit of its elements . . . the tensor effects a kind of transitivization of the phrase . . . An expression as simple as AND . . . can play the role of tensor for all language. In this sense AND is less a conjunction than the atypical expression of all of the possible conjunctions it places in continuous variation."[24] Deleuze takes such care in creating figures that describe his modus operandi vis-à-vis Guattari because in them he is uprooting restrictive configurations of the relation between the two authors, emphasizing variability and redistribution, and collective enunciations. Deleuze defines the conjunction AND: "Neither a union, nor a juxtaposition, but the birth of a stammering, the outline of a broken line which always sets off at right angles, a sort of active and creative line of flight."[25] Stumbling over and . . . and . . . and is a way of creation for Deleuze.

For Parnet, AND is a multiplicity and, as such, it is never alone: "And, And, And—stammering. And even if there are only two terms, there is an AND between the two, which is neither the one nor the other, nor the one which becomes the other, but which constitutes the multiplicity."[26] The line—a "narrow stream"—between sweeps both away undoing dualisms from the inside (as they become about "successive choices.") All the ANDs of a collaboration "would appear as so many distorted images in running water."[27]

ASIGNIFYING CREATIVITY

Another strap-on: "I'm strapped to this journal. Grunt. Heave." At this point in 1972, *Anti-Oedipus* had been out for about eight months, and Guattari was supposed to be contributing to "volume 2" of *Capitalism and Schizophrenia*, but keeping his journal had become a burden, and he was experiencing anxiety at reading the proofs for his own collection of essays, *Psychanalyse et transversalité*. He had become an author, publishing two books in one year, his first and second. Guattari engaged in a protracted self-analytic assessment of his strategy of writing during this period, and whenever the occasion arose thereafter. He expressed his worries about not producing and being accountable for Gilles; that he was just "fucking around"; yet that was how he worked because the energy was in the mess: mayhem, bad spelling, poor expression, arguments to hide behind; multiple beginnings. "I'm a sort of inveterate autodidact, a do-it-yourself guy, a sort of Jules Verne—*Journey to the Centre of the Earth*. In my own way I don't stop . . . But you can't tell. It's the never ending work of reverie. Lots of ambitious plans. Everything in my head, nothing in the pocket."[28] Another character comes to mind: Mr. Cavor in H. G. Wells's *First Men in the Moon*: cloaked in a "haze of 'abstruse phrases' and 'possible substances.' "[29] Guattari's explanations are full of denials—"I'm not a philosopher"—and colourful characterizations and alignments. Circa 1982 while in Brazil, Guattari explained how he worked in contrast to Deleuze: "I try out ploys, like people who try to rob banks—I venture into manoeuvres of expression in a certain context, in a certain situation. Later, I abandon it all and go and do something else."[30] Guattari's reticence about producing meaning effects is worked through in his diagrams. A plan without the heist; an outline without a text. "I stole Félix, and I hope he did the same for me," Deleuze once said, invoking constructive thievery in the conceptual realm.[31] Scrunched up papers in a dustbin. Restlessness at his writing desk. These deterritorialized, machinic signs conjoin directly with other signs and objects and affects, but without the crutches of representation and signification and the anchor of an individuated subject: "Desire is the system of a-signifying signs out of which unconscious flows are produced in the socio-historical field," wrote Deleuze.[32] Guattari's diagrams operate whether or not anybody, including Deleuze, can make sense of them. They generate ideas and objects: little machines of invention that relate to one another by triggering interactions.

ETHOLOGICAL BECOMINGS

Ethology is the scientific study of processes of animal behaviour, favouring field observation, and a subdiscipline of evolutionary biology. The ideas of its Austrian founders Nikolaas Tinbergen and Konrad Lorenz were influential in post-war anthropology and spread via Lévi-Strauss in France. In *The Machinic Unconscious*, Guattari approaches ethology in order to criticize its mechanistic behaviourist assumptions and hierarchical arborescent logics by means of the insertion of refrains (rhythms of temporization and territorialization and facility traits like silhouettes) that precipitate innovations (rhizomic mutations) in and between the semiospheres of animals, and animals and plants. Guattari further rethinks territory in nonhuman animals by describing the open assemblages of components some of which become non-passively expressive and give consistency to social relations between the same and different species. Instead of explaining territory by means of innate mechanisms and the need to satisfy the big drives (hunger, sex, flight, aggression), Guattari turns to expressivity as surplus value of code (beyond the sum of genetic encoding, ecological adaptation, and social communication) as a source of innovation, that is, as art, which "perhaps begins with the animal, at least with the anima; that carves out a territory and constructs a house. . . . The territory-house system transforms a number of organic functions—sexuality, procreation, aggression, feeding. But this transformation does not explain the appearance of the territory and house; rather, it is the other way around."[33]

To the extent that Guattari's *The Machinic Unconscious* may be read as a workbook for *A Thousand Plateaus*, the emphasis on ethology plays a vital role as a "very privileged molar domain for demonstrating how the most varied components . . . can crystallize in assemblages that respect neither the distinction between orders not the hierarchy of forms. What holds all the components together are transversals, and the transversal itself is only a component that has taken upon itself the specialized vector of deterritorialization."[34] Famously, the a-parallel evolution of the wasp AND the orchid has become for some[35] a description of Deleuze and Guattari's work together. Guattari writes:

> It is known that the wasp, effectuating a simulated sex act with a morphological and olfactory lure constituted by the rostellum of the orchid, afterwards releases and attaches the pollen that it transports onto other plants. . . . The ensemble of the transcoding systems authorizing these round-trip tickets between the vegetable kingdom and the animal kingdom appears completely closed to any individual experimentation, training, or innovation. . . . Nothing would be gained by reducing a symbiosis like that of the wasp and the orchid to a simple "attachment" between two heterogeneous worlds. This encounter produces what I called elsewhere a "surplus-value of code . . . the new symbiotic assemblage actually functions like a mutant wasp-orchid species evolving on its own account and redistributing the genetic and semiotic components selected from both original species according to its own standards . . . thus a new evolutionary line of flight is launched on the bio-ecological rhizome which is in other respects immediately masked by the genetic encodings which delimit it."[36]

Borrowing from studies of the wasp and the orchid, baboon troop communication, and tool usage by various birds, Guattari interpolates freedom, in the form of semiotic expansion, into closed behavioral sequencing. Improvisation and individual initiative help to deterritorialize a given assemblage (i.e., courtship rituals) and establish new transversal co-relations between the most and least deterministic components. Guattari wanted to expose ethology's misunderstanding of linear causality (higher to lower) and its binarisms (inhibitors-innate releasing mechanisms) through the non-transcendent entanglements of components of assemblage. Guattari's goal was to complexify ethological logic rather than simply reverse its priorities or substitute one hierarchy for another. He accomplishes this task in part by levelling the differences between animal and human desire and by injecting psychoanalytic, semiotic, and political concepts as explanatory principles into points of rupture.

The relationship between the wasp AND orchid does not adequately describe the work of Deleuze and Guattari. The selectivity is far too exclusive. The emphasis is on *and* hence on the new lines thrown out into the rhizome beyond the conjunction; on what *each becomes* and on *that which becomes*; the bestiary required to account "for the AND" is enormous. After all, Deleuze found many animals in Guattari: "In Guattari there has always been a sort of wild rodeo, in part directed against himself."[37] This is the menagerie that one encounters in conversation and collaboration: a wild rodeo, a happening, a growing solitude populated with animal becomings. A-parallel evolution happens between animals, between ideas, not between persons.

FLYING PAPERS

In a review of Guattari's *Anti-Oedipus Papers*, philosopher Charles T. Wolfe remarked:

> What exactly is in this book? Most notably, the "matrix" for one of the most unusual intellectual collaborations in the 20th century: *Anti-Oedipus*. Deleuze once described this collaboration, disarmingly, as follows: "If I told [Guattari] that at the centre of the earth there was redcurrant jelly, his role would be to find what might support such an idea (if it is an idea!). It's the opposite of a series or exchange of opinions" . . . And when Deleuze was asked in the same interview to describe the method of their collaboration, he answered: "It's a secret." So the texts in this volume shed light for the first time on the nature, not just of the "creative process" of the two-headed monster that produced *Anti-Oedipus*, but of the invention of a collective language.[38]

Enter the matrix: this non-book is a disparate collection of materials cobbled together by editor Stéphane Nadaud from archival materials and assembled around the process of composing *Anti-Oedipus* with Deleuze. These writings include annotated notes and clarifications written by Guattari to Deleuze and then corrected and revised, reminders to himself, autobiographical and theoretical journal entries (1971–1972), and a glossary of concepts. Meta-comments on letters between Guattari and Deleuze as well as the former's entreaties to the latter and his partner Fanny appear throughout. These papers provide scattered and suggestive insights into how Guattari and Deleuze worked together, apart, and lay bare some of the conceptual challenges faced by the authors in fine-tuning their investigations: how to read Marxism unconventionally by focusing on its conceptualization of capitalism, how to extract from psychoanalysis schizoanalytic principles, and how to be done with representational semiotics. Guattari's conceptual and practical struggles are front and centre; diverse theoretical skirmishes are punctuated by practical examples from Guattari's practice at La Borde and criticisms of bad psychoanalytic clinical habits. Guattari often responds to Deleuze's requests for clarification with intense explanations marked by exclamations, name-calling, and asides. Brief characterizations of how Guattari approached concepts punctuate explanations: surf their crests and make messy outlines. Guattari's journal entries provide insight into his self-analysis and how he thought about his relationship with Deleuze. When we look for answers and find sketches, the dynamic diagrammatic thought of Guattari is thrown into relief. The principles of affirmation, transformation, metamodelling (singular automodelization), and "mad drawings"[39] are affirmed in a wild diagram of still restless papers.

KAFKA EFFECT

If *Anti-Oedipus* "stands apart" in a number of ways from Deleuze and Guattari's other collaborations because "they themselves are made other in that work,"[40] what is the character of the alterity initiated by the Kafka book? Deleuze treads carefully and expresses concern in other worldly terms, when describing how he and Félix approached Kafka: "My ideal, when I write about an author, would be to write nothing that could cause him sadness, or if he is dead, that might make him weep in his grave. . . . So many dead writers must have wept over what has been written about them."[41] Respect for the dead mingles with a double refusal of the familiar (identifying with him) and the object of scholarship: "I hope Kafka was pleased with the book that we did on him." Experimenting with Kafka through the concepts of rhizome, assemblage, missing people, and minor literature, Deleuze and Guattari proceed with respect and care so as not to disturb the rest of the great author. AND Kafka: for Guattari, finding new means of alterification to join the Kafka assemblage became a lifelong preoccupation. His first effort was to co-curate with Yasha David an exhibition at the Centre Pompidou (*Le siècle de Kafka*, 1984) on the occasion of the Kafka centenary in 1983. Guattari collected Kafka's dreams; he organized performances around this theme; he even envisaged a film by as opposed to about Kafka during this period that could be shown on television in the form of a cultural series that would minorize television, a modernist strategy undertaken by directors from Godard to Lynch. Despite Guattari's mistrust of television, it was in this instance a choice medium for forging a potential public and connecting it with independent Kafka affects, precipitating becomings-Kafka. The film would build highly abstract and lyrical sequences around molecular elements such as bowed heads: heads bursting through windows, doorways, even ceilings, and the wall that is at the heart of the project operates as a machine that both breaks up and connects movements of characters. It is a screen, a molecularized face, bearing geological strata, vegetal becomings (moss), and receptacle for men's urine. Guattari described a "Kafka effect" based on the appreciation of a richly processual "chronic precarity" that makes his work perfectly suited to the twentieth century.[42] Both Deleuze and Guattari were caught up in Kafka effects that fascinate and that bring about experimentation across media (books, essays, film, theatre, curation), and both express tender constraints with regard to their favourite author (certainly Guattari's). This movement is a multimedia stuttering. And it was already evident to some degree in *Anti-Oedipus* as examples borrowed from Kafka—machines, the eminent character of the state, and the law—are qualified as unequalled in relevance.

CONCLUSION

The many examples and details discussed in this chapter may be connected together by a number of ANDs in order to create the kind of rhizome with a particular logic discussed throughout, in addition to the limitations on connectivity in the defence of practical, juridical reason. The lines of connective alliances include the authorial collaborations of Deleuze and Guattari, which are themselves modified and expandable by other ANDs. The logic of AND is a war machine, not a contraption, a strap-on, a Marxo-Freudo remake. Yet the war machine has both positive and negative sides: affirmation and reaction.[43] The former is often integrated into the collaborative books themselves as a statement of how Deleuze and Guattari understood their collaborations (subjects do not enunciate; collective assemblages enunciate); at other times their explanations are reactive in the sense that they answer the questions of those looking for secrets, for evidence, for the statement that will make an interview, for the bare author-subject. There are some very ugly moments in the universe of reception that clog the collective assemblages, but also some remarkable creations (as we have seen, figures of the sumo, ocean waves, running water, thievery). Why is it important to continue considering the ways in which the relationship between Deleuze and Guattari has been characterized by the authors themselves and others? Simply put, because of the unresolvable tension between the name, signature, and identity, and the desire to escape authorial pairing, division, separation, and the erection of contrived (dis)unities. Recourse to a movement from the name as pseudonym for philosophical conceptual characters is no guarantee—there is no escape from the disaster of sales promotion. Performed successfully, this escape operation may give rise to new names, like the one suggested by Ronald Bogue for Deleuze: "Alice H. Challenger."[44] Some of these names are playful; others are raw, like Guattareuze, and still provocative, like writing Guattari and Deleuze and . . .

It would be an exaggeration to claim that the use of Guat(t)areuze to preface this discussion of figurations of Deleuze and Guattari constitutes a method in its own right. However, recourse to graphic art as an approach is not unknown, and may put me, in fact, in good company. After all, Charles Stivale takes a "relaxing" approach to the question of the folds of friendship by reading Martin tom Dieck and Jens Balzer's bande dessinée *Salut, Deleuze!*[45] While wonderfully "offbeat," Stivale qualifies his choice in terms of how the graphic artists engage both seriously and playfully, creatively doing philosophy while offering an homage to the late philosopher. Compared to the "gentle fun" of the scenario in which Deleuze is delivered by the boatman of the dead to the eagerly awaiting trio of friends Barthes, Foucault, and Lacan, a similar description for Lauzier's comic would not be possible to offer, as the humour is vicious. Nevertheless, recourse to the medium shows some promise as a new tool in the philosopher's cultural rootkit for connecting heterogeneous materials.

NOTES

1. François Dosse, *Gilles Deleuze and Felix Guattari: Intersecting Lives*, trans. D. Glassman, New York: Columbia University Press, 2010, pp. 10 and 424.
2. Ibid., p. 595, n. 3; Gérard Lauzier, "Enfin le cri," in *Tranches de vie*, vol. IV, Paris: Les Editions Dargaud, 1978, p. 21.
3. *The Guattari Reader*, p. 38.
4. Ibid., p. 60.
5. Nick Thoburn, *Deleuze, Marx and Politics*, London: Routledge, 2003, p. 134.
6. Collectif A/Traverso, *Radio Alice, radio libre*, Paris: Laboratoire de Sociologie de la Connaissance, 1977, p. 71.
7. Guattari, *Anti-Oedipus Papers*, p. 404.
8. Gilles Deleuze, "Deleuze and Guattari Fight Back," in *Desert Islands and Other Texts 1953–74*, trans. M. Taormina, Los Angeles: Semiotext(e), 2002, p. 217.
9. Julian Bourg, *From Revolution to Ethics: May 1968 and Contemporary French Thought*, Montreal and Kingston: McGill-Queen's University Press, 2007, p. 36, n. 1.
10. Franco Berardi, *Félix Guattari: Thought, Friendship, and Visionary Cartography*, trans. G. Mecchia and C. Stivale, Basingstoke: Palgrave Macmillan, 2008, p. 43.
11. "Deleuze and Guattari Fight Back," p. 219.
12. Patricia T. Clough, "Introduction," in *The Affective Turn*, Durham, eds. P. Clough and J. Halley, NC: Duke University Press, 2007, p. 14.
13. Slavoj Zizek, *Organs without Bodies*, London: Routledge, 2004, p. 20.
14. Nicolas Bourriaud, *Relational Aesthetics*, trans. S. Pleasance and F. Woods, Dijon: Les presses du réel, 2002, p. 87.

15. Deleuze, "Three Group-Related Problems," in *Desert Islands*, p. 193.

16. Deleuze, "Letter to Uno: How Félix and I Worked Together," in *Two Regimes of Madness: Texts and Interviews 1975–95*, trans. A. Hodges, Los Angeles: Semiotext(e), 2007, p. 237.

17. Deleuze, "For Félix," in *Two Regimes of Madness*, p. 382.

18. Gilles Deleuze and Claire Parnet, *Negotiations*, trans. Martin Joughlin, New York: Columbia University Press, 1995, p. 7.

19. Deleuze and Guattari, *Anti-Oedipus*, p. 7.

20. Guattari, *Anti-Oedipus Papers*, pp. 318–19.

21. Dosse, *Intersecting Lives*, p. 192ff.

22. Barbara Godard, "Deleuze and Translation," *Parallax* 6/1 (2000): 60.

23. Deleuze and Parnet, *Dialogues II*, pp. 98–99.

24. Ibid., p. 99.

25. Ibid., pp. 9–10.

26. Ibid., pp. 34–35.

27. Ibid., p. 35. See also Rodrigo Nunes, "Politics in the Middle: For a Political Interpretation of the Dualism in Deleuze and Guattari," *Deleuze Studies* 4 [Supplement] (2010): 104–26.

28. Guattari, *Anti-Oedipus Papers*, p. 400.

29. H. G. Wells, *First Men in the Moon*, New York: Ballantine, 1964, p. 17.

30. Guattari (with Suely Rolnick), *Molecular Revolution in Brazil*, trans. K. Clapshow and B. Holmes, Los Angeles: Semiotext(e), 2008, p. 449.

31. Deleuze and Parnet, *Dialogues II*, p. 17.

32. "Four Propositions on Psychoanalysis," in *Two Regimes of Madness*, p. 81.

33. Gilles Deleuze and Félix Guattari, *What is Philosophy?* trans. H. Tomlinson and G. Burchell, New York: Columbia University Press, 1996, p. 183.

34. Deleuze and Guattari, *A Thousand Plateaus*, p. 336.

35. Dosse, *Intersecting Lives*, p. 15.

36. Guattari, *Machinic Unconscious*, pp. 121–22.

37. Deleuze and Parnet, *Dialogues II*, p. 11.

38. Charles T. Wolfe, "Review of *The Anti-Oedipus Papers*," *Metapsychology Online Reviews* II: 35 (August 28, 2007). http://metapsychology.mentalhelp.net/poc/view_doc.php?type=book&id=3790&cn=452.

39. Watson, *Guattari's Diagrammatic Thought*, p. 6.

40. Fadi Abou-Rihan, *Deleuze and Guattari: A Psychoanalytic Itinerary*, London: Continuum, 2008, p. 37.

41. Deleuze and Parnet, *Dialogues II*, p. 119.

42. Guattari, "1984—Kafka: Procès et Procédés," in *Les années d'hiver 1980–85*, Paris: Les Prairies Ordinaires, 2009, p. 271.

43. Eugene Holland, "Affirmative Nomadology and the War Machine," in *Gilles Deleuze: The Intensive Reduction*, ed. C. Boundas, London: Continuum, 2009, pp. 218–25, and p. 219.

44. Ronald Bogue, *Deleuze's Wake: Tributes and Tributaries*, Albany: SUNY Press, 2004, p. 26.

45. Charles Stivale, *Gilles Deleuze's ABCs: The Folds of Friendship*, Baltimore: Johns Hopkins University Press, 2008, pp. 7–9.

Chapter 8

Do It! Negri and the Yippies

> Do. Do. Do. The movement gets its unity around tactics. We become a community through collective action.
>
> —Jerry Rubin[1]

Jerry Rubin's contributions to micropolitical analysis may be excavated from Guattari's statement in *The Machinic Unconscious* that " 'Do it!' could be the watchword of a micropolitical schizoanalysis."[2] Guattari revisits this position in *Lines of Flight* to the effect that it brings into play a pragmatics of modifying a set semiotic assemblage: "Rather than agreeing to remain prisoner of the redundancy of signifying tracings, one will endeavour to fabricate a new map of competence, new a-signifying diagrammatic coordinates."[3] And the Yippies tried to diagram the forces of free love, free speech, student and anti-war movements, and eventually phone phreaking, too. Guattari's thesis survives in some measure in Michael Hardt and Antonio Negri's *Empire*, in the analysis of the multifaceted values of social experimentation and resistance to the "disciplinary regime" by youth countercultures.[4] Resistance to a normalized disciplinary regime is irreducible to simply dropping out or to mere cultural experimentation. Proliferating refusals of all sorts force a reevaluation of labour that from this moment would come to be identified as immaterial, affective, cooperative, and cognitive. "We are," Rubin concludes in *Growing (Up) at Thirty-Seven*, "redefining the value of society, from marriage to family to work to love and death."[5] The consequences of these creative redefinitions form the basis of the mutual imbrication of the economic and cultural, the emergence of immaterial labour, and the theory of semiocapital.

In 1976, Antonio Negri wrote the introduction to the Italian translation of Jerry Rubin's *Growing (Up) at Thirty-Seven*—trans. *Quinto: uccidi il padre e la madre*—the book that followed his iconic Yippie manifesto *Do it* (trans. In

Italian as *Fallo!*). Out of print for some time, the former (with Negri's introduction) was reprinted in 2009.[6] In this introduction, Negri draws a parallel between the transformation of a culture that had flourished in the late 1960s with the Yippies (the Youth International Party) and the culture that emerged in Italy after 1968. In both cases, these cultures advocated new forms of activism, notions of labour, sexuality, and production of subjectivity through technological forms of resistance. This is the same culture of action and resistance that later converged into the young upwardly mobile professionals known as Yuppies. Rubin admits he grew up in 1976 as a washed-up radical, after which he wandered through the mystic lands of pop therapy, reinventing himself in the 1980s as a "born-again capitalist and self-proclaimed spokesman for the yuppies."[7]

The re-publication of Rubin's book, along with Negri's introduction, should not come as a surprise. Despite its outdated content, and somewhat maudlin tone, the text immediately establishes a connection between those early years of struggles and social unrest and the fragmentation of identity and political dissipation that characterizes today's global (dis)order. Negri assesses the then new culture arising in the mid-1970s. This culture was the expression of many disenfranchised youth and independent groups in opposition to the heavily bureaucratized politics of the PCI (Italian Communist Party) and its historic compromise with the Christian Democrats (DC). Because of its inability to come together and create a cohesive group, and in the light of the violent repression that followed, this new movement was seen as a failure, as a sign that the "labyrinth of utopian bifurcations that followed the creative explosion of 1968 [had turned] into their opposite."[8] Despite being labelled as the "appendix of the working class struggles of the twentieth century,"[9] Negri's reading of this emerging culture is not pessimistic. While 1976 represents Rubin's embrace of maturity with "positive illusions"[10] to sustain him, in 1976–1977 Italy was traversed by a massive repression of student and labour protests and deadly episodes of police brutality. These episodes were read in negative terms as the product of the increasing disintegration of the extra-parliamentarian Left. Writing before these facts happened—that is when these movements seemed to give renewed confidence to an increasingly disaffected movement—Negri documents the refreshing emergence of pockets of underground resistance, one that was leading the working class to a "positive and constructive opposition to the capitalist irrational drive to produce both during crisis and during development," a new opposition that constituted itself dialectically as "creative moments through the refusal of labor, into perception of the proletarian possibility of a new world order."[11] Through this fragmented, yet constructive opposition, Negri appears to see the potential for a true transformation of the conditions brought about by the monolithic and managerial system of the official parties and of the tenets supporting the ethics of labour.

In his "introduction," Negri fondly figures the new "youth underground" as a brother, a younger, sillier, and less well-equipped sibling. This little brother was a comrade in arms, yet took different routes: he didn't work for the organization; he pulled out "anti-authoritarian discourses" from our political writings and took off to the Far East to expand his consciousness, and started to smoke pot. Negri's examples are dated as he mentions, for instance, postwar events and the Piazza Statuto protests by young disaffected workers at Fiat in the summer of 1962. Now in the mid-1970s, he witnesses a new wave of events, less compact and cohesive, yet not less meaningful. Rather than dismissing the emerging youth underground, Negri welcomes this apparent lack of cohesion and established principles as a joyful and vital movement. This movement didn't "unfold through management but through action"; its configuration could not be equalled to "a new party, but a revolutionary power"; its "organizational process materializes out of the growth of all the comrades and in the re-articulation of material conditions, desires and short term commitments."[12]

Referring back to the same social and historical context, but speaking well afterward, and to the way in which the underground groups expressed themselves creatively through the dissemination and manipulation of media, Berardi sees the same underground movement that arose in the mid-1970s as anticipating today's media activism. He recommends that "revisiting and reassessing that movement may be interesting if within those times you can find the premonition of what is happening nowadays, the premonition of an anthropological mutation that is unfolding in the new century that we inhabit. Moreover, that movement also created some antidotes to today's problems and some possibilities for looking in another direction."[13] Thus, revisiting Negri's introduction and relocating it into the semiocapitalist context described by Berardi, Negri's interest in the Yippies and their transient passage, yet still on the radar of autonomist Marxist theory, anticipates a number of elements that characterize the current hybrid status of labour, the dispersed multiplicity of the political, and the formation of heterogeneous alliances among unlikely bedfellows. Negri's commentary sheds a new positive light upon the chaotic interventions practised by the underground scenes in the mid-1970s in the US and in Italy, revealing a number of dynamics that characterize contemporary social and political articulations. Such analysis also explains today's emergence of a certain type of media action, whose legacy originates in the creative work and the pranks of the Yippies as well as the Italian movement described by Negri and Berardi. Surely it is not fortuitous that a number of recent media interventions such as the pranks of the Yes

Men, the short-lived and humorous whimsy of the Liens Invisibles and Paolo Cirio, among others, contain elements inspired directly from the interventions and antics of those cultures that produced the initial youth underground described by Negri and Berardi and in which Rubin played a significant role. The pranks of the Yes Men clearly evoke the early campaigns and actions of the Yippies, in using a combination of traditional and recent media (TV, documentary, or the Internet) to package laughable, yet deceitfully credible and well-orchestrated stunts. The Yes Men have become known for their dissemination of semi-false information that simultaneously jams, ridicules, and denounces the shady politics of multinationals and major corporations, and for impersonating CEOs and WTO officials at corporate gatherings to which they had been mistakenly invited. At these gatherings, posing as the legitimate representatives of these corporations, they would announce absurd business plans as the products of "innovative" entrepreneurship or would deliver scruple-free, a-moral speeches. Other recently emerged creative groups have embraced the art of the fake and the unclear, and directed it to unveil the hidden politics and the exploitative bias of online social networks, a space where distinguishing between the deceitful and the trustworthy is already a challenge and is becoming increasingly difficult. For instance, the Liens Invisibles have become popular among online art critics for promoting tools that function as artistic divertissements, as social experiments, and as satire. These operations, often in the form of semi-serious online services offered to the user, challenge his or her attachment to, reliance on, and trust of Web 2.0 platforms: they propose that users commit "Facebook suicide" by deleting their profiles from the popular social network permanently, or to assist armchair activists to create custom petitions that would generate as many signatures as needed in just a matter of days. More complex projects such as Paolo Cirio's Gift Credit Card aims at subverting the current financial order by producing and sharing wealth through a new peer-to-peer credit card system that operates at the margin of what is legally permitted. In trying to generate and redistribute money within a new subverted system that is no longer pyramidal but network-based, Cirio's endeavour is inscribed in the same DIY tradition that produced the Yippies' credit card exploits or phone phreaking, and the autonomous media produced out of military radios (Radio Alice) or other found objects by the "centri sociali" in Italy.

Indeed, re-reading Negri's "introduction" allows us to reassess the relationship between him and Berardi. The received wisdom is that a split occurred between Berardi and Negri within Autonomia. It would be incorrect to insist, in the light of Negri's self-understanding of his welcome and positive outreach as blasphemy, on a hard and fast distinction between more traditional workerist political spaces and organizations and countercultural, underground squats and hangouts with their fragile post-media experiments.

Negri's positive description undermines his supposed scepticism towards the less organized and intentionally chaotic practices supported by Berardi, and partially erodes the categories that distinguished Autonomist movements between organized workers' autonomy, diffuse autonomy, creative autonomy, armed autonomy, and so on. While divergences between different fringes of the movement, and Berardi's critique of certain orthodoxies of Autonomy endorsed by Negri, have been well documented, one should note that these distinctions didn't become evident until later and sometimes can be very subtle. Looking beyond alleged disagreements for the sake of seeking common threads, Negri's informal and honest piece doesn't refer to a specific set of practices or tactics, or to labour issues. Rather, he fondly writes of a generalized spirit that comprised all groups of disenfranchised individuals roughly united around a common restlessness, a spirit that knew neither formal hierarchy nor priority of action, yet it infused and energized an entire generation. This description seems to evoke what Berardi calls the "existential demand," a "desire to liberate time and the body from the chains of industrial labour,"[14] and by and large echoes Rubin's Yippie manifest: "The left demands full employment for all—we demand full unemployment for all."[15]

In examining the 1976 piece by Negri and his identification of points of contact between the Italian underground in those years and the American Yippies, vis-à-vis the more recent media analysis of the same movement undertaken by Berardi, two elements jump to our attention: the refusal of labour and the subversive use of media. In both cases these two aspects run parallel, mirroring each other and reflecting the culture and the discourses they wished to subvert and with which they no longer identified. Rubin's book was originally published in Italian translation with a different title, which means literally "Kill Your Father and Mother." The title refers to a famous buzzphrase used by Rubin—"Kill Your Parents" that overthrows the "honor" of the fifth commandment. In *We Are Everywhere*, Rubin reflects on this phrase: "Do you mean take a gun and literally shoot them or destroy their way of life and symbolically 'kill' them? *I smile*. If I said it was symbolic, I'd take all the bite, all the oomph, all the sex out of this statement. . . . Is it literal or symbolic? I don't know myself. *I guess it depends who your parents are*."[16] The title, a tribute to Jerry Rubin, also elucidates some of the motivations behind the rise of the youth underground. The refusal of labour; squatting and petty crime, with often sophisticated pre-electronic "hacks" of credit cards and telephones; and embracing drugs and overtly reinventing sex were subversive, and thus metaphorically "killed" the principles that had informed the previous generations. These principles were only virtually unifying a group of individuals under the same society or under the same party. Negri observes how in this society "elements of the whole are all unified [only] in a technical sense,"[17] that is merely according to conventions, as this system is operating under the assumption that the entire society agrees with these principles. The myriads of different subjectivities that existed were hardly taken into consideration, or they were interpreted as blasphemous, the product of some maladjusted individual.

The dissent of the new underground groups didn't materialize as a direct critique of the general system or, more specifically, of the traditional Left, nor was it carried on in traditional fashions. These dada-and-yippie-inspired absurd activities were far from being the product of passive refusal or examples of meaningless dissent. They emerged as the affirmation of a generation of disenfranchised youth faced with a disastrous unemployment rate (which in Italy had reached almost 15 per cent), and with a generalized absence of representation of their subjective needs. The creation of alternative pockets of creativity resulted as the expression of a variety of subjectivities against the official bureaucratic system of union and political parties that not only did not represent them but that would also accuse them of betraying it by contributing to its dissolution.

While in the US the Yippies would organize provocative guerrilla theatre—like Rubin and Abbie Hoffman's attempt to levitate the Pentagon in the fall of 1967—or running a Mr. Nobody as presidential candidate in 1976, in Italy the Metropolitan Indians would declare "self-reduction day" and invite everybody to a restaurant from which they would walk away without paying the bill; they would publish DIY fanzines whose titles were anagrams (*OAKS* = Kaos) and whose content would consist of non-linear mash-ups and collages of which *A/Traverso* is a fine example; free radio station Radio Alice would broadcast delirious programmes and would open its microphones to the public at large, accepting live phone calls from whoever wanted to contribute; Judith Malina's Living Theater would entertain with its controversial street performances. The previous nontraditional interventions and performative expressions combined a refusal of labour and media subversion. In general, they never voiced demands for more work, but for no work at all. This refusal carried the potential for a transformation of the way in which generations before these new underground groups had conceived of labour. As Illuminati explains, a tradition that goes back to Hegel has historically conceived of labour dialectically as a path to freedom.[18] In capitalist society, the worker is subjected to the owners of the means of production. However, more recently, the worker is subjected to his or her own labour before he or she is to the owners of the means of production. In other words, the worker is afraid to take any action towards emancipation because he or she is too afraid to lose his or her job, and, thus, his or her only way of survival. Refusing to work is a way to break the vicious circle that eternally traps the worker.

Thus, living at the edge, often consensually without a fixed residence, surviving through small real-world hacks and using makeshift means was a way to resist the regimented culture that had betrayed these young militants. During this period and later into the 1980s Italy witnessed the dissemination of a large number of squats, called "social centres" where various activities—like the creation of free radios—were carried on using found materials and practising self-teaching. This mode of survival echoes the way of life of the Yippies: they had engaged in the same myriad of small illegalities quite similar to those technically described in their newsletters; first, in the Youth International Party Line (YIPL) founded in 1971 and later renamed the Technological American Party circa 1973, eventually morphing into the Technological Assistance Program in 1979, a clearinghouse of micropolitical hacks, devices, and diagrams. These were dedicated to phone phreaking, tapping power and gas lines, demanding freeware for personal computers, and agitating against the monopolies of Bell and Con Edison.

A founder of Radio Alice, Berardi describes the agglomeration of young students and working class youth as fragmented, yet cohesive. This free radio was founded in 1976 and constituted one of the most successful examples of this creative wave, until it was closed by the police in 1977 after a violent university confrontation that left student Francesco Lorusso in Bologna and Giorgina Masi in Rome dead, the Bologna episode being broadcasted live thanks to members' telephone calls from public phones to the radio. According to Berardi, what made the groups involved with Radio Alice or the Metropolitan Indians united was not a programme, or a manifesto to which everybody had agreed, but their "desire to breathe together, to express and cultivate subjectivity, to refuse labour."[19] All these activities were combined and communicated through radical rhetoric, simulation, and parody. The subversion of the conception of labour was accompanied by a subversion of the traditional contents and conception of media. In a posthumous reflection on the Metropolitan Indians, Torealta writes: "Since all the 'real contents' (the referents of production, affect, signification) that ballasted the sign with a kind of useful force of gravity are no longer effectively communicated, the signs are now exchanged among themselves without any commerce with some object in reality. . .(and the question of wages, by definition, is the general referent of all signs), the 'pangs of conscience' and discourses on 'political economy' are completely useless; one cannot struggle against transience and dispersion with the blows of purpose and conscience."[20]

The goal of these groups then was not to distribute communiqués or leaflets that would explain their intentions in a lengthy and linear fashion, but to "replace the bearers of truth that divided unions, political groups with their identifying signs and their banners with intelligence and shrewdness." By doing so, they hypothesized a series of interventions that jammed and disjoined the traditional link between signified and signifier, "based on the social possibilities of falsehood, on the technological possibilities resulting from the destruction of rules, on the free exchange of products, simulation, the game, the nonsense argument, the dream, music."[21]

Such interventions, often short-lived and semi-spontaneous, according to Berardi, helped pave the way to the "social dynamics, cultural and communicative that would develop in the following decades."[22] In fact, he sees the realization of the predictions described earlier as the anticipation of the new language that characterizes the "sphere of video-electronic communication," where critique, following what the Metropolitan Indians and the other underground groups had envisioned, "becomes progressively substituted by a form of mythological thinking in which the capacity to distinguish between the truth and falsity of statements becomes not only irrelevant but impossible."[23]

Shortly after the movement of 1977 (or the demise, as it has been defined), Negri wrote the essay "Dominio e Sabotaggio." In it he acknowledges the significance of the movements that arose in the mid-1970s and that he had welcomed in his "introduction" to Rubin. While addressing a more specific set of activist practices emerging from, and operating within, a context of struggle focused on labour, rather than on the persuasive and deceptive potential of media evoked by the Indians or Radio Alice, his text addresses the entirety of small movements as factions that criss-crossed and animated the political spirit of those heated years. The chaotic and dysfunctional rise of the multiple subjectivities expressed through the underground had been a pleasant surprise for Negri. Now, he appears to use the failure and the suppression of the movement as a warning against the obsolescence of the discourses disseminated by a party-monolith: "It is no longer possible to invent indeterminate macro-economic equilibria which are independent of short-run variations and independent of the micro-economic components which are variable within the unforeseeable timing determined by the struggles of the collective worker."[24]

The same dilemmas appear to repeat themselves again today: not only is the worker still oppressed by labour itself, but this situation, thanks to the massive normalization of precarious, part-time, or contract labour, has become institutionalized, reinforced by a media frenzy that heaps guilt and anxiety upon workers so they guiltily hang onto their precarious jobs because of an alleged "global economic crisis." The dissociation of truth and statement has become a norm that has turned what once constituted an ironic gesture into a mere cynical routine. Paradoxically, today's interventions by the aforementioned recent figures seem to utilize similar tactics or deception, simulation, and irony that were popularized in the 1970s, this time to reveal, rather than to jam, the furtiveness that lies behind glossy and deceptive media.

NOTES

1. Jerry Rubin, *Do It! Scenarios of the Revolution*, New York: Ballantine Books, 1970, p. 125.
2. Guattari, *Machinic Unconscious*, p. 176.
3. Guattari, *Lines of Flight*, p. 171.
4. Hardt and Negri, *Empire*, Cambridge: Harvard University Press, 2000, pp. 274–75.
5. Jerry Rubin, *Growing (Up) at Thirty-Seven*, New York: M. Evans and Co., 1976, p. 199.
6. Antonio Negri, "Prefazione," in *Quinto: Uccidi il Padre e la Madre*, ed. Rubin, Milano: Mimesis Edizioni, 2009, pp. 7–18. All translations from the Italian are by Roberta Buiani.
7. See Marty Jezer, *Abbie Hoffman: American Rebel*, New Brunswick, NJ: Rutgers University Press, 1992, p. 291.
8. Franco Berardi, *Precarious Rhapsody: Semiocapitalism and the Pathologies of the Post-Alpha Generation*, London: Minor Compositions, 2009, p. 8.
9. Negri, "Prefazione," p. 16.
10. Rubin, *Growing (Up)*, p. 188.
11. Negri, "Prefazione," p. 12.
12. Negri, "Prefazione," p. 14.
13. Berardi, *Precarious Rhapsodies*, p. 15.
14. Berardi, *Precarious Rhapsodies*, p. 22.
15. Rubin, *Do It!*, p. 86.
16. Rubin, *We Are Everywhere: Written in Cook County Jail*, New York: Harper & Row, 1971, pp. 194–95.
17. Antonio Negri, "Domination and Sabotage," in *Semiotext(e)* III/3, Italy: Autonomia: Postpolitical Politics, 1980, p. 64.
18. Augusto Illuminati, *Per Farla Finita con l'Idea di Sinistra*, Roma: Derive e Approdi, 2009.
19. Berardi and Emanuela Biliotti, "'La Rivoluzione della Creatività. Il contesto storico in cui appaiono I fogli transversali. Fogli e movimento; tecnologia e comunicazione 'A/traverso,'" *Riscoprire* 2 (December/January 2011): 42.
20. Maurizio Torealta, "Painted Politics," *Semiotext(e)* III/3 (1980): 102.
21. Ibid., p. 103.
22. Berardi, *After the Future*, p. 25.
23. Berardi, *Precarious Rhapsodies*, p. 15.
24. Negri, "Domination and Sabotage," p. 68.

Chapter 9

Epilepsy, Speed, and Affect

This chapter focuses on the role epilepsy plays in the theories of Paul Virilio and Guattari. Beginning with a discussion of Virilio's deployment of childhood petit mal crises (picnolepsy) as a model for the implosive effects of speed, I then move to a detailed study of how another conception of epilepsy shaped Guattari's theorization of existential affects, showing how he derived the concept from phenomenological psychiatric sources, and explaining how this illness informed his delineation of different kinds of affects. I transit from Virilio to Guattari through an interpretation of some pertinent features of the graphic novel by David B, *Epileptic*, and eventually turn Guattari's work towards an analysis of how epilepsy functions cinematically through a deathly epileptoid atmospherics that confirm affect's dangerous autonomy. To this end two films are considered: Marco Bellocchio's *Fists in the Pocket* (1965) and Anton Corbijn's *Control* (2007). Guattari's overriding concern was with the production and composition of subjectivity in a pathic mode, and my critical task is to show how epilepsy contributed to this theorization, and to explore it through select cultural materials.

My selection of cultural materials is guided, in the first instance, by the overt content of the graphic novel in question, but also in virtue of what a low-tech example brings to Virilio's thinking—undertaken in a high-tech register—about absences in the theory of the perceptual organization of the space and time of the medium of graphic novels. Secondly, for Guattari cinema was a privileged medium for the exploration of minor becomings that had the content of anti-psychiatric struggle, in the broadest sense so as to include films exploring epilepsy within the disabling environments of the family and in terms of its constraints on public performances. My main concern is with the organization of key scenes, that is, how bodies are shown to be affected on the screen, rather than the communication of affect along a-signifying vectors to an audience in formation or yet to come. However, my ethical concern is that in both cinematic examples affect in its nuanced appearances linked to complex refrains is overpowering and unwinds violently in dramatized deterritorializations that lead to on-screen deaths. I am not conflating an unowned intensity with the actualization of convulsion in immediate or mediated death (the opposite of creation is a death-dealing shock upon a body seized by convulsions). Rather, I am questioning after Guattari's founding of affect on a certain conception of epilepsy that is autonomous and atmospheric (viscous and immobilizing) but in the absence of what philosophers of affect have detected as the "positive connotations" of affect's unassimilable, uncapturable, vital, and open characteristics, for instance, as may be found in Massumi's *Parable of the Virtual*. The rhythmic transductions of epileptic seizure in *Fists in the Pocket* and *Control* reveal only the misery of affect's void as bodies careen towards decomposition. What is positive about affect's epileptic foundation? In order to calibrate affect's much-vaunted transformative potential, I will conclude by considering that epilepsy is not something that befalls a body and has a diminishing effect by way of restraint. Living with epilepsy opens onto a diversity of the ways of being affected, enhancing sensitivities, and even productivity in the case of artists whose attempts to visualize their intense experiences have attracted the attention of curators and neuroscientists alike.[1]

PICNOLEPSY

Virilio built his theory of disappearance as an implosive dimension of everyday life in the age of the hegemony of speed on epilepsy, to be precise, on picnolepsy, or frequent, slight epileptoid episodes. His book *The Aesthetics of Disappearance* begins on the subject of loss, lapse, absence, "missing time" and meditates on the active memory that the young picnoleptic brings to patching over, inventing what cannot be remembered from the course of existence: "There is a tendency to patch up sequences, readjusting their contours to make equivalents out of what the piconoleptic has seen and what he has not been able to see, what he remembers and what, evidently, he cannot remember and that it is necessary to invent, to recreate, in order to lend verisimilitude to his *discursus*."[2] But Virilio's move here is not designed to ghettoize and stigmatize the picnopelptic: he or she may not be an epileptic at all, as this diagnosis is controversial. For "childhood absences" are sometimes classed as partial and subject to criticism because "loss" is not adequate to their epileptological description.[3]

Still, Virilio's main point is that this condition raises an awkward question, posed on the basis of the characteristics of a *petit mal* crisis, that is perceived neither by the sufferer nor always by observers: "Who is picnoleptic? We could possibly respond today: who isn't, or hasn't been?"[4] Inverting the paradoxical sleep of rapid eye movement with the paradoxical waking of the picnoleptic in a state of "rapid waking," Virilio probes the aesthetic and technological (for film and photography in the nineteenth century) implications of this experience for how reality is constructed through formally similar "stop tricks" that render visible the hitherto invisible. These implications are profound for Virilio because ontologically the lost moment of the non-seen is captured, illumined, by early inventions like Etienne Marey's chronophotographic rifle, and this speaks of the fascination with absences and the struggle to master them as key to understanding contemporary speedscapes dominated by technologies of visibility and mobility.

It is not that all of us have been picnoleptics; rather, all of us have been adolescents struggling to master the childhood that slips from our hands in the passage of time, and with it goes the picnoleptic experience, at least according to Virilio's sense of the epileptiform's unfolding and puberty's interferences. As picnolepsy wanes, bad habits arise "as attenuated adaptations of the vanished epileptic process."[5] These derivations are numerous (drugs, gaming, sex, rock 'n' roll, extreme sports) but all amount to the dissimulations of ageing itself. Picnolepsy is known "typically" as a childhood disorder that often slowly ceases with maturation.[6] This is the specific type of seizure that interests Virilio because of its slightness and non-convulsiveness. Indeed, it also lacks a pronounced aura or premonitory symptom—which can be a disturbance in the field of vision, or take the form of an auditory distortion or change; sensory twitchings or numbness in a limb, intensification of olfactory sense, peculiar tastes, vertigo, malaise.[7] This lack of a distinctive gestural semiotic lends picnolepsy to both strategies of appearance and disappearance, but suggests a passage within the theoretical deployment of epilepsy by Virilio towards the more overtly framed attack. Yet even here this notion of the framing of an attack is speculative, and it will take a diversion from medicine into graphic novels to better understand it.

In many literary accounts of epileptic seizures, like those by Fyodor Dostoevsky in a number of novels, especially Prince Myshkin in *The Idiot*, but also in detailed autobiographical descriptions like Margiad Evans's *A Ray of Darkness*, one finds acute renderings of the moment of the onset of crisis, what is known as a prodrome or more commonly as aura, which Virilio also describes as "a special state of happiness" (à la Myshkin) and "inexplicable enthusiasm."[8] The moment before time is evacuated and opens onto a disjuncture between the event and one's apprehension of it, the latter always out of step, a little behind: "It travels, like sound, behind the jet airplane" as Evans put it in quite a Virilian manner.[9] Surprise and suddenness are the essential attributes of this experience of the unfamiliar as a breach in the familiar. Virilio elsewhere considers this as the general consequence of departure that precipitates loss (of direct contact with experience). In Virilio's thought connections are made between speed and epilepsy, and between speed and senescence.[10] Clearly, though, Virilio switches from picnolepsy to grand mal types of seizures in introducing aura. Generally, Virilio regains the "gaps" of "intermediate times" as original moments irreducibly singular in temporal terms, a kind of personalized duration not beholden to rhythm or clock symmetry, but radically unpredictable and asymmetrical (although this is also a contested point in the predictive modelling of extreme events in the brain, like epilepsy).[11] These diverse dimensions of time may be retrospectively patched together in a way that corresponds for Virilio to the management of absences in the arts and in his own writing.[12] But these "intermediate times" are liberatory and unleash forces: "A latitude given to each man to invent his own relations to time."[13] There is a subtraction that animates Virilio's apprehension of epileptic absence that scientific reason tries to reconstruct and test clinically by digging into EEGs, for instance, and trying to pin down the slippery onset moment of an absence, but only in order to rob it of its mystery by making it common, known, and predictable, a struggle that still goes on today to produce epilepsy "know how," in short to master surprise by integrating it into knowledge production itself.

Consider, then, another set of frames between which one may jump in the form of the graphic novel *Epileptic*, drawn in black and white, of Pierre-François Beauchard, pseudonym David B. Centred around namesake Pierre-François, and told from his point of view, his younger sister Florence, and his older brother Jean-Christophe, this novel recounts the family's struggle with Jean-Christophe's seizures and the "endless round of doctors" that come to define their lives together from childhood forward into adulthood. Faddish macrobiotic treatments, hopes and letdowns, guilt and escape merge in Pierre-Francois's entry into the world of drawing comics, a missing dimension populated with totem animals and magical beings where he finds some respite. Inspired by May 1968 as an epic scene of violence seen through the pages of *Paris-Match*, young Jean-François at nine years defines his drawing style in densely detailed battles, indebted to the psychedelic mysticism of middle-brow French journal *Planète*. At the same time, his parents struggle with another hope—the leading lights of the anti-psychiatry movement: "The anti-psychiatry movement begins, propounded in France by people like Gilles Deleuze, Félix Guattari, Roger Gentis." Sitting in bed his mother states: "These are the kind of people Jean-Christophe should be seeing. And his father replies: 'You think?' "[14] Nothing comes of it. In passing it is interesting to note that comics have become a refuge of sorts for anti-psychiatric ideas, taking Chester Brown's use of Thomas Szasz's and Laing's critiques of schizophrenia in his strip "My Mom Was a Schizophrenic."[15]

Adolescent revolt turns to violent outbursts as Jean-Christophe's seizures continue unabated, spiralling into a kind of psychosis punctuated by severe seizures and feelings of oppression[16] giving rise to the need to arm himself with knives, punch his father, battle with his younger brother, terrorize everyone, and so on; later, Jean-Christophe suffers from terrible paranoid hallucinations ("bad omens") brought on by a new medication. These series of frames are almost completely black. The two male siblings also beat each other up. It is, after all, a family. The young boys once enjoyed a mutual love of graphically representing violent scenes, that is, until Jean-Christophe gave up drawing altogether. Later, the guilt and anger-ridden (only a "sick man's brother") Pierre-François attends commercial art school in Paris but fails the final exam. At the end of the novel, which is presented first as a device framing the time-scale from 1964 to 1994, the man that Pierre-François encounters one morning in his parents' bathroom during a visit home turns out to be his brother, bloated, scarred, and toothless.

Much of *Epileptic* explores the intersecting structures of misrecognition in the family, as well as the stereotypes of the series of alternative communities and healers they come into contact with, produced in response to Jean-Christophe's epilepsy. This exploration takes place beyond the level of framed content and narrative in-between the panels, in the gutters, as it were, to which readers bring certain kinds of closure, patching together the absences that the form delivers while providing signposts for their continuous navigation.[17] Virilio has most often addressed "the landscape of images" through high-tech examples borrowed from videography, cinematography, and post-scanning technologies, in terms of the systems that support the surpassing of the representation of images and the rapidity of their transmission. His abiding concern is with shifts in perceptibility in the "aesthetics of disappearance" when physiology falls further and further behind or to the side of image technologies, and conscious perception is eluded.[18] What if we plug the graphic novel into this drive towards disappearance? Isn't it, despite a rather low-tech profile, one future of the book and another example of going beyond direct observation and exploring the gutters and panels? But that would be too simplistic to align the gutters between panels with the absences of epilepsy. Rather, as one reader of David B's *Epileptic* notes, "every panel of the book is a little world-deforming explosion."[19] Pierre-François's childhood passion—"rage"—for creating comics featured page-saturated scenes of medieval battle and carnage, and he renders this rage in a style of drawing as his "own form of epilepsy."[20] Further, it is possible to detect in the "panel-to-panel transitions" how the relationship between the worlds of Pierre-François and Jean-Christophe is ultimately "remedied" in a fantasy of mutual understanding.[21]

GLISCHROIDY

Like many intellectuals of his generation, Guattari read Eugène Minkowski's important book *Lived Time*, first published in 1933 but reprinted in the late 1960s. *Lived Time* is one among many intersections between psychiatry and phenomenology. There are traces of this reading in Guattari's challenging essay on "Ritornellos and Existential Affects" (collected in *Schizoanalytic Cartographies*) as he suggests at the outset that, borrowing from Minkowski's writing on epilepsy, affect adheres to the subject in a "glischroidic" manner.[22] Affect is sticky; it is also non-discursive and pre-personal and has a transitivist character that makes it transferable or sharable between subjects but not bound to dyadic representations such as speaker-listener or tied down to specific emotions (or other functional anchors). In fact, as Massumi has clarified, emotion is subjectively "owned," whereas affect is an "unowned" intensity.[23] "Somewhere," Guattari wrote, "there is anger" that is available communally as it circulates through a dimension that may work itself out through, by analogy, objects of value that an individual's or clan's influence ("mana") finds to express itself.[24]

What is significant is that the search for philosophical precedents for this view of affect in Spinoza, Bergson, and elsewhere has underplayed Minkowski's contribution and overlooked the fact that some of the character given to affect is borrowed from epilepsy. What I propose to do in this section is to excavate glischroidy in Minkowski in order to expose epilepsy's role in Guattari's thinking not only of affect, but how it works in the cinema, as well. Of course, one could say that the intersection between Guattari, Minkowski, and affect is found in the precursor of Henri Bergson as Minkowski's psychiatric phenomenology of time was Bergsonsian in inspiration, with a number of important qualifications and deviations.[25] While undoubtedly accurate as far as line of influence is concerned, I want to emphasize that Guattari's path was slightly different from Deleuze's more overt Bergsonianism, and he notes as much referring to the affective "atmospherics" (hazy yet comprehensible) borrowed from phenomenological psychiatry on his thinking; specifically, Guattari gleaned this from Arthur Tatossian's overview *Phénomenologie des psychoses*.[26] While this tradition is not as well known as the many variants of Dasein analysis, it is decisive for Guattari's construction of affect with reference to pathology, which will be somewhat familiar to readers of Maurice Merleau-Ponty in his use of the case studies of brain-damaged patient "Schneider" in describing the body's spatiality and motility in *Phenomenology of Perception*. Merleau-Ponty borrows this example from Kurt Goldstein's studies of brain-injured soldiers during the 1940s, in this instance a man in his twenties whose vision and ability to perform abstract movements were impaired by a shell splinter at the back of his head.[27]

One finds in Massumi's writings on virtuality epileptoid phenomena of gaps, lags, and missteps ("something that happens too quickly to have happened") that have always concerned the thinking of infolding, psychopathological or otherwise. I am not suggesting in these remarks that affect has been psychopathologized in being ascribed to individuals as clinical entities. On the contrary, one of the hallmarks of Minkowski's approach is that he considers the epileptoid character in the context of a world of objects and others, especially families (throughout which illnesses are unevenly distributed), social situations, intergenerational relations, and biological issues around heredity. Readers of *Anti-Oedipus* are familiar with the non-clinical entity—the schizo process—that involves a dismantling of the ego, escaping the imposition of a breakdown by the capitalist mode of social production: "Society is schizophrenizing at the level of its infrastructure."[28] Deriving affect from epilepsy, like creating schizoanalysis from the ruins of capitalism's schizophrenia, is turned into a positive task.

Merleau-Ponty reflected on his use of Schneider in terms of the role of pathology in phenomenological analysis of the body in movement and in space: he argued that normality could not be deduced from pathology. It did not suffice to grasp lack and then recover it in the normal. For Merleau-Ponty, the world of illness is no less a world than that of a so-called normal person. The role of the pathological case "has enabled us to glimpse a new mode of analysis—existential analysis—which goes beyond the traditional alternatives of empiricism and rationalism, of explanation and introspection."[29] In other words, there is something more basic at issue than a description of Schneider's failures (of representation, of objectifying schemas, and symbolic intermediaries of experimental simulation) for Merleau-Ponty, and it is that the intentional arc of consciousness that unifies our sensory world, intelligence, and motility "*goes limp* in illness." Although Merleau-Ponty is not discussing epilepsy, his approach to the pathological is foundational within the phenomenological tradition. Here is one of the sources of Guattari's sense of the pathic (affective) foundation of experience and the tangibility of pathological existential transferences.

Minkowski relies upon the family-centred research of Françoise Minkowska on epileptic character in his discussion of glischroidy. Minkowski first rejects the older view that epilepsy, that is, grand mal delirium, is intimately linked with thoughts of death, God, ecstasy, and mysticism brought on by the trauma of the seizures. The problem with this view is that, for Minkowski, there is a false transposition between the trauma's "brutality" and the reaction taking the form of "morbid religiousity." Minkowska's research published in the 1920s showed, on the contrary, that "explosive reactions" to trauma are secondary to a more basic disorder described as "a slackening and a particular viscosity."[30] Minkowska filled out the epileptoid constitution (glischroidy) further as involving: loss of mobility; incapacity to remove oneself from one's environment; lack of initiative; lack of productivity; clinging to what one has; unattractiveness of change; love of order, especially details, to the loss of a big picture; admiration of stability; concentration of emotional energy on one's family or general ideas (world peace); intellectual slowness; and morally informed missionary zeal. She specified that the "viscous affectivity" of this constitution appears in the epileptic's inability to detach himself or herself from objects when change requires it. Thus, "the epileptoid is the paradigm of the affective personality . . . this emotion is viscous and lacks mobility."[31] Ultimately, the suffocating stasis and immobility eventually combust and the consequent explosion leaves an anguished psyche beset by delusions.

Minkowski reads this characterization of a "general slackening" and saccharine emotional life through a three-pronged strategy of backgrounding trauma and its effects (the "falling sickness" of the pre-moderns), rejecting single causation (inability to interact), and resisting reduction to certain unexamined expectations (squandering an opportunity to emigrate, denigration of a strong cultural attachment to native soil, or praiseworthy tenacity). Instead, he recalls the difficulty of interpreting viscidity as it may erroneously show as insincerity, or, again falsely, as egotism. While viscosity steers clear of explosiveness and mysticism, it runs into other phenomena such as contemplation, which is only allegedly immobile and "completely different from real immobility."[32] There is a syntonic element of epileptoidism that suggests the nuances of thinking through any kind of unity with the environment as sympathy, for example, thinks Minkowski, has a viscous side. So, just as the personal élan (the withdrawal from reality that the accomplishment of a personal project requires before re-engaging with becomings beyond the subjective) has a schizoid element, contemplation and sympathy have epileptoid nuances in their characteristics of engagement.

TWO AFFECTS

Guattari separates affect (open and full of potential) from emotional anchors (limits of embodiment). This separation is relative because although affect lacks an obvious origin and destination, it can and does find an existential footing in intersubjective phenomena like commiseration where it is sharable. Affect still retains a vagueness, an irreducible qualitativeness against efforts to bind it to some quantity (this is its virtuality, its openness, and its autonomy—unassimilated and unanchored). Affect has the capacity to fade out and escape from its most intense footings.[33] But it also has the capacity to invade, disorient, and breakdown subjectivation, carried by a death-dealing ritornello of sound and seizure.

In order to characterize sharable affect as an extra-personal phenomenon that "speaks through [one]," Guattari borrows from the tradition of the anthropologically tinged phenomenological psychiatry of Hubert Tellenbach the idea of an "atmospheric diagnostics" relevant to schizophrenia developed in the late 1960s. Guattari quotes Tatossian's overview on this point about diagnosing schizophrenic alienation not symptomatically but through phenomena embedded in a communicative situation of intersubjective encounters, and thus "atmospheric"; unlike the symptoms which, for Tellenbach, an illness shows itself and thus is not present but must be diagnostically inferred, phenomena revealed by the bracketing of the empirical are given directly and fully, not through inference or interpretation. The characterization of phenomenological diagnostics involves "ascertaining the dissidence between the atmospheres proper to two partners."[34] For his part, Tatossian wonders whether phenomenological diagnostics is pre-semiological and thus naïve and non-psychiatric, or simply post-semiological, thereby "integrating but moving beyond the cataloguing of symptoms."[35]

Guattari is indebted to the conceptualization of vitality affects in the work of psychologist Daniel Stern, and it is the non-categorical or non-discrete character of such elusive qualities to which he turns in particular for important clues about expression without specific categorical colouration and sensory specificities.[36] For instance, a vitality affect like soothing need not be experienced by an infant (whose sense of self is still emerging) as linked to a specific modality of expression (vocal or gestural) or even anchored in a response to discrete stimulus categories (fright or sadness). The supramodal character of vitality affects makes them rich in transversal potential for matching, transferring, and assembling sensory experiences between and among different modalities of expression and behaviour. Freeing affect from arousal and how it is experienced enhances its transversality. For Guattari, affect is pre-personal: literally experienced before a category of person may be used to describe selfhood's integrated networks organized under identifiable principles. For instance, Stern describes the emergent self in an infant immersed in vitality affects, and these consist of multiple transferences across sensory domains prior to the hierarchies of semiology with language at the centre and all other semiotic modes subject to translation by the central mode but not vice versa. Transference-transitivist-transversal: these terms employed by Guattari in rapid succession indicate the dynamic and abstract features of affect. Whose semiotic polyvocity remains incomplete, thus not yet yoked to one semiotic-sensory modality.

Affect circulates, thought Guattari, like "spirit," which is shared in common and in its own right a sort of medium through which its influences are distributed or shared. This meant, for Guattari, that affect was far removed from its analysis as discourse, from quantification, and from extensional categories in general. Affect is collective. It "speaks to and through me," Guattari wrote, yet it is not language.[37]

Affect sticks to a subject in production, a processual subject defined provisionally: "The ensemble of conditions which render possible the emergence of individual and/or collective instances as self-referential existential Territories, adjacent, or in a delimiting relation, to an alterity that is itself subjective."[38] Guattari describes an existential territory in which his subjecthood is given shape as a tributary of the following scene: "The somber red colour of my curtain enters into an existential constellation with nightfall, with twilight, in order to engender an uncanny affect that devalues the self-evidences and urgencies which were imposing themselves on me only a few moments earlier, plunging the world into a seemingly irremediable void."[39] Guattari qualifies this example by distinguishing it from the lingering influences (emotive and cognitive) of affects that reach beyond the confines of a localized and immediate scene like that involving his red curtain and twilight. These other sorts of affects are called *problematic* against immediate *sensory* affects; problematic affects are spatio-temporally ungrounded and in flight (more than just associative, but fading and thickening) and for Guattari more ontologically basic than situationally bound sensory affects in terms of the latitude given to their influence; the residues of signifier and signified are evident enough, and Guattari reinscribes them as sensory (ritornello) and problematic affect (abstract machine) or form of expression and form of content (their mutual relationship is what Guattari calls the sign function, and this becomes the existentializing function when form finds substances of expression and content). For subjectivity as a tributary of a number of diverse components assembled in a "scenic dis-position" announces a relation of dependency: "I find myself subject to a multi-headed assemblage of enunciation: the individuated subjectivation which in me is authorized to speak in the first person is no more in fact than the fluctuating intersection, and the conscious 'terminal,' of these diverse components of temporalization."[40] This subject is composed from heterogeneous components that achieve a certain consistency, but it is not an effect of structure (signifying operations), Guattari having displaced the signifying chain of linguistics and reinscribed the scene in terms of non-discursive affects, guaranteeing semiotic heterogeneity in the process. The attainment of consistency in subjectivation through a heightened affectivity is achieved without threatening the latter's autonomy. But affect sticks to subjectivity nonetheless. It is a "glischroid matter" that gives texture to the existential constellation of components and the temporalities that cross and catalyse them (i.e., like iterative ritornellos understood as emergent motifs that cluster the components and adhere them to the subjectivity in process). Further, in order to describe the "inchoate dimension" of affects that have not achieved consistency or consummated their existentialization (but have not lost the capacity to influence) Guattari turned to a cluster of concepts borrowed from phenomenological psychiatry and psychopathologies of temporality (i.e., reversals—history bathed in guilt—and shrinkages of time—classic symptomatology of disruptions in lived continuity—from melancholia and autism). He makes a point of not, however, producing a distinction between orderly and harmonious temporal components of subjectivation and discordant componentialization, which would erroneously uphold a further distinction between normal and abnormal (one wouldn't deny the profound difference between the pathic temporalizations of a maniac whose accelerations fan out and an obsessive whose inhibitions retain and circumscribe); instead, diverse, livable temporal modes that are crossable constitute normality, while only one mode dominates in abnormality (i.e., a " 'hardened representation' like an obsessive ritual").[41] This is not a diagnostics but a way of presenting a more general perspective on problems of enunciation, not to mention an appreciation of its precariousness, irreducible to both psychopathology and linguistic semiology (the tyranny of the signifier becoming in this light abnormal with regard to enunciation).

Reiterative phenomena like ritornellos congeal by giving substance to sensory affects in music or intonation, and open the fields of reference of problematic affects, as in the feeling of ambiance or atmosphere for those attuned to such environmental features. In terms of semiotic functions (sensory affects), ritornellos concern the relations between enunciation and the form of expression, and abstract machines (problematic affects) concern the relations between enunciation and the form of content. In these terms, semiotic functionality involves: the existentialising function of enunciation engages both "functives" of the sign understood as two mutually presupposing forms—expression and content—which are projected onto unformed matter in order to create substances—expression and content substances. Substances are ordered by or subsumed by form, with the expression substance finding a medium like sound and content substance performing conceptual labour. Guattari advocated for greater attention to be paid to how ritornellos "fix [that is, extract or detach something from the significational chaos and congeal it in a substance] the existential ordering of the sensory environment and . . . prop up the most abstract meta-modelizing scenes of problematic affects."[42] For Guattari, ritornellos intersect both types of affects, just as abstract machines involve sensory affects as well. Enunciation is not anchored to a speaking subject but exhibits a certain degree of autonomy and "foliatedness" (*feuilletage*),[43] exhibiting growth as in an arrangement of leaves, in consisting of a number of heterogeneous voices (social and pre-personal) in which semiotic components are assembled in an open-ended way and through which subjectivity takes and changes shape. The entire territory of subjectivation is pathically perfused. The existential function of enunciation opens a territory for subjectivation to emerge through the imperfectly and non-structurally and multicentred (multi-headed lay-out) intersecting affects.

SOUND AND SEIZURE

Marco Bellocchio was one of Guattari's favourite directors. His first film *Fists in the Pocket*[44] is set in an isolated family villa in a small Italian town. The story revolves around the interactions of the adult children—three brothers and their sister—and a blind mother. Although considered crazy by the townspeople, the children struggle for independence in a claustrophobic environment over which hangs the terrible legacy of the family illness, a debilitating epilepsy, distributed unevenly among the children; Alessandro is in-between attacks and seems to have his epilepsy under pharmaceutical control, even if the rest of his actions lack such control, while brother Leone is brain-damaged and subject to uncontrollable seizures. Elder brother Augusto's narcissism seems manageable enough for him to contemplate marriage, while Guilia's fragility threatens to disintegrate at any moment. The film catalogues the misplaced enthusiasms of the split Ale/Sandro (a familial schizz splitting the name) as he plots and executes the murder of his mother and brother Leone, attempts to seduce and/or smother his sister, arrange a suicidal car ride to his father's gravesite for his siblings, and even follow in Augusto's footsteps beyond the family with hopeless schemes. It is the final scene of Ale/Sandro's massive and deadly seizure that features the work of a notable ritornellizing expression-substance, Verdi's *La traviata*. Throughout the film Bellocchio has Ale/Sandro retreat to his bedroom and play his Verdi record, to which he moved and mimed and performed strange signal-like gestures, sometimes simulating suicide, other times gleefully play-singing an aria like a massive baritone. His bedroom has hitherto served as a protective, infantile territory, the soundtrack to which is always the same. The Verdi ritornello conducts the final bedroom scene and fills it with sound, yet it is not the only expressive substance as Ale/Sandro's gestures and movements; these include singing-miming-dancing-bouncing on his bed, laughing, and thrashing around—all of which agglomerate and induce in him a kind of ecstatic experience. Bellocchio shows us in one violent edit, a blurry close-up of Ale/Sandro's mouth followed by a quick cut—what is about to occur, as he has throughout used, as one critic astutely observed, "aggravated editing, with sequences jerking spasmodically from one to another . . . like epilepsy itself."[45] This edit drags us across a threshold and intersects with problematic affect—that glishroidic affect that oppressed the household, colouring everything, until the film's climactic scene. The seizure that kills Ale/Sandro enters upon the scene from "somewhere" and reorganizes it, turning ecstasy inside out, reconnecting ecstasy with its neo-platonic twin epilepsy.[46] Suddenly the rapturous experience animating Ale/Sandro's gestures becomes unbearable as he thrashes violently on the floor, and the aria changes face as a new component introduces itself beyond the music—the seizure clashes with the singularizing effects of the music, and the scene becomes tense and disharmonious—seemingly heightening and prolonging his suffering. What happens to a ritornello whose content is a seizure? Time can no longer be kept, a vast gulf opens up between the record that plays on and the seizure that continues but turns the drama in a different direction and brings it to a brutal end. This is not all external; from inside the seizure Ale/Sandro calls his sister for help—"hold my head," a request he used earlier when he felt a seizure coming on and sought comfort from his sister. But Giulia remains in her bed and does not move, listening with a certain satisfaction to the horrible events, as the massive seizure opens a territory with which she is familiar and which she permits to run its course because through it she explores her own share of atmospheric immobility in relation to the murderous intentions of her brother.

If Bellocchio dramatically cultivated the psychotic episodes that sometimes accompany and alternate with epileptic events—in this case interictally or between seizures in Ale/Sandro's character whose behaviour becomes more and more bizarre[47]—then Corbijn works the post-ictal terrain where the resulting psychopathology not only increases the risk of suicide but also exemplifies it.[48] The final scene of *Control*[49] in which the actor Sam Riley playing Ian Curtis hangs himself in his kitchen on the support rope of a clothes' rack after a night of heavy solitary drinking, failure to reconcile with his spouse—to passages from Werner Herzog's *Stroszeck* (1977) on a black-and-white television and Iggy Pop's (and not Dostoyevski's) *The Idiot*[50] on the turntable—is conducted by the seizure that announces itself with an auratic hand tremor that loosens the suicide note from his hand, as his body follows the note to the ground. All the components of territorialization and temporalization at play in the final scene—night gives way to morning (by which time he "will be gone"), the television broadcasting day ends in static, his passing out accompanies a fade-out, the record ends—constellate around an impending end, his suicide, which is never seen, only heard in a muffled sound behind a black screen. The black screen is the threshold across which the suicide, pushed by the seizure, carries viewers, who are its tributaries. And with his spouse's discovery of the body the hollow, insistent strains of Joy Division's "Atmosphere"[51] emerge to count off the final moments of the film, her pleas for help giving way to the black smoke rising from the chimney of a distant crematorium.

In *Control* the ritornelloization is accomplished by means of the recurrent and unpreventable seizures that haunt the singer's private and public lives (his on-stage seizures are remarkable for the confusion they create in his band mates and audiences). He slows down, he cannot accept change in his family situation, and the atmosphere with his partner is complicated by his heavy drinking, nicotine loading, emotional inability to accept that his spouse wants a divorce because he has taken a lover, whose capacity to stick to him he rather lethargically laments. The Joy Division soundscape of pain, disillusion, and persecutory energy catalyses the existential affects that assemble like ominous clouds waiting to strike discordant chords—the unpredictable seizures whose debilitating effects earlier led him into an attempted suicide by means of overdosing on his medication. Their virtuality is sinister.

Between Bellocchio and Corbijn there are at work in the two films under discussion complementary intersecting ritornellos of sound and seizure, each in a different order of priority—in *Fists* the ritornellos of *La traviata* are subject to the contingent emergence of the final seizure, which finds Ale/Sandro in a state of paroxysmic joy whose content is revealed as the unpreventable, crushing seizure; while in *Control* the seizures conduct numerous sensory scenes, finally becoming intolerable and precipitating suicide. Both filmmakers insert the somewhat residual, gendered machinic technology of the record player as one vector along which subjectivation takes place, the vinyl record serving as a controllable palette for subjectivity's self-positioning, even if what is put on does not make a sound in, as Guattari put it, "eventful compositions" of sounds and seizures that damage processual subjects. The repetitive, ritualized action of putting on a record is a machinic ritornello that helps carve out a territory, not only concretely, but abstractly as well as it is the crossing-point for a number of worlds. The soundless record reverts to an a-signifying ontological disqualification. Here a counter-Guattarian question is posed: it is not so much "how are sounds . . . going to be arranged so that the subjectivity adjacent to them remains in movement, and really alive"?[52] but how is the silencing of such life accounted for?

IS THIS THE END?

Across media (graphic novel and cinema) there is a tendency to fuse into the formal expressive material some feature of epilepsy—through style, editing, and even iconicity, as in David B's *Epileptic* where an epilepsy-serpent coils around Pierre-François's head and chases him,[53] quite unlike the Aesculapian snake coiling around a staff that is a universal icon for medical assistance. In the cinematic examples under discussion, the self-enunciative potential of the key characters is put at risk by their seizures, as the components of partial subjectivation seem to indicate that only an action undertaken to conquer what is unmanageable is valid, in the case of suicide; but in Ale/Sandro's situation, the sonic ritornello cannot guard against the threat of a seizure, whose convulsiveness is final, but the effects of which have already hardened into psychotic violence directed against his family. In *Control* the final episode intersects with a musical ritornello by delay because, unlike *Fists*, the seizure carries us into an intensive time where the record, while apparently playing (the needle is in the lead-in groove and later found in the lead-out area), is not heard; whereas the music in Ale/Sandro's bedroom is heard all too well. In both films, the content affects—seizure and suicide—give a definitive consistency to the sensory affects, but one whose hopelessness is brutal (even in the graphic novel Jean-François tries to vanquish the epilepsy-serpent by recourse to drawing scenes of violence).

Affect tonally coloured by epilepsy attaches to what ends badly: in these films the result of epilepsy is death. It deterritorializes rapidly and effectively: the joy and comfort of Verdi reverses, and Bellocchio reveals its capacity to abolish: "music," wrote Deleuze and Guattari, "has a taste for destruction."[54] Epilepsy deterritorializes the ritornello towards death, unwinds it too quickly and with ferocity, and Guilia refuses the line it sends out for help. And in the situation of the characterization of Curtis, his epileptic ritornello territorializes with precision, as we see in his relationship with his child whom he cannot pick up and hold but only stare at through the playpen's bars; and in his relationship with his bandmates whose gigs his seizures violently interrupt. It is only when all the lines of flight and fields of reference converge/collapse on the same content that the ritornello contracts intensely around a single reference and the subject plunges down into suicide—lost in affect's void.

It is worth noting as a final comment that the distinction between the sensory and problematic affects, in which the latter is more determinative because more transversal, disappears from the period of the *Schizoanalytic Cartographies* to *Chaosmosis*, where together these affects become hypercomplex ritornellos/refrains—the first crystallizing existential and territorial assemblages and the latter catalysing transversal connections among incorporeal universes (the non-discursive dimensions of Guattarian ontology: Universes and Territories). Therefore the pre-eminence given in the cinematic examples to ritornellos that shut down enunciation and hurl subjects into the void presents epilepsy as a kind of death sentence. To be the tributary of an assemblage that is epileptoid, in the theories we have reviewed, creates heterogeneous implosive temporalizations ("missing time") which eventually compromise lifelines. This approach thrusts one back into diagnostics. If affect is epileptoid, then we are all perhaps epileptics to the extent that our bodies have the capacity to be affected and actualize such potential. Of course, my cinematic examples are extreme and do not admit of lines of differentiation distributed in directions that lead to other outcomes. But the point about the negative transformative effects of affect upon subjectivity stand as a counterweight to more positive versions of affect's alleged positive plenitude.

In order to regain epilepsy from the cultural telos of death, passivity, and degradation, it is useful to revisit Guattari's remarks in *Chaosmosis* about pathic apprehension and apply them to seizures, discovering what it means to pass through them.[55] Guattari underlines the importance of *enlarging* openings to the event, in order to access and excavate the material and energetic traits of experience. This has been accomplished by Australian media artist Isabelle Delmotte who attempts to attune herself to internal changes during seizures and regain body knowledge by inhabiting the chaotic openings and closing of them. It is also significant to *increase* the means available for one's existential recomposition. In this process one hopes to avoid hard-and-fast attachments to tired symbols, like the Christian religious tradition of St. Valentine as an intercessor of demons (the "falling sickness") with its ponderous European pedigree.[56] Additionally, Guattari advocates a therapeutic approach that *engages and discerns* a variety of "semiotic vectors" that impact and intersect the complex experiences of epileptics, not only in terms of their interfaces with the medical establishment, especially diagnostic routines, the gathering of histories, and physical exams. The goal is to release them from any "existential entrapments" by introducing materials of expression that could be used to gather from the depths of their facticity source materials for subjectivation. This is not an argument for the post hoc analysis of children's seizure drawings, for example, from an art therapeutic perspective, in order to see how they adjust and cope to their epilepsy, despite their underutilization.[57] It is rather an approach that pays attention to potential, even transitory, becomings across the spectrum that are disclosed in what might be called, after Guattari, the *epileptic real*, that provide the foundation for consistency, coordination, and finding ways to inhabit the specific pathic relations of an epileptic with his or her seizures, which is also a way to avoid standardized "deficit alterations of normal subjectivity . . . glischrogeny for epilepsy," interestingly enough,[58] and the clichés of epilepsy in popular music, particularly in rap and heavy metal.[59] Instead, Guattari's approach points us in the direction of the filmic archive of Paul Sharits, whose films such as *Epileptic Seizure Comparison* (1976) enhance his flicker method with a soundtrack of scratches, abstract colored squares, and documentary stills, and the performance artist Rita Marcalo's *Involuntary Dances* that investigates both involuntary convulsions and the effects of the drugs that control them on her body. Within the more popular music spectrum, there is Antony and the Johnsons's expressionistic fairy dance in the video for the song *Epilepsy is Dancing* (Wachowski Brothers, 2009). Perhaps the more aggressive and technologically dystopian video performances of Neoist Monty Cantsin (Istvan Kantor), on the "spasmo" theme, such as *Seizure Aktivity* (2001), expose the intensities of existential chaosmotic immersion, and confront their strangeness.

NOTES

1. Steven C. Schacter, "The Visions of Artists with Epilepsy: Implications for Neuroscience," *Epilepsy & Behavior* 14 (2009): 12–14.
2. Paul Virilio, *The Aesthetics of Disappearance*, trans. P. Beitchman, New York: Semiotext(e)/Autonomedia, 1991, p. 10.
3. Andrea E. Cavanna et al., "Epilepsy and Consciousness," in *New Research on Epilepsy and Behavior*, ed. K. J. Holloway, New York: Nova Science, 2007, p. 300.
4. Virilio, *Aesthetics of Disappearance*, p. 14.
5. Ibid., p. 20.
6. John M. Sutherland and Howard Tait, *The Epilepsies*, Edinburgh: E&S Livingstone Ltd., 1969, pp. 31–32.
7. Manfred Sakel, *Epilepsy*, New York: Philosophical Library, 1958, pp. 24–26.
8. Sutherland and Tait, *The Epilepsies*, pp. 32–33.
9. Margiad Evans, "Epilepsy," in *The Inner World of Mental Illness*, ed. B. Kaplan, New York: Harper & Row, 1964, p. 352.
10. *Negative Horizon*, London: Continuum, 2005, p. 44.
11. Lehnertz Klaus, "Epilepsy: Extreme Events in the Human Brain," in *Extreme Events in Nature and Society*, eds. S. Albeverio et al., Berlin: Springer, 2006, p. 138.
12. Steve Redhead, *Paul Virilio: Theorist for an Accelerated Culture*, Toronto: University of Toronto Press, 2004, p. 160.
13. Virilio, *Aesthetics of Disappearance*, p. 22.
14. Jean-François Beauchard (David B.), *Epileptic*, trans. Kim Thomson, New York: Pantheon, 2005, p. 36.
15. Chester Brown discusses his mother in "The Chester Brown Interview," *The Comics Journal* 135 (1990). http://www.tcj.com/the-chester-brown-interview/.
16. Perminder Sachdev, "Schizophrenia-Like Psychosis and Epilepsy," in *The Spectrum of Psychotic Disorders: Neurobiology, Etiology and Pathogenesis*, eds. D. Fujii et al., Cambridge: Cambridge University Press, 2007, p. 270.
17. Scott McCloud, *Understanding Comics*, Northampton, MA: Kitchen Sink Press, 1993, p. 74ff.
18. Paul Virilio, *Lost Dimension*, New York: Semiotext(e), 1991, p. 36.
19. Douglas Wolk, "David B.: The Battle against the Real World," in *Reading Comics*, ed. D. Wolk, New York: Da Capo, 2007, p. 144.
20. David B., *Epileptic*, p. 20.
21. Susan M. Squier, "So Long as They Grow Out of It: Comics, the Discourse of Developmental Normalcy, and Disability," *Journal of Medical Humanities* 29 (2008): 80.
22. Félix Guattari, "Ritornellos and Existential Affects," trans. J. Schiesari and G. Van Den Abbeele, *Discourse* 12.2 (1990): 66. See also "Refrains and Existential Affects," in *Schizoanalytic Cartographies*, trans. A. Goffey, London: Bloomsbury,

2013, pp. 203–14. And Eugène Minkowski, *Lived Time: Phenomenological and Psychopathological Studies*, trans. N. Wetzel, Evanston, IL: Northeastern University Press, 1933.

23. Brian Massumi, "The Autonomy of Affect," in *Deleuze: A Critical Reader*, ed. P. Patton, Oxford: Blackwell, 1996, pp. 221–22.

24. "Ritornellos," pp. 66–67.

25. See Herbert Spiegelberg, *Phenomenology in Psychology and Psychiatry*, Evanston, IL: Northeastern University Press, 1972, pp. 243–46.

26. "Ritornellos," p. 67; Arthur Tatossian, *Phénomenologie des psychoses*, Paris: Masson, 1980. Watson in her *Guattari's Diagrammatic Thought* explains Guattari's debt to Tatossian in terms of how pathic experience remains "immediate, intuitive, preconceptual" and a matter of "existential consistency" (pp. 133–34).

27. Maurice Merleau-Ponty, *Phenomenology of Perception*, trans. C. Smith, New York: Routledge & Kegan Paul, 1962. And Kurt Goldstein, *Aftereffects of Brain Injuries in War*, New York: Grune & Stratton, 1948.

28. Guattari, *Anti-Oedipus*, p. 361.

29. Merleau-Ponty, *Phenomenology of Perception*, p. 136.

30. Minkowski, *Lived Time*, p. 203.

31. Ibid., p. 209.

32. Minkowski, *Lived Time*, p. 65; Sutherland and Tait, *The Epilepsies*, 113; Walter J. Friedlander, *The History of Modern Epilepsy: The Beginning, 1865–1914*. Wesport, CT: Greenwood Press, 2001, pp. 220–23.

33. Massumi, "Autonomy of Affect," pp. 228–29.

34. Tatossian, *Phénomenologie des psychoses*, p. 42; "Ritornello," p. 79, n. 4.

35. Tatossian, *Phénomenologie des psychoses*, p. 42.

36. Daniel Stern, *The Interpersonal World of the Infant: A View from Psychoanalysis and Developmental Psychology*, New York: Basic Books, 1985, p. 54ff.

37. "Ritornellos," p. 68.

38. Guattari, *Chaosmosis*, p. 9.

39. "Ritornello," pp. 68–69.

40. "Ritornello," p. 69.

41. Guattari, *Chaosmosis*, p. 17.

42. "Ritornellos," p. 73.

43. Ibid., p. 72.

44. Marco Bellocchio, *Fists in the Pocket*, 1965. DVD. Doria Film/The Criterion Collection.

45. Peter Cowie, *Revolution! The Explosion of World Cinema in the Sixties*, New York: Faber and Faber, 2004, p. 170. And Giuseppe Verdi, *La traviata* [1853]. Libretto by F. M. Piave, 1852.

46. Oswei Temkin, *The Falling Sickness: A History of Epilepsy from the Greeks to the Beginnings of Modern Neurology*, Baltimore: Johns Hopkins University Press, 1971, pp. 160–61.

47. Sachdev, "Schizophrenia-Like Psychosis and Epilepsy," p. 270.

48. R. Pompili et al., "Suicide Risk among Epileptic Patients," in *New Research on Epilepsy and Behavior*, ed. K. J. Holloway, New York: Nova Science, 2007, pp. 147–48.

49. Anton Corbijn, *Control: The Tragic Tale of the Singer of Joy Division*, 2007. DVD. The Weinstein Company/The Miriam Collection.

50. Iggy Pop, *The Idiot*. Produced by David Bowie. RCA Records, 1977; Fyodor Dostoyevsky, *The Idiot* [1869], trans. R. Pevear, New York: Vintage, 2003.

51. Joy Division. "Atmosphere," *Unknown Pleasures*. Factory Records, 1979.

52. Guattari, *Chaosmosis*, p. 133.

53. David B., *Epileptic*, p. 143.

54. Deleuze and Guattari, *A Thousand Plateaus*, p. 299.

55. Guattari, *Chaosmosis*, pp. 68–70.

56. Gerhard Kluger and Verena Kudernatsch, "St. Valentine—Patron Saint of Epilepsy: Illustrating the Semiology of Seizures over the Course of Six Centuries," *Epilepsy & Behavior* 14 (2009): 219–25.

57. Carl E. Stafstrom and Jancie Havlena, "Seizure Drawings: Insight into the Self-Image of Children with Epilepsy," *Epilepsy & Behavior* 4 (2003): 43–56.

58. Guattari, *Chaosmosis*, p. 83. Guattari's ambivalence about Minkowski surfaces here.

59. Sallie Baxendale, "The Representation of Epilepsy in Popular Music," *Epilepsy & Behavior* 12 (2008): 165–69.

Chapter 10

Micropolitics of Hope

Anthropologist of micropolitical hope Barbara Glowczewski is among the vanguard of key global Guattarian thinkers. Deploying Guattari's three registers of ecosophy to understand the foliatedness of disaster in the anthropocene, she excavates a range of examples, from artists' responses to crises and neo-liberal betrayals, collective intelligence marshalled against the violence of privatization, experimentations leading to micro-social innovations challenging the criminalization of asylum seekers, and political actions against the ongoing endo-colonialist policies of settler states. Eschewing victimal discourses traded like stocks by big media, she additionally eviscerates the dehumanizing logic of humanitarian care in the form of "assistancialism" and, as some Aboriginals know it, "sit down money."[1]

Glowczewski's unique voice speaks from her fieldwork among the Warlpiri in Australia that began in the late 1970s, and her interpretations of dreaming as a kind of becoming caught the eye of Guattari in the late 1980s. The struggles of Aboriginal individuals and families to mount convincing cases for land titles against a state not above dirty tricks, like destroying ministry archives, form part of her criticism of state interventions and bureaucracies against the background of what the Birmingham school cultural studies theorists, referring to youth subcultures, once called "resistance through rituals."

However, it is attention to the problems of social scientific method that highlight her Guattarian concerns. Guattari wanted to develop a new method of analysis that would not rehearse the centrality of linguistic semiology that marked structuralism and reduced the unconscious to language. Schizoanalysis became a meta-model that criticized all inherited analytic models of interpretation and sought to look on events as the bearers of the potential for automodelisation that yield new maps of subjectivation. For Guattari, "Schizoanalysis . . . is not an alternative modelization. It is a meta-modelization. It tries to understand how it is that you got where you are? 'What is your model to you? It does not work?'—Then, I don't know, one tries to work together. One must see if one can make a graft of other models."[2] Guattari's inventive and hybrid sense of the possibilities of modelling for singularization goes hand-in-hand with his critique of method, in particular, the old and new testaments of psychoanalysis (Freud-Lacan), and how this secondary religion preaches false freedoms under a "pitiless semiotic control."[3] For Guattari, the "ultimate reductionist model"[4] was psychoanalysis, as it surpassed both mass media and literature in its flattening effects.

Guattari explains in *Lines of Flight* that "in the present study we have no other ambition than to attempt to appreciate what could be the *conditions* of a new analytic method whose task would not be limited, in this domain, to an external exam and 'expert' interventions, but which would facilitate a collective care-taking in a specified micropolitical field."[5] Guattari is explaining here how the collective production of research reports, of which *Lines* is an instance,[6] can help address fundamental challenges when faced with the overwhelming elimination of real political options by massive institutional constraints. The proviso he sets out is that despite such limits on political choice, the formation of new micropolitical groups remains not only possible but desirable, but neither on the foundations of universals, nor even on the refounding of conquered territories.

Paying close attention to the specificities of the objects studied, namely, desiring productions in their collective manifestations, requires adherence to a methodological principle that is not neutral: "Only desire can read desire. We therefore cannot emphasize enough the necessity of a certain *transference of enunciation*: the subject undertaking a study must be 'enmeshed' in one way or another with the mode of enunciation of the subject of the study."[7] In this vein, then, Glowczewski observes the effects of distanciation typical of social science methods and points out that "the traditional academic recommendation regarding the need for a scientific distance in order to remain 'objective' in social sciences has opened curious filiation tracks in disciplines where the civic, and even political engagement, as well as the utopic spirit that prevailed at their beginning now seem to be frowned upon by many colleagues in France and elsewhere."[8] She directs us towards acknowledging the importance of respecting indigenous singularities, and of acknowledging political options, for instance, in the emergence in 2011 of the short-lived First Nations Political Party (renamed in 2013 and de-registered in 2015 for failing to meet the membership floor). Avoiding sterility and refusing to serve as a handmaiden of power, as disciplinarity in the service of social control, are two goals set out by Guattari.

Glowczewski states: "I believe that anthropology is particularly called to engage in analyses that consider all those relations [natural and social disasters, memories, histories, responses to the agency of victims] in a critical way in order to trigger local and global reflection towards new social alternatives."[9] She cites David Graeber on anarchist anthropology, but we could just as well go to Eduardo Viveiros de Castro, who writes in *Cannibal Metaphysics*: "Anthropology is ready to fully assume its new mission of being the theory/practice of the permanent decolonization of thought."[10] Not everyone agrees, of course, De Castro is not naïve. It is evident though that transferences of enunciation are at work in the shift regarding the sources of anthropology's most imaginative concepts, namely, those societies it studies. Indigenous practices and styles of thought make anthropology run, but whether change on the order of that announced in *Anti-Oedipus* will occur is anyone's guess, even though the "cycle" of colonialism and exoticism is coming to an end and the era of ontological partition is being remapped.

Guattari's revision of the transference relation in psychoanalysis, what Freud once suggested in his papers on technique as an "unexpected novelty" arising in the treatment of neurotics and hysterics; this is a "special interest" the analysand shows in the analyst for a time, and vice versa if the countertransference is taken into account. Indeed, when transference becomes resistance, a problem arises. Transferential relations are recoded by Guattari as beyond "any actual dual relation"[11] as they are group-based, collective, involving minimally a third element that can be detached, and the avoidance of alienating models that re-establish the social status quo. The encounters of subject groups and subjugated groups greatly interested Guattari in his clinical practice and form the practical scene of his deployment of transferential relations. Collective assemblages of enunciation may be transferred between groups, with their different degrees of agency, but specifically also transferred across the subject-object divide in a research setting. The alienating model of social science extraction of knowledge from a study group, and anthropology's comfortable and entrenched misrecognition of the source of its own inventiveness, may be overcome if new relations are opened up and more robust transversal connections are admitted that modify the relations at stake. This is not a recipe for instant cooperation, but it is a clarion call for the bypassing of institutional structures and dogmas of ideology. It does not guarantee mutual understanding. The machinic expression highlights the necessity for co-production of knowledge, but also respect for the amount of play the "teeth" of a situation will tolerate as seen from the inside. Guattari did not much concern himself with official academic research, with its alienating procedures, but if we take to heart his suggestion, then transferences of enunciation build capacities for new organizations and alliances where collective work can be undertaken that involves mixtures of participants with the courage to cast off their blindness (separation, reification, extraction, idealization, etc.). Transference, as Freud stated, involves love. Love of the relationship in research is, as militant-researchers remind us, not intellectual, not objectifying, not capitalistic, but rather consists of intensities with which a new collective bond is composed.[12] This is the future road of an anthropology animated by social justice that Glowczewski advances along, directed by the signposts planted by Guattari among others. It may be too much to ask of an academic discipline that it collectively semioticizes in a non-formal way new assemblages; it is at least possible for it to reset priorities and actively resist becoming an accomplice to the general givens that arrange its hierarchies and apparently ineluctable combinations.

NOTES

1. Barbara Glowczewski, "Resisting the Disaster: Between Exhaustion and Creation," *Spheres* 2 (December 2015): 17. http://spheres-journal.org/resisting-the-disaster-between-exhaustion-and-creation.

2. In this radical post-psychoanalysis the schizoanalyst attempts to discern the emergence of something that might get a patient moving again, by scouting out opportune potentialities among nuclei of autopoesis, and activating cross-componential hatchings of subjectification by means of found (extracted) or placed (created) elements, enriching (onto-logic) rather than reducing (logic of sets) them. See *The Guattari Reader*, pp. 132–33.

3. Guattari, *Schizoanalytic Cartographies*, p. 44.

4. Ibid., p. 45.

5. Guattari, *Lines of Flight*, p. 36. Translation modified.

6. *Lines of Flight* is the infamous "lost" report written by members of the Centre for Institutional Study, Research and Development, to satisfy a French government research contract, and dates from an important period in Guattari's intellectual life, as it straddles the publication of both *A Thousand Plateaus* and *The Machinic Unconscious*. Much of the material contained in it will be familiar to readers of the other two books.

7. Guattari, *Lines of Flight*, pp. 38–39.

8. Glowczewski, "Resisting the Disaster," p. 19.

9. Glowczewski, "Resisting the Disaster," p. 19.

10. De Castro, *Cannibal Metaphysics*, trans. P. Skafish, Minneapolis, MN: Univocal, 2014, p. 40.

11. Guattari, *The Guattari Reader*, p. 63.

12. Collectivo Situaciones, "On the Researcher-Militant," www.situaciones.org (September 2003), p. 7.

Part IV

SEARCH FOR A METHOD

INTRODUCTION

The title of this part indicates the theoretical debts of Guattari to Jean-Paul Sartre (his *Questions of Method* is sometimes translated as *Search for a Method*), especially his theory of groups, but also the links between militant political struggles against capitalism and advocacy for the mentally ill, both thinkers highlighting the struggles of the Socialist Patients' Collective (SPK) in Germany; both Guattari and Sartre played important roles in the appeal of French intellectuals against state repression in Italy in 1977. Sartre's ghost haunts much of Guattari's early theoretical work, and he attributes to Sartre direct lines of influence for a number of his own key concepts:

> Everything I have said and done is I some way marked by him. His reading of nothingness, and of detotalization, became in my work, deterritorialization. His conception of seriality, of the practico-inert, influenced my notion of the group subject. His understanding of freedom and the type of engagement as well as intellectual responsibility, which he incarnated, have remained, for me, if not imperatives, then at least immediate givens. . . . Sartre is a verb who is conjugated in the present.[1]

Sartre was for Guattari an antidote to postmodernism and the "subsidence of social practice."[2] His example helped Guattari get through the "winter years." It may also have steered him in the direction of writing scripts, a literary passion that Guattari pursued but did not publish during his lifetime. But Guattari's Sartre was a thinker he reimagined as an ecosopher, or at least as someone who would be an advocate for the importance of the three ecologies in reinventing the social.

Chapter 11, "The Search for Non-Meaning," is not a parody of the classic popular study in phenomenological psychiatry by Viktor Frankl, but a combination of two lines of flight from meaning, that is, from structuralism, semiology, discursivity, and linguistics: Guattari's theories of a-signifying semiotics and conceptualization of affect as pathic experience.[3] The production of subjectivity was separated by Guattari from speech and writing, in an existentializing gesture that made use of fragments of language to create new references and recalibrate its relation to the socius, escaping the minimally operational subjectivity of capitalism, at the very least by exploiting its machinic potentialities. This was the goal of his development and refinement of "the grid" at La Borde: to found an analytic relationship that could produce new subjectivations, by means of strange local languages, constitutive meanings, and affects (sharable and unsharable). It was the curious confluence of semiotics and psychoanalysis, the two great intellectual loves of my early career, that not only brought me to Guattari's thought in the first instance but kept me there as well.

Chapter 12, "Dissident Organ: The Three Billion Perverts Issue of *Recherches*," answers the question: why study a journal? Journals are sites of collective production and the formation of groups. These micro-institutional spaces of auto-production were constants in Guattari's intellectual life, from his earliest experiences in the youth hostel movement through the lessons of the Freinet School delivered by Fernand Oury, learning about the role of auto-critique in auto-production, and participating in the collectivities that coalesce as editors, readers, volunteers, printers, funders assume their roles. Journals engender institutional matter not only in their pages but also in the meetings, the review process, editing activities, trips to the printer, and so on. Collective journal publishing was a constant in Guattari's life, especially *Recherches*, which spanned two formative transdisciplinary groups, which it helped to produce and sustain. Journals are not mere products. They are universes of reference for the groups that are formed by them. The Three Billion Perverts issue of *Recherches* is an example of collaboration (CERFI and the Front homosexual d'action révolutionnaire) in a milieu unfiltered by social scientific methodological distanciation. A landmark in French queer history, and certainly the touchstone for queer Deleuze studies, Three Billion Perverts was subtitled a Grand Encyclopedia of Homosexualities. As Stéphane Nadaud remarks upon the occasion of the posting of an edited online reissue, the self-censorship and amputation of chapter four concerning "pédo-philie" (a rerouted boy scout manual) raises the question not of the correctness of the decision, which is not in doubt, but about forgetting and remembering and by whom: "This is why they [editors of the web site criticalsecret.com] have orchestrated a dynamic of *restitution* which, in a remarkable fashion, is to be accomplished by way of a *disappearance*. To be more precise, this is a *restitution which hides a disappearance* . . . this is a false restitution."[4] Readers are asked to remember something about which they know nothing, to become passive, disappointed, disillusioned. Still, this is the enduring power of Three Billion Perverts. It is effectively provocative whether it is 1973 or 2012. Despite a court order for the destruction of all remaining copies, hard copies remain in circulation.[5] This is the context of my reading of the figure of the Arab in the pages of the original journal, a problem of representation that persists across the chapters and the registers of informal and academic languages.

One of my early forays into schizoanalytic method involved an attempt to embed Guattari's understanding of transdisciplinary research into contemporary discussions of the concept, but by respecting both his commitment to elaborate a immanentist metamethodology adequate to the hypercomplex objects of the contemporary universe of things, and to posit the need for the passage from modelling to metamodelling via diagrams and non-representational forces such as a-signifying signs and affects.[6] Later, I integrated Guattarian transdisciplinarity into the study of journals and their editorial assemblages.[7]

NOTES

1. See my *Félix Guattari: An Aberrant Introduction*, London: Continuum, 2002, p. 65.

2. See Guattari's essay "Plutôt avoir tort avec lui," *Libération* (Samedi 23 and Dimanche 24 Juin, 1990). Guattari found *Libération*'s invitation to rethink the "operationality" of Sartre's concepts a little embarrassing, but contributed a stirring, and unfashionable, endorsement of Sartre nonetheless.

3. My efforts to explain Guattari's a-signifying semiotics culminate in a chapter of my recent book, "From Information Theory to Félix Guattari's A-signifying Semiotics," in *Critical Semiotics: Theory, from Information to Affect*, London: Bloomsbury, 2016, pp. 13–53. Chapter 11 is largely unpublished and was presented under the title of "Can Semiotics Make the Affective Turn?" with a response by Ian Angus, at Simon Fraser University, Institute for the Humanities, Vancouver, spring 2017. The section on pathic apprehension owes much to the essay "Pathic Transferences and the Contemporary Japanese Arts," that I included in my co-edited volume (with Jay Hetrick), *Machinic Eros*, Minneapolis, MN: Univocal, 2015, pp. 119–35.

4. S. Nadaud, "Whatever Happened to Chapter Four of Three Billion Perverts?" *Paragraph* 35/2 (2012): 293.

5. This chapter is a revised version of the essay I published under the title "The Figure of the Arab in Three Billion Perverts," *Deleuze Studies* 1/1 (2007): 60–78.

6. This chapter borrows from my essay "Félix Guattari: Towards a Transdisciplinary Metamethodology," *Angelaki: Journal of the Theoretical Humanities* 8/1 (April 2003): 129–40. Five years later I co-edited and introduced with Andrew Murphie a special issue on "Models, Metamodels and Contemporary Media," *Fibreculture* 12 (2008). http://journal.fibreculture.org/issue12.

7. Chapter 13 also borrows from my essay "Transdisciplinarity and Journal Publishing," in *Valences of Interdisciplinarity*, ed. Raphael Foshay, Edmonton: Athabasca University Press, 2011, pp. 231–49. This essay hints at a larger project that I have completed with the research assistance of Kristina Marcellus in which the transversality of the editorial structure of the American political theory journal *Telos* is investigated in relation to its diasporic editorial composition with Canadian critical and cultural theory journals. The unpublished manuscript is titled *Back Issues: Journals and the Formation of Critical and Cultural Theory in Canada.*

Chapter 11

The Search for Non-Meaning

Dear semionauts, Daniel Chandler writes in his introductory text *Semiotics: The Basics* that "we seem as a species to be driven by a desire to make meanings: above all, we are surely *homo significans*—meaning-makers."[1] Rather, perhaps it is the search for non-meaning that defines an immersion in general semiosis that is not anchored irreducibly by a human maker. Yet immediately a quandary arises: what sorts of engagements other than interpretation are at issue, and which sorts of semiosis might these entail? I am not, of course, referring to phonemes or graphemes that taken by themselves do not have meaning, although they, as Roman Jakobson reminds us, are at its "service," but "devoid" of it, consisting of "mere otherness."[2] Neither is the search for non-meaning framed as an anti-phenomenological effort that completely rejects the existentiality of semiotic acts, and the becoming of signs. Indeed, keeping one's distance from the pose of the semiotic nihilist is the order of the day, since the nihilist accepts the sign's representative function and its relations of subordination that open a gap between one sign standing for another, and then uses meaning-making to paper over it, remaining silent about this power.[3]

The search for non-meaning advances beyond nihilism. A critical semiotic theory may be found stirring in the heterogeneous forces of plural and hybrid semiotic entities. These constitute signposts pointing towards the affective turn within contemporary critical thought that seeks to apprehend and embrace the intensities that have the capacity to disrupt and open experience, without then arresting and limiting them. If critical semiotics has a credo, it would be that grasping signs as conductors of intensities opens new pathways leading to the displacement of meaning for the sake of a dynamic and processual semiosis. There are numerous ways to state the problem of the relationship between flows and signification, between change and structure.

One need only return to Jacques Derrida's comments about the conditions affecting force and signification: for him, force is defeated by structure, or at least neutralized by it, even if this too is a force of sorts.[4]

Although for affect theory it is doubtful that change and movement can enter into structure, what interests me is the question of how to recognize that structure has the potential for change and movement. One of the clearest statements of this problematic is found in Brian Massumi's book, *Parables for the Virtual* that announces an ambitious plan to refresh cultural theory by regaining the bracketed middle of movement/sensation between bodies and change. For him, cultural theory (including semiology) lacks processual awareness and is too grid-like in the way it pins down bodies in its mode of apprehension, especially in the identification of local manifestations and resistances. Massumi wants to give matter and motion, potentiality, processuality, dynamism, intensity, and becoming back to bodies: "rethink body, subjectivity, and social change in terms of movement, affect, force, and violence—before code, text, and signification."[5]

Massumi's call to resist and reject pre-existing interpretive grids that arrest motion because such grids bracket becomings echoes Guattari's statement that the "theorising which stems from structural linguistics forbids us from entering the real world of the machine."[6] Structures can smother events. Language can dampen affective intensities by prefigured codes and invariant rules.[7] Process must come before signification and semiogenesis. The general problem Massumi elucidates is the effort to put movement back into code: "After all is signified and sited, there is the nagging problem of how to add movement back into the picture. But adding movement to stasis is about as easy as multiplying a number by zero and getting a positive product."[8] Despite all of the richness and nuance in the development and execution of Massumi's project, the absence of a sustained reflection by him on the contributions of post-structuralism and its efforts, from Derrida to Lyotard, to think intensity, force, and signification, leads to a further problem: that movement may not have been completely missing in the first place from codes, structures, and discourse. In other words, Massumi overheats the distinction between affect and structure, and it sits awkwardly in his theoretical system; he is at once aligned with a search for processuality yet rejects it as long as it concerns signs. This overheated concern then becomes strangely attractive for affect theorists.

Certainly, the search for non-meaning must avoid a "stalemate"[9] resulting in semiotic stasis. Affect theory's "generic rejection"[10] of semiosis and structure, with some exceptions, requires correction. The key insight is that it matters a good deal where language's alterity is situated. If what is dynamically visceral and eventful is opposed to semiotic states, the potential for mutual influence and conditioning is, however, limited. Inspired by Guattari, it is useful to examine the mutual conditioning of discourse and affect. Simply, supplies of discourse are found in the pathic or affective, non-discursive domains, despite discourse's tendency to bracket and annex intensities. Pathic intensities can work to either engage discourse to make something discernible when required or divert discourse from its overt purposes, uses, and ends by manipulating its contents, and in so doing triggering further affects. Indeed, the complex relationship between machine-structure and subjectivation was at the core of Guattari's theorizing about machinic disruptions of the stable differences inside of structure. First then Guattari's sense of pathic apprehension will be discussed; second, the semiotic typology that he used to search out two kinds of a-semiotic entities; and finally, how he characterized the encounter between machine and structure.

PATHIC APPREHENSION

Peter Pál Pelbart opened a trail in recognizing that the pathic dimension, borrowed from Viktor von Weizsäcker's theorization of pathic vitality, is a mode of lived experimentation intimately connected with the self-founding, and moving Guattarian subject living "more on the modalities of 'existensifying' than on ontic determinations."[11] Through this insight Pelbart introduces a fundamental distinction for von Weizsäcker between pathic and ontic determinations of being and Guattari's rewriting of the complex relations between these categories. Pathic intensity is by definition non-discursive, and used in conjunction with affectivity, while ontic is discursive and semiotic. Quoting Guattari, "the delimitation of affect is not discursive . . . not founded upon the systems of distinctive oppositions inflected according to sequences of linear intelligibility and capitalized in memory banks that are mutually compatible."[12] Affect is neither semiological nor digital data, and thus pathic experience is not obviously recognizable in these terms. Why this matters is that ontology can be one of the ways in which pathic intensity is pacified or qualified, which means that in Guattari's diagrams of ontological functions he is extremely careful not to trap it, or at least to intentionally build in escape routes that allow it to be just hazy, unqualified, sticky, and critically self-referencing. In order to vouchsafe this, he needs to shed the semio-linguistic baggage of expression-content, not reducing them to signifier-signified relations, resist privileging one term over the other, keep open transversal bridges across them, and not universalize the distinction.[13]

It is helpful to recall that Guattari's schizoanalytic cartography is built around four ontological functions (Flux/Phylum/Territory/Universe). One of the major divisions of these functions is drawn between a domain that is discursive, involving real contingent actualization on the plane of expression, and one that is non-discursive, that is, virtualization on the content plane. (See Table 11.1). The two functions associated with the discursive order are the fluxes and machinic phylum. Both of these are sources or roots of expressions like machinic propositions of logic or computer code; whereas existential territories and incorporeal universes belong to the non-discursive domain and are intensive rather than strictly objectal. Further, discursive relations are exo-referred models, and non-discursive meta-models are endo-referred. Guattari defines discursivity as "synonymous with sequential order exo-referenced to Energetico-Space-Time (EST) coordinates."[14]

Whereas non-discursivity is by definition pathic, pathic apprehension of being-in-the-world is, however, inevitably discursive, that is, not forever so, but secondarily so. This is a key qualification that itself requires sub-qualifications. The relationship between discourse and non-discourse is complex and abstract and more like a mutual solidarity, but not harmonious.

Consider this example. Readers of *A Thousand Plateaus* will recall that the discursive is already in the body-without-organs,[15] which is basically non-discursive, that is, non-interpretive, and that discourse introduces significance and subjectification, both kept in "small supplies." Similarly, Guattari positions the infinite speeds of the virtual as already loaded (inhabited) with finite speeds[16] of the actual (slows down, organizes, crystallizes);[17] thus, grasping finitely is possible only if an infinity upon expulsion from its virtual domain bears a quality that is graspable. Discourse is pre-loaded (it inhabits chaos and the bwo), is not in short supply, but in small supplies in every assemblage: "It is part of our apprehension of the world," Guattari states:

> It is linked to the fact that one is thrown into time, thrown into space, thrown into energetic fluxes. . . . The question is one of knowing if they [fluxes] found being, of knowing whether these energetico-discursive beings are things which are of the weft of being or on the contrary refer to an existential function which is this grasping, which is not a being that "edits" relations between beings but which is a projected being . . . multidimensional, heterogenetic, and which corresponds to singular constellations.[18]

The non-discursive is able to birth the discursive, because it already in some sense contains an element of it, and the maieutic may be achieved through a

Table 11.1

	EXPRESSION	*CONTENT*
	Actual discursive	Virtual enunciative nuclei non-discursive
Possible	*Phylum*/machinic discursivity	*Universe*/incorporeal complexity
Real	*Flux*/energetico-spatio-temporal discursivity	*Territory*/chaosmic incarnation

relative consistency gained in something akin to thrownness; obviously, the recourse to *Geworfenheit* is disclosed through objective processes of deterritorializtion, described by Heidegger as Dasein's facticity.[19] It is not as if Guattari substitutes discourse for thrownness. His use of discourse does recall Heidgegger's characterization of the calling of conscience as discourse by contrast to the distracting "hubbub" of "they" and what is "listening-away." In Guattari's nomenclature, the pathic is giving and the discursive is given; there is a solidarity between them, even though the phrase "there is the Given, thus there is the Giving" suggests an order or prority or implication. Nevertheless, what these terms primarily describe is the kind of discursivity in the non-discursive and how it manifests as blending that respects heterogeneity; and between the domains of F and P, their fusion through "relative delimitations." Discourse is a mode of disclosure, yet discourse for Guattari reveals a countervailing penchant for delimiting non-discursivity, which allows consistency to plant signage and build fences—that is, manifest itself. Likewise, it cannot be claimed that pathic life is unlocalizable.

Understood as markers of discursivity, the aforementioned "small supplies" include within the domains of flux (fluctuations) and phylum (the formation of fluxes) extrinsic elements of discursive ordering (exo-references) such as space-time coordinates and the linguistic formation and deformation of unformed matter,[20] that is, transformations of contingent fluxes into possible occurrences (abstract machines). And the endo-references of the pathic intensities are accessible phenomenologically, Guattari thinks, in analyses of nausea (overwhelmingly thrown), and megalomania (an overestimation of world-founding).[21]

Guattari further clarified that not all discourse was the enemy. Rather, only discourse that contributes to capitalistic subjectivation, with its infantile attachments, segregational attitudes, and inane enthusiasms, is the enemy because the more it proliferates in the spread of information, the further it diminishes and slows down enunciative capacity by making it less collective, more standardized, and exchangeist.[22] "What is a cancer is not discursivity as such, [but] the discursivity that deals with standardized, distinctive oppositions, with exchange currencies: capital, energy, the signifier, etc."[23] Discourse provides support in discernibilizing non-discursive virtual enunciative content. Guattari describes the promise of this support as a "diversion of narration."[24] As long as discourse aids in the production of non-equivalent, singular, auto-modelizations, it may be kept relatively free of capitalistic prerogatives. Pathic knowledge is enunciated through a narrative that no longer proves something or explains it rationally but, instead, is a diversionary path supporting more "lines of the possible."

The discursive and non-discursive domains, which Guattari is describing in terms of bi-directional interfaces at infinite speeds (with qualifications) between complex actualized Fluxes and hypercomplex chaosmic Territories, as well virtual Universes and the machinic Phylum, underlines a basic principle, as stated in *Chaosmosis*:

> What gives consistency to . . . discursive systems, what authorizes the erection of enunciative monads should be sought on the side of Content; that is, on the side of this existential function which, taking support from certain discursive links, diverts them from their signifying, denotational and propositional incidences, making them play the role of a refrain of ontological affirmation.[25]

There is a diversion of discursivity from its significational entrapment in denotational and connotational semiological strata by the insurgent forces of chaomosis that lead them, perhaps ride them, into richer and more heterogenetic enunciations that do not get stuck in discrete signifying economies, but can themselves receive grafts that highlight enriching "wild flights" and maximize "new charges of complexity."[26] Still, they need to support themselves on something, to acquire consistency, and a refrain serves this purpose. It is "pathic temporalization," a term borrowed from the description of psychopathological phenomena within phenomenological psychiatry without valorizing discordance and binarizing normal and abnormal.

The two vertically embedded categories of expression and content are for Guattari not mechanically layered like the signifying (morphemes) and non-signifying elements (phonemes) of linguistic double articulation. Their assemblage is partial and their enunciation "open, chaotically determined."[27] Most importantly, we may recall from *A Thousand Plateaus* that they exist in some way in one another and in intermediate states, and even their names are relative.[28] There is no priority given to either expression or content. They are functors that contract their functions. All species of discursivity, encompassing "phonological, gestural, spatial, and musical" examples, are irreducible to semio-structuration and to homogenetic reduction to transcendent entities. On the content or non-discursive side, an existentializing function—which needs to be identified in one or more contingent "concrete operators" and/or abstract machines—will cross over to the expression side in search of a discourse that will give it support, only to divert it from its "significational perspectives." Support and divert: these are two ways that pathic intensity self-enriches through discursivity. Anne Querrien, who worked with Guattari at the Centre for Institutional Study, Research and Training, explains in terms of writing as a bureaucratic form of expression that it "becomes a desiring-machine if what is written is placed in a position adjacent to the process that it serves, and begins to draw the tangency of its existence on the body-without-organs and not in the service of the writers' insurance company or ministry."[29] Deterritorialized writing engenders sideways exits. For Guattari, the breakdown of sense, a collapsus, "will always be associated with the promotion of a-signifying links of discursivity dedicated to the ontological weaving of an autoconsistent world."[30]

PATHIC PROTO-SUBJECTIVATION

Guattari posed the following semiotic question: "How do certain semiotic segments achieve their autonomy, start to work for themselves and to secrete new fields of reference?"[31] This is a basic question firstly about how such segments escape being reductively beholden to structural organization and the linguistic signifier. Remember, one of the goals of schizoanalysis is to depart from signifying interpretation. But, secondly, it is in addition a question about autonomization in an aesthetic sense. Mixing conceptual languages sifted from Lacan (gaze and voice), Bakhtin (content fragment), and Duchamp (onlooker's experience of an aesthetic echo) Guattari settles on "partial enunciator" to express how a fragment of a work's content becomes detached from its expressive material and is seized upon by a "creative subjectivity" in the process of assembling itself—a process that involves entering a new universe that is incorporeal as it is coming into existence. Such a universe doesn't pre-exist entry into it. Guattari borrows an example of this fragment of content from Bakhtin's analysis of poetry where "the feeling of movement" such as rhythmical elements become "attractors" that send processes of subjectivation down untried paths rather than back to pre-established coordinates. This "feeling of movement" is a vitality affect in the late psychotherapist Daniel Stern's (1934–2012) terminology, that is, a feeling unanchored to a category signal of emotion (i.e., due to anger or surprise).[32] For Guattari, the detached fragment of semiotic content is a point of origin that effects a "poetic-existential catalysis" towards the emergence of "nuclei of subjectivation" and is not peculiar to either creator or audience but, rather, is "quasi-synchronically the enunciative crystallization of the creator, interpreter and the admirer of the work of art."[33] Guattari underscores the dynamic affective relations between these figures and how they are put to work creating a "new existential edifice."[34]

The figure of von Weizsäcker appears as a footnote in *The Machinic Unconscious* that warns against the tendency to fall back upon hard-and-fast distinctions like that between "pathic" and "ontic," between the personal-vital-fluctuations and the physical-objective world of causal relations and quantities, to which Guattari himself is sometimes prone, he readily admits. "Certain distinctions that seem relevant in a given context can function elsewhere [when they are imported from the sciences] as concepts that binarize the assemblages while aborifying the problems."[35] This is to be avoided, and one of the functions of the molar-molecular or tree-rhizome dyad, without privileging either term, is to prevent hardening from occurring that drains away all interaction. An additional point for Guattari is that the reuse of imported concepts from science cannot preserve the heterogeneity, that is, the "machinic creationism" that he finds at every level of the cosmos.[36] Guattari regains the pathic from von Weizsächer's opposition and finds it at work in all processes of subjectification. Thus, by the period of *Chaosmosis*, Guattari restates his position in this way: rationalist and capitalist subjectivations can crowd out pathic knowledge by "bracketing" it as in scientific modelling.[37]

One of the most compelling implications of decentring is that it permits "enunciation [to] become correlative not only to the emergence of a logic of non-discursive intensities, but equally to a pathic incorporation-agglomeration of these vectors of partial subjectivity."[38] Guattari's shift to the non-discursive not only escapes models of subjectivity built upon discursive logics, individuation, and personhood but also pushes past the subject-object opposition. Yet drawing upon both phenomenology and psychoanalysis, Guattari looks for fusions of subject-object poles in "subjective transitivism" or "non-discursive transitivism" that do not exist outside of some relation to the discursive, but are not fixed by it or anything else for that matter. Discursivity is not an enemy done away with once and for all—it is precisely this kind of thinking that Guattari wants to avoid (likewise, a-signifying semiotics do not forgo once and for all signifying semiologies). Guattari instead focuses on the pathic knowledge of non-discursive experience that he mentions briefly may be seen in hypnosis and in the experience of duration in the encounter with nuclei of subjectivation that pre-exist the subject-object relational division. Subjectivation comes to exist alongside the subject-object relation in due course as it attempts to self-actualize. To do this it eventually needs spatio-temporal coordinates and semiotic mediations, namely, discursive operators (fluxes and phyla). But Guattari notes that this recourse to discourse has a peculiar character since while it allows for the apprehension of subjectivity's autoformation, it additionally reveals an element of pseudo-discursivity and pseudo-mediation installed at the foundation of the subject-object relationship.[39] The paradox, as he calls it, is that the foundation of all modes of subjectivation is the pathic, even though the pathic tends to be squeezed out of discourse, especially by reductionistic sciences and rationalist subjectivities, even by badly botched narrative refrains like those of consumer culture; yet Guattari's insight is that discourse rests on the very thing it attempts to evacuate, namely, non-discursivity. And conversely, the non-discursive requires discursivity along the way to making discernible lines of heterogeneity.

Non-discursive, pathic, universes of reference are virtual: deterritorialized and incorporeal. The virtual (complex incorporeal Universes) brings about actualization (real chaosmic existential Territorizations) by finding an interface (a complex, heterogenetic refrain, that is limitless) between them. The operator between these two orders, that is, territory and universe, is called "pathic"—its role is to translate back and forth their endo-references to existential and virtual striations and in so doing mix them (i.e., mixed speeds); whereas, the "ontic operator" hinges flux and phylum with exo-referenced coordinates that generate intermediary mixtures of consistencies including regularities, moulding, and processual elements as well.[40] The search for nuclei of enunciative consistency involves a "diverting" deployment of discursivity (i.e., using narrative to establish complex refrains as opposed to offer explanations). Pathic knowledge does not generate objective descriptions and circumscribed fields of references with regard to external objects. For Guattari, "pathic expression is not placed in relations of discursive succession in order to situate the object in the basis of a clearly delimited referent. Here we are in a register of co-existence, of crystallization of intensity."[41] Pathic relationships are neither fixed by signification nor structural coordinates nor metaphysical dualisms. A virtual universe cannot be only identified in its existential incarnation; it cannot be solely described in the discursive register it deploys, fixed by its referents. The deployment of discursivity against its tendency to evacuate pathic knowledge gives to it a certain against the grain texturality as narrative, especially mythically rich theories like Freudianism, that can become the existential supports for intensive refrains and thus for mutant subjectivations. Nevertheless, in directing pathic intensity towards a distinctly formed and fixed entity, it may be converted into an anchor. This is the main failure of the Lacanian signifier, thinks Guattari, which inherits linearity and misapplies it, overweights it in a homogenizing manner to the "pathic, non-discursive, autopoetic character of partial nuclei of enunciation,"[42] reducing the diverse components of any assemblage by means of structural logic and limiting subjectivation under the crushing influence of the symbolic order.

How does awareness of partial enunciators arise? Pathic consistencies are becomings. They are not apprehended through representation but through affect and a constantly changing field of forces that display various degrees of differentiation: "They start to exist in you, in spite of you." They transport, that is, sweep you away, Guattari thinks, into a universe of reference: "I find myself transported into a Debussyst Universe."[43] This happens all at once, before the traits of the affects enter into representational discourse. The "transversal flash" across subject and object is described by Guattari in terms of the "agglomeration" of affects before representation—it is "existence" pure and simple. Agglomeration becomes something of a technical term in *Chaosmosis* as it specifies the amassing in a jumbled, non-sequential way of components into assemblages of subjectivation. Returning to the aesthetic example of the fragment of content discussed earlier, there is a dovetailing of the transversal flash and manner in which such a fragment " 'takes possession of the author' to engender a certain mode of aesthetic enunciation."[44] The transversal flash is a complex refrain that has multiple powers: "plunging" (into sadness) or "imploding" (personality).

TRANSITIVIST AND FUSIONAL

Guattari's passing reference to von Weizsäcker's *Le cycle de la structure*,[45] translated into French by Michel Foucault, ends with a discussion of the pathic-ontic distinction. In addition, I turn to Von Weizsächer's *Pathosophie*, again in French translation, under the impetus of Jacques Schotte, who attended the latter's seminars in the early 1950s. It was the Belgian psychiatrist Schotte who convinced Guattari to rethink the transference relations by emphasizing transport in the sense of *transport amoureux* to be precise, a kind of love or sensual rapture.[46] And it was through Schotte that Pelbart accessed theory of the pathic; Guattari, too, accessed Von Weizsächer through Schotte.[47] Von Weizsäcker explains his conception of the pathic in terms of five categories constituting an interdependent pentagram of verbs: may, can, will, must, shall.[48] Pathic experience finds expression through the categories modelled on verbs. The expression is fixed by verb categories which von Weizsächer describes as akin to cages in which the passions have been imprisoned. Noting, however, their abstractness, he insists that such fixity is not to the exclusion of fluidity (after all, verbs can be conjugated and qualified by auxiliaries), but that "the imprisoned bird can take flight with its cage or the cage can take flight with the bird."[49] Pathic becoming-giving stands against ontic givenness-ordinariness. This becoming defined by cagey verbs indicates a volitional striving, that is, drive-based categories, whereas Guattari abandoned the drives for machines and rejected the nosological categories of psychoanalysis (neurosis, psychosis, melancholia, hysteria), as well as the aforementioned affective categories for amodals (not tied to a specific sensory mode). It is not hard to imagine Guattari's further objections to these statements: both the construction of a grammatical "axiomatic" for pathic intensity and the definition of pathic striving that is based on lack, for what is not (yet): "on ne peut vouloir que ce qui n'est pas,"[50] denounced in a global refusal in *Anti-Oedipus*: "nothing can be defined as a lack."[51] For von Weizsäcker pathic intensity appears to be stratified grammatically in which the categories are "coagulated abstractions"[52] that are only fluid as encumbered wholes (the flight of the bird with its cage). The five categories, von Weizsäcker specifies, "are to the logic of language what the axioms are to geometry."[53] The semiotic overcoding at work here takes language as the dominant model of realization, and the postulates as accepted and stable can only flow as wholes and in accordance with existing rules of combination, in other words, with the imperatives of grammar as a model of *subjectification* beginning in childhood. In fact, Guattari states that the pathic categories "mask one another by mutual disguise,"[54] yet he considers Von Weizsächer, via Schotte, an inspiration for his own theorizations.

Despite these differences, von Weizsäcker's thinking of the pathic is indexed to becoming. In *Cycle de la structure*, he advances a number of remarkable definitions of pathic becoming as potential: "The being in a state of crisis is nothing at the moment, but everything in potential."[55] Reading this in a Guattarian way, the emphasis is on passage and controlled proliferation. Intensive movements of the pathic erase the ontic: "The pathic state is basically a synonym for disappearance of the ontic; the crisis of transformation reveals the struggle to the death engaged in between pathic and ontic attributes."[56] This disappearance is for von Weizsäcker indicative of the non-translatability of the pathic experience into those of the ontic like space, time, and causality.[57] Put differently, it is not possible to resolve categories of desire and obligation in ontic motivations or causes. Guattari rejects this and other typical antagonisms (pathic/ontic; eros/thanatos) and develops a domain with "ontic" attributes in his cartography. For his part, Pelbart emphasizes a link between the erasure of the ontic in von Weizsäcker and Guattari's sense of a "de-differentiated" chaosmotic immanence that exists before so-called coordinating "ontic" attributes like space and time.[58] Submersion into a chaosmotic state—described as a pathological spectrum by Guattari including psychosis, autism, mania, and epilepsy. Drawing on Schotte's explication of von Weizsäcker, Pelbart first establishes that the parallel between Guattari's chaosmotic immanence and Schotte's sense that "in critical moments [crisis], life goes to 'the depths'; it resurges from the depths."[59] The indeterminable depth, like the unrepresentable chaosmosis, is inhabited at specific nodes Guattari calls "umbilical," and these are where existential territories are incarnated and incorporeal universes are constituted as subjectivity begins to be established in and around these "points of intensification" as it re-emerges.[60] Every depth has its own specific texture, and every inhabitation has its own "signed and dated event."[61] Pelbart characterizes von Weizsäcker's approach as a *science of suffering*: "the pathic being, after all, is the being which is able to feel—be it pain or pleasure."[62] Moments of crisis expose the pathic dimension more than others, especially when illness initiates a new set of coordinates as well as possibilities: "Illness is the moment when this ground erupts."[63]

TOWARDS A POST-SEMANTIC HORIZON

An interest in a-signification gets off the ground by dissociating itself in some manner from a meaning component and considers meaning to be an irritant.

This approach has an approximate birthdate in the post-war years of the late 1940s in the work on information and communication beyond semantic content by Claude Shannon and Warren Weaver among others. While Shannon announced the irrelevance of meaning for the engineering problem of communication, Weaver, a popularizer of science and consummate Cold War bureaucrat, tried to put meaning back into the bottle by claiming that the primary technical problems at issue overlapped the secondary semantic problem. He addressed the problem through the insertion of extra components, including a semantic receiver and a semantic type of noise, into the point-to-point transmission model of communication. These "skirmishes with meaning," as Guattari referred to them,[64] show that what may be regrettable about the transmission model from a cultural perspective is promising from a machinic perspective. In other words, the critical semiotic search for non-meaning formulated by Shannon and Weaver fundamentally displaced signs for the sake of signals, a kind of technified semanteme.[65] This displacement is what I am identifying as one possible starting point for a-signification. However, the minimum communicational condition that corresponds to the predominance of signals should not be taken as a diminishment. Signals are in some respects scapegoated as the poor semiotician's stock-in-trade. What makes them less than signs proper is, as Umberto Eco explains in *A Theory of Semiotics*, that they "can be computed quantitatively irrespective of their possible meaning."[66] Signals thus on this view occupy "the lower threshold of semiotics." In my view, the lowly status of signals is unearned and unfortunate. Even if they slip under the semantic horizon, this gives them not only quantitative but lively connective qualities worth exploring in depth. Signals may be revivified semiotically, rather than restored to full semiological status, through their a-signifying characteristics. The distinction between signals and signs is fundamental for Guattari. He distinguishes between hormonal signals and linguistic signs: "The former produces no signification engenders no sable system of redundancy that would make it possible for anyone to see it as identical to any representation."[67] Signals (a-semiotic and a-signifying) operate without generating significations, although they may function adjacently and incidentally to them.

SIGNALS	SIGNS
Asignifying semiotics: technoinformatic; musical; mathematical	Signifying semiologies
Proliferate in delirium: excess semiosis	Linguistic (central)
A-semiotic: viral, bacterial, cellular; outside the signifying strata	Symbolic (peripheral but still translatable into semiology)

Still, overcoming semiotic prejudices against signals does not lead us into a mono-semiotic landscape. Guattari insisted that a-signifying semiotics subsists alongside the signifying semiologies (around language) and symbolic semiotics (around non-verbal and ritual performances). A-signifying semiotics are defined relationally by Guattari against signifying semiologies, beyond which—outside the strata defined by content and expression planes and form-matter-substance relations—are a-semiotic encodings (genetic and other codes involving purely signaletic communication among viruses, cells, bacteria that are stripped of any projected "writing" onto them). Independent of language, then, a-semiotic codes consist of signals that "do not generate significations, do not engender stable systems of redundancy that someone might mistake as being identical to a representation."[68] A-semiotic and a-signifying semiotics both deploy signals—but only the former a-semiotic is truly independent from representation and is manifested in a living being of some kind, taking on numerous substances (aminoacids in proteins). Whereas the latter is never done with signifying semiologies, especially the semiological triangle at the summit of which is a mental point of reference; it is simply that they are crutches a-signification can sometimes do without.

Signifying semiologies concern well-formed substances (formed matter with a double planar articulation) situated on the stratified planes of expression and content, with the proviso that the transits among these strata are "centered on a single signifying substance" such as a sonorous substance of expression.[69] Symbolic semiologies are a species of signifying semiologies and concern multiple substances of expression (gestures, ritual acts) that are neither completely translatable into linguistic terms nor are they overcodable by any one substance of expression among them. This rule of non-translatability and non-linearity keeps at bay "the semiological linearity of the structural signifier which imposes itself despotically over all other [non-linguistic] modes of semiotisation."[70]

It is not difficult to appreciate Guattari's typologizing efforts: a-semiotic phenomena are purely signaletic and the furthest removed from human meaning-making; a-signifying semiotics are akin to this in that they may forgo human-centred and representational models of meaning, but neither completely nor indefinitely; the linguistic contents of signifying semiologies play a centralizing and controlling role within semiotic thought; and the non-linguistic semiotics are secondary but resistant in terms of translatability into language, yet they, too, like signal-using semiotics, may be marginalized on the basis of their alleged deficiencies, refusals, or incompatibilities with dominant systems. By the same token, but in the opposite direction, signifying semiologies can find useful resources in less well-formed and decentred semiotics, and put them to work in blurring the territories of the body or dismantling certain institutional power relations or eluding certain preset classifications and social sorting mechanisms. The idea of a-signification as arising in delirium and taking off in all directions is not-reducible to "talking nonsense," although this has been a tendency and for this reason is aligned across from dominant linguistic signs.

By the time he wrote his final book *Chaosmosis*, Guattari had become much more focused on a-signifying info-networks and the devices used to engage with them, namely bank and debit cards. He had always shown an interest in examples drawn from the banking sector and economic institutions of capitalism, such as "the a-signifying grids [indexes, charts, data tables] of the Stock Exchange [Bourse]."[71] Playing the market, or just as well being played by it, so to speak, was for him just a matter of "manipulating the a-signifying workings of the system" by any number of trading strategies, many of which are now recognized to be purely machinic involving the competitive advantage of high-speed computing like flash trading. A-signification becomes for him essentially automated and informatic. Guattari consistently describes the assembling of partial or particle-sign components (parts that do not lack wholes and are fundamental and not grammatical particles) as a-subjective and machinic, in other words, as taking place without the mediation of subjectivation and mental representation at all and without forming a single semiotic substance. Guattari did not always reduce his machines to technical devices, yet his repeated description of how a-signifying semiotics trigger processes within informatic networks highlights the interactions initiated with a plastic card bearing a magnetic stripe in activating automated access to a bank or credit account and engaging in an elaborate authorization process at a distance, which makes it clear that we are dealing with a complex, info-technological network. Guattari clarifies that this has a direct purchase on material machinic processes of magnetic stripe technologies like "a credit card number which triggers the operation of a bank auto-teller,"[72] algorithmically digit-checks the card number, opens access to resources through remote machine-to-machine communication and anonymization routines. This return to information does not eschew politics. The question of control and conquest of space that communication theorist James Carey identified with the transmission model,[73] which he contrasted non-exclusively with the cultural perspective he introduced under the name of ritual-symbolic elaboration of social reality in time, does not entail that machinic explanations are devoid of political analysis. The work of particle-signs at the technomaterial level without psychical entities and prior to representation, the actions of iron oxide particles, of their conversion in swiping, working flush with material fluxes makes available the questions of who owns the tracks on the magnetic stripe, and who profits from the network in which they are used. This is the Guattarian, not exactly post-human, but a more and more artificial humanity in contact with partially enunciative recommendation software "a new kind of communicational actor," says Ganaele Langlois in her book *Meaning in the Age of Social Media,* making quasi-discursive statements "inspired by your browsing history."[74]

Although the rejection of meaning in the transmission model has been considered in various ways vulgar and reductionistic within contemporary communication theory,[75] Guattari revalorized and positively expressed this deficit in a novel semiosis adapted to the age of the algorithm. Of course, Guattari never rejected meaningful signification outright, but decentred it in an acute criticism of the alignment of its prerogatives with dominant significations and persons. Guattari did not restage what is sometimes popularly described as "the sacrifice of meaning"[76] in information theory. Rather, he made meaning a crutch that, tied to existing, compromised conceptions of subjecthood, semiological regimes, and representations, could be set aside because of the opportunities he found in machinic enfoldment and the important roles played by a-signifying semiotics therein.

The human-machine assemblage at the core of a-signifying semiotics is at once the site of capitalist exploitation, with its engineered subjectivities such as the economic and moral subject of debt,[77] and the promise of new collective formations that can act against capitalist subjectivations. For Maurizio Lazzarato in *Signs and Machines,* Guattari discovered in a-signifying semiotics post-representational machinic relationships that surpassed social categories of identity—national, racial sexual, and classist—and announced the promise of a post-identitarian politics freed from the subjugations that result in alienation. Lazzarato cites the "multiplicity of modes of subjectivation" available in machinic assemblages wherein humans become components in ways that position them as parts of integrated functional ensembles.[78] The ontological implications of this position are profound: "The ontological barrier between subject and object established by social subjection is continually blurred not because of language but because of a-signifying semiotics."[79] This blurring occurs because a-signifying signs work flush with the real, they forgo passage through individuated subjects and its avatars and attune themselves directly without detours to flows vaguely attributable to larger aggregates. And in this lies their promise, and risk. A-signifying signs including affects permit non-human, machinic proto-enunciations. The intensity of this unimpeded circulation is illustrated in Lazzarato's book *The Making of Indebted Man* by an automated bank teller that activates a 'dividual cog rather than a subject in a sociotechnical apparatus: "The individual makes 'use' of money, the 'dividual is adjacent to the credit-machine, s/he does not act, does not use, s/he functions according to the programs that use him as one of its component parts."[80]Affect is assigned to non-identities; it is pre-personal, difficult to locate, that is, anchor. It remains somewhat vague. It flows across human-machine functional assemblages. Lazzarato deploys the figure of the trader as an example of "machinic subjectivity" that is only a "terminal" for affective mixed rational and sign-flows, both signifying (like the tropes of belief and ways of reading the market) and a-signifying semiotics (flash trading by means of automated algorithms, but also the amodal experiences of surging and bullishness), in a kind of post-cognitive capitalism that places more emphasis on operationality than on meaning generation.

MACHINE AND STRUCTURE

One of Guattari's first theoretical innovations was to outflank the restricted forms of subjectivation available within structural psychoanalysis by conjoining desire and machine in order to trouble the enclosure of subjectivity by structure and its restriction by signification. By turning Lacanian psychoanalytic concepts against themselves, Guattari was able to reinscribe the *objet petit a* as a disruption of sorts in the relationship between structuration and subjectivation. Emphasizing the little object's detachment in the process of the subject's constitution by splitting (speaking/spoken; conscious/unconscious), Guattari aligned it with machinic forces that are embedded in an ongoing, that is, evolving relationship between machine and structure. The object falls out of this relationship, Guattari underlining how it is disequilibrating for structure, as it causes perturbations in the stable references inside of it and between structures. It falls away from the signifier[81] towards a more decentred conception of a-subjective and a-signifying machinic potentialities for a more and more artificial subjectivation (hyper-mediations, post-natural materials, algorithmic solutions, bio-engineered futures);[82] but it additionally indicates an opening to history, which is how Guattari conceived of the march and replacement of machines by machines on a vast planetary machinic phylum. Just as the *objet petit a* may be grasped psychogenetically beginning with the child-mother relationship, so too in its machinic incarnation can a diachronic approach be applied to machines; a good example is Guattari's attachment to the concept of megamachine in its ancient (tyrannical) and modern (molecular) forms. Guattari's "machinic evolutionism"[83] has diachronic (of machines displaced and machines anticipated by their substitutes) and synchronic axes (contingent contextualizations), but also what he calls, undoubtedly referring, from the perspective of the late 1980s to his own thinking in the late 1960s, "the older view" of an opposition between machine (surplus, possibilistic) and passive structure (exo-determined like discourse).

It is worthwhile revisiting this "older view." While the essay "Machine and Structure" is saturated with Lacanian nomenclature and the bold theoretical reinscription of certain concepts, there is another argument at play that warrants scrutiny. Guattari took care to distinguish his use of machine as either a concrete or abstract thing from sociologists such as Georges Friedmann who saw in *machinisme* workers' alienation.[84] Guattari contrasts the dialectic of master and apprentice, initiation into a skilled trade, and the geographic embeddedness of guilds, against the castrating, de-skilling, and de-institutionalizing experience of labour under industrial capitalism and some socialist states that cling to the notion of the "model worker."[85] His argument is that human labour is residual in the age of machinic production: "Human work . . . is only the residue that has not yet been integrated into the work of the machine."[86] As a consequence human action becomes a "residual sub-whole" of the machinic order, and thus desire, too, is machined. Machines disrupt the structural equilibria provided by historical organizations and experiences ("security of ritual" attached to repetition, like sowing seeds)[87] of human labour: "This residual human work represents no more than the point of the machine's imprint on the imaginary world of the individual."[88] From this perspective, then, scientific discoveries threaten and efface even those individuals who make them, rearranging entire fields and their relationships in the process. Guattari pursues the implications of such effacement, as machines assume what individuals and groups had previously, and for him this unconscious subjectivity of the de-skilled worker who must of necessity start again from scratch when faced with new technologies of production is specifically unrepresentable. On one hand, it would be delusional to insist that one could regain an imagined lost unity of the pre-mechanistic kind described earlier. On the other hand, Guattari writes: "The essence of the machine is precisely this operation of *detaching a signifier* as a representative, as a 'differentiator,' as a causal break, heterogeneous to the structurally established order of things."[89] From the unconscious structural chain a signifier is detached that acts as a "*representative* of the representation of the machine."[90] Here Guattari repeats Lacan's formula about the subject's sliding among signifiers, as an effect, of what a signifier represents to another signifier. But as a representative, the detached signifier bounds the desiring subject to both the machine and structural orders. For Guattari, "the human being is caught where the machine and the structure meet."[91] Elsewhere, Guattari noted that this relationship is less a predicament than an "embrace."[92] No matter how soft the interlacing, machinic intrusions result in a sphere of anti-production that manages change through phantasy. Guattari calls this "transitional," as it has a foothold in the external world of the shop floor, managerial prerogatives, workers' culture, as much as in dreams and fiction.

For Guattari, the *objet petit a* behaves like an "infernal machine"[93] that disequilibrates individuals and brings the kind of change that cannot be absorbed into structure (self-representation), leaving neither a place for refuge nor a transit to otherness. While for Guattari "individual phantasy represents this impossible merging of different levels . . . a group has no such 'hitching posts' of desire."[94] Group phantasy finds nothing but dead ends, meaningless circularities, mirror reflections, endless substitutions of events. No signposts. It is doomed, Guattari thinks, to repetition, and without a way to get a grip on the *objet-machine petit a,* as the unconscious cause of desire, the desiring-machine. Watson puts the matter bluntly: "Guattari is suggesting that the subject survives as a subject thanks to its *objet petit a*, the object-cause of desire, whereas structure leads to the death of the subject."[95] Likewise, self-destruction is the end of group phantasy as well.

Although in his early writings Guattari tended to dichotomize his concepts, and here machine and structure seem to divide between a force that ensures the subject's access to history and the real as opposed to a continuum that begins with masking potentialities of subjectivation (reduced to a signifier) and ends in a death sentence in the symbolic order. The *objet petit a* prevents abolition in a "pure and ideal structure."[96] Guattari reworks Lacanian concepts in order to semiotically excavate hitherto constrained forces of escape from structure and its anti-production. Object-machines catalyse uncontainable changes in structured relations, and it is reassuring to find in *Anti-Oedipus* almost verbatim sentences from "Machine and Structure" regarding the *objet petit a*'s "erupt[ion] at the heart of the structural equilibrium"[97] in the spirit of a Lacan who schizophrenized, and not structuralized, psychoanalysis. The Guattarian theory of desire as a machine must, then, appear attractive for a critical semiotic approach to how change gets into structure, and connects with social production inasmuch as desire and the social field are coextensive.[98]

WHITHER PROCESS?

The skirmishes with meaning that take place like tactical engagements within the search for non-meaning suggest a transitoriness and occasionality. Pathic knowledge's diversion of discourse recalls the spirit of selective resignification; whereas the struggle to put meaning back into the communicational bottle, and the acknowledgement that a-signifying semiotics is never done with signifying semiologies, both resist in different ways an absolutely independent machinic position beyond meaning. The disruptive action of a part object may disturb the repose of a structure, but for how long? It seems that getting change and intensity into structure is less of a problem than ensuring that it remains there and keeps working, before fizzling out. This is a problem discussed by theorists of process signs such as James Williams. In *A Process Philosophy of Signs*, Williams emphasizes the *ongoing* character of the intensive processes that unfold in a sign: he begins with the selection but not detachment of some elements (emphasizing certain of them) from an array of all elements (allowing others to recede into a background), thereby introducing multiple changes in intensities of relations, among all elements, and the openness of these to revaluations arising from evolving interactions among them.[99] The life of signs is ongoing and irreducible to contingently introduced disturbances, that is, to a machine that confounds structure only at some moment or moments and at certain pressure points and not others without other ramifications; such life is also *ubiquitous*, as it is neither confined to a zone of permanence nor permitted in a zone of impermanence. All relations are in play; there are no such static zones. Process philosophy places structure in a secondary relation to the sign, but considers structure to be a selectable element that may be included in the process, and thus change, the sign exposing structure's fluidity and dynamism, giving rise to competing diagrams of those relations.[100]

NOTES

1. Daniel Chandler, *Semiotics: The Basics*, 2nd edition, London and New York: Routledge, 2007, p. 13.
2. Roman Jakobson and Morris Halle, *Fundamentals of Language*, The Hague: Mouton, 1957, p. 22.
3. Oliver Gerland, "Lyotard and the Theatre of Energy," in *The Semiotic Bridge: Trends from California*, eds. I. Rauch and G. F. Carr, Berlin: Mouton, 1989, p. 24.
4. Jacques Derrida, *Writing and Difference*, trans. Alan Bass, Chicago, IL: University of Chicago Press, 1978, p. 4.
5. Brian Massumi, *Parables for the Virtual*, Durham: Duke University Press, 2002, p. 66.
6. Guattari, *Chaosmosis*, p. 48.
7. Massumi, *Parables for the Virtual*, p. 27.
8. Ibid., p. 3.
9. Steven D. Brown and Ian Tucker, "Eff the Ineffable: Affect, Somatic Management, and Mental Health Service Users," in *The Affect Theory Reader*, eds. M. Gregg and G. Seigworth, Durham, NC: Duke University Press, 2010, p. 234.
10. J. S. Hutta, "The Affective Life of Semiotics," *Geographica Helvetica* 70 (2015): 295.
11. Peter Pál Palbert, "The Deterritorialized Unconscious," in *The Guattari Effect*, eds. E. Alliez and A. Goffey, London: Continuum, 2011, p. 75.
12. *The Guattari Reader*, ed. G. Genosko, Oxford: Blackwell, 1996, pp. 158–59.
13. Guattari, *Schizoanalytic Cartographies*, p. 59.
14. Guattari, *Schizoanalytic Cartographies*, p. 70.
15. Deleuze and Guattari, *A Thousand Plateaus*, p. 160.
16. Guattari, *Chaomosis*, p. 112.
17. On this point see Simon O'Sullivan, *On the Production of Subjectivity: Five Diagrams of the Finite-Infinite Relation*, London: Palgrave Macmillan, 2012, pp. 99–100.

18. Guattari, "The Vertigo of Immanence," *The Guattari Effect*, eds. E. Alliez and A. Goffey, London: Continuum, 2011, p. 36.
19. Martin Heidegger, *Being and Time*, trans. J. Macquarie and E. Robinson, New York: Harper & Row, 1962, p. 276. See also pp. 270 and 314.
20. Guattari, *Schizoanalytic Cartographies*, p. 131.
21. Ibid., p. 156.
22. Guattari, "The Vertigo of Immanence," p. 36.
23. Ibid., p. 36.
24. Guattari, *Chaosmosis*, p. 61.
25. Guattari, *Chaosmosis*, p. 60.
26. Guattari, *Chaosmosis*, p. 111.
27. Guattari, *Chaosmosis*, p. 59.
28. Deleuze and Guattari, *A Thousand Plateaus*, pp. 44–45.
29. Anne Querrien, "Maps and Refrains of a Rainbow Panther," in *The Guattari Effect*, eds. E. Alliez and A. Goffey, London: Continuum, 2011, p. 90.
30. Guattari, *Chaosmosis*, p. 82.
31. Ibid., p. 13.
32. Genosko, *Aberrant Introduction*, pp. 52–53.
33. Guattari, *Chaosmosis*, p. 19.
34. Guattari, *Chaosmosis*, p. 20.
35. Guattari, *The Machinic Unconscious*, p. 149.
36. Guattari, *Machinic Unconscious*, p. 155.
37. Guattari, *Chaosmosis*, p. 26.
38. Ibid., p. 22.
39. Ibid., p. 26.
40. Guattari, *Schizoanalytic Cartographies*, p. 112.
41. Guattari, *Chaosmosis*, p. 30.
42. Ibid., p. 72.
43. Ibid., p. 93.
44. Guattari, *Chaosmosis*, p. 14ff.
45. Viktor Von Weizsäcker, *Le Cycle de la Structure*, trans. M. Foucault and D. Rocher, Bruges: Desclée de Brouwer, 1958.
46. Guattari, *Psychanalyse et transversalité*, p. 45.
47. Guattari, *Schizoanalytic Cartographies*, pp. 109–10.
48. Von Weizsäcker, *Pathosophie*, trans. J. de Bisschop, M. Gennart, M. Ledoux, B. Maebe, C. Mugnier, and A.-M. Norgeu, Grenoble: Millon Jérôme Editions, 2011, p. 54.
49. Weizsäcker, *Pathosophie*, p. 55.
50. Weizsäcker, *Pathosophie*, p. 65.
51. Deleuze and Guattari, *Anti-Oedipus*, p. 60.
52. Deleuze and Guattari, *A Thousand Plateaus*, p. 144.
53. Weizsäcker, *Pathosophie*, p. 54.
54. Guattari, *Schizoanalytic Cartographies*, p. 109.
55. Weizsäcker, *Le Cycle de la Structure*, p. 220.
56. Ibid.
57. Ibid., p. 222.

58. Guattari, *Chaosmosis*, p. 80.
59. Schotte quoted in Pelbart, "Deterritorialized Unconscious," p. 75.
60. Guattari, *Chaosmosis*, pp. 80 and 82.
61. Ibid., p. 81.
62. Peter Pál Pelbart, *Cartography of Exhaustion: Nihilism Inside Out*, trans. J. Laudenberger and F. R. Palazuelos, Minneapolis: Univocal, 2015, p. 119.
63. Ibid., p. 120.
64. Félix Guattari, *La révolution moléculaire*, Fontenay-sous-Bois: Encres/Recherches, 1977, p. 335.
65. Tiziana Terranova, *Network Culture: Politics for the Information Age*, London: Pluto, 2004, p. 16.
66. Umberto Eco, *A Theory of Semiotics*, Bloomington: Indiana University Press, 1976, pp. 20 and 33.
67. Félix Guattari, "Meaning and Power," *Molecular Revolution: Psychiatry and Politics*, p. 171. In media theory, Wolfgang Ernst picks up this emphasis by contrasting signals and signs, investigating the former's "chronotechnical complexity" as opposed to the latter's "culturally emphatic signification." See *Chronopoetics*, trans. A. Enns, London: Rowman & Littlefield, 2016, p. 89.
68. Félix Guattari, *La révolution moléculaire*, Paris: Editions 10–18, 1978, p. 227.
69. Guattari, *The Guattari Reader*, p. 150.
70. Guattari, *Chaosmosis*, p. 49.
71. Guattari, *La revolution moléculaire* [Encres], p. 237.
72. Guattari, *Chaosmosis*, p. 49.
73. James Carey, *Communication as Culture*, Boston: Unwin and Hyman, 1989.
74. Ganaele Langlois, *Meaning in the Age of Social Media*, New York: Palgrave, 2014, p. 52.
75. See Steven Maras, "On Transmission: A Metamethodological Analysis (After Régis Debray)," *Fibreculture* 12 (2008). http://twelve.fibreculturejournal.org/fcj-080-on-transmission-a-metamethodological-analysis-after-regis-debray/.
76. James Gleick, *The Information: A History, A Theory, A Flood*, New York: Pantheon, 2011, p. 416.
77. Maurizio Lazzarato, *The Making of Indebted Man*, trans. J. D. Jordan, Los Angeles: Semiotext(e), 2012, p. 146.
78. Lazzarato, *Signs and Machines: Capitalism and the Production of Subjectivity*, trans. J. D. Jordan, Los Angeles: Semiotext(e), 2014, p. 90.
79. Ibid., p. 83.
80. Lazzarato, *The Making of Indebted Man*, p. 149.
81. Guattari, *Anti-Oedipus Papers*, p. 186.
82. Guattari, *Schizoanalytic Cartographies*, pp. 11–12.
83. Ibid., pp. 73–74.
84. Félix Guattari, "Machine and Structure," in *Psychoanalysis and Transversality*, trans. A. Hodges, Los Angeles: Semiotext(e), 2015, p. 319.
85. Ibid., p. 320.
86. Ibid., pp. 320–21.
87. Ibid., p. 321.

88. Ibid.
89. Ibid., p. 322.
90. Ibid.
91. Ibid.
92. Guattari, *Anti-Oedipus Papers*, p. 51.
93. "Machine and Structure," p. 323.
94. Ibid., p. 324.
95. *Guattari's Diagrammatic Thought*, p. 146.
96. "Machine and Structure," p. 328.
97. Deluze and Guattari, *Anti-Oedipus*, p. 83.
98. Ibid., p. 30.
99. James Williams, *A Process Philosophy of Signs*, Edinburgh: University of Edinburgh Press, 2016, pp. 75–76.
100. Ibid., pp. 102–3.

Chapter 12

Dissident Organ: The Three Billion Perverts Issue of *Recherches*

Why write about a journal issue? The notoriety of the issue in question is one thing, but the value in returning to the scene of the crime, as it were, provides valuable historical, philosophical, and political context within Deleuze and Guattari scholarship. This focus on a dissident organ is situated within the life and work of Guattari in particular, as his involvement in the collective production of journals by transdisciplinary editorial assemblages was a constant from his teenage years: from the time of the founding with Lucien Sebag of *Tribune de discussion* to his writing and editing of *La Voie communiste*, writing under the pseudonym Claude Arrieux, from 1959 to 1965.[1] The journals with which he is associated, *Recherches* and *Chimères*, and all of the other little experiments in which he participated, in print and otherwise, make a journal a favoured micro-institutional matter for the collective realization of projects and the creation of new worlds of reference. Founding a journal provides a site for the existential refrain of serial issue production; it is a place where desiring-flows, tendencies, schisms, breakaway groups, collaborations, and reassessments can take place; and these flows become tenable for young militants against the backdrop of the traditional phyla of unions, parties, employers, and so on. What is called a labour of love is the name given to many small publications, a statement of existence, no more, no less, an enunciated universe of possibility for a small band of dissidents.

Three Billion Perverts underlines the challenges of collective production and quasi-anonymous authorship, exacerbated by the volatile subject of sexualities in the plural. It additionally demonstrates something about which Guattari constantly reminded his readers: that it is not possible to exclude the worst excesses of multiplicity. Since this journal, to the extent that it survives, is the kind of enduring micro-institutional substance available for revisiting, unlike all of the drafts and meetings and so forth lost to time, it provides an opportunity to study how one of the figures that recur in its pages, that is, the figure of the Arab, appeared to catalyse the collective self-production of the Centre for Study and Research into Institutional Functioning (CERFI), an organization whose proposals, as Anne Querrien recalls, "were always directed towards the life of the group rather than strengthening the ego of the few."[2]

In March 1971, CERFI published in its house journal *Recherches* a special issue #12 devoted to homosexuality in France, "Trois milliards de pervers: Grande encyclopédie des homosexualités." Guattari was listed as director of the publication and held legally responsible for it. The events that followed its publication are summarized thus in Guattari's "Liminaire" in *The Guattari Reader*: "The March issue . . . had been seized, and Guattari, as director of the publication, was fined 600 francs for affronting public decency. Number 12 . . . was judged to constitute a 'detailed display of depravities and sexual deviations,' and the 'libidinous exhibition of a perverted minority.' All copies of the issue were ordered destroyed."[3] Paper copies of the issue are still in circulation and found in private libraries, and an edited and adapted issue was posted on the French website Critical Secret. The print copy I used had been sitting on a shelf in Paul Patton's office.

HOW MANY PERVERTS?

Slightly less than the earth's population in 1973, three billion of which were perverts. The journal issue mixed politics with pleasure, amateur with academic debate, journalism and diaristic writing; the photos, mostly snapshots, and drawings of a delightful lasciviousness were often ribald and ridiculous, playful and silly. The original list of contributors runs to at least thirty-five persons. Many of the best-known contributors have since passed away: Guattari, Deleuze, Foucault, Sartre, Châtelet, Genet, Hocquenghem. The issue retains an aura of mystery. Though the story of its creation has been recounted by Querrien, Guattari never failed to mention it when looking back on the highlights of *Recherches*. In 1972, several members of Front homosexual d'action révolutionannaire (FHAR) crossed over into CERFI and, eschewing funding or the quaint term *commissions* from the French state, produced the issue and thus "with them CERFI became what we wanted, and feared, from the outset: a gathering place for resistances and interconnecting singularities."[4] Querrien adds that it took six months to put the issue together, with the assistance of Guy Hocquenghem.

What exactly caught the attention of the court? In an interview, Guattari explained that at the time "among the things that most shocked the judges was one of the most original parts of this work—a discussion of masturbation. I think that a work devoted to homosexuality in a more or less traditional manner would have had no difficulty. What shocked perhaps was the expression of sexuality going in all directions. And then there were the illustrations—they were what set it off."[5] The wide-ranging section on masturbation, occupying pages 64–94, meditates on a range of pertinent options across the sexes—the use of lubrication and, if so, with which substance, and from what source? What is the relationship between masturbation and lack? Between lack and guilt? Solo or assisted? Gilles and Guy (first names only) explore these and other themes in a speculative mode, while their discussion is punctuated by interjections by two frisky interlocutors, and then turned away from its overt phallicism by Anna. The line drawings inserted into the dialogue stage all kinds of psycho-sexual scenes: the question of size, a penile film projector, prisoners' masturbating, and so on. There is no hint of the scaffolding of sexology and objective social science. One cartoon by Copi is a noteworthy parody of "what's on a man's mind?" type psychobabble, but with small line drawings showing other men are on a man's mind and for women, other women.[6] Number 12 is staged as a game, a bit of Snakes and Ladders, suitably queered, and viciously parodied: what else can one say about a little hand-drawn penis the head of which is wrapped in a turban and bears a sultanate moustache ("Sexe Arabe"). What about the high-rise HLM (council estates) penis?

Other sections of the publication are equally candid yet visually diffuse the discussion through art historical references, in the example of lesbian culture, and by means of graphic novel formats, in the case of paedophilia. However, running through the sections of the journal may be found contributions regarding a volatile sexual dimension of French colonialism in North Africa. Indeed, if there is an issue that the journal tackled across its different sections, it is that of the Arabs who populate certain articles and are the displaced subjects of several of the submissions which sought to reckon with the racist and fascist desiring-machines unleashed in the publication. My strategy of critical reading follows the movements of race across the journal's sectional-sexual specificities. In this way the figure of the Arab serves the unrestrained expression of desire, providing the basis for a myriad of statements and observations, from the overtly racist to meta-editorial wrangling about which articles are in and that are out. This figure informs readers about the transversal dimension of the journal and the group desire that it unleashed and conducted towards diverse referential worlds: autobiography (Arabophilia in French gay cultures), socio-historical specificity (the legacies of French colonialism in North Africa, understood at various historical junctures), and the journal's self-criticism (writing about Arabs yet without them). What is it to write, as one contributor put it in identitarian terms, "on Arabs, but without Arabs?" This is one of the lessons of Deleuze's "Letter to a Harsh Critic" as it concerned issue number 12, especially Michel Cressole's contribution "Us and the Arabs," soundly criticized as "completely Oedipal—more Oedipal than my daughter" by Deleuze in his comment on the text "Sex-Pol en Acte."[7]

As the subject of critical reflection, the status of the Arab in the pages of the journal did not cancel other flights of fancy, such as the masturbatory phantasies of several contributors who cruised immigrant neighbourhoods in urban France, or enjoyed sex junkets to Morocco or Algeria. The field of desire is heterogeneous and complex and, keeping in mind the kinds of statements and sentiments in circulation in the late 1960s and early 1970s with regard to French-African relations, requires some reconsideration of the early and neglected work from French sociologists and philosophers in North Africa. Who is an Arab, anyway? What would Frantz Fanon have said? After all, Fanon diagnosed the racist character of French culture and exposed psychoanalytic apologists for colonization. Problematically, he also fell back on simplistic Freudian symbolic equations—"the Negrophobic man is a repressed homosexual."[8] Even the red psychiatrist and founder of institutional psychotherapy François Tosquelles recalls with honesty and naively how in his first encounter with Fanon at St. Alban he had to consciously minimize his surprise at the colour of Fanon's skin, in relation to the white faces to which he was accustomed. And their veiled abstract exchange about differences was brought to a head when Fanon offered Tosquelles a copy of his book, *Black Skin, White Masks*. Tosquelles' sense of masks was non-racial. He listened to Fanon who recounted the story of how in Lyon he was harassed by the police when walking out with his white fiancé, and Tosquelles later recodes this as another instance of sexual jealousy, a matter raised at a later dinner meeting in which some of the physicians in attendance were jealous of the dexterity of how Fanon danced with their wives.[9] The crude interpretation of homosexual desire was not rehearsed.

ON THE STAND

Guattari's defence of *Recherches* before the 17th Magsitrate's Court in 1973 was not a matter of giving voice to minority voices. Rather, he rejected outright the "formal and Jesuitical" version of "giving voice" to so-called research subjects under the guise of a problematized pseudo-objectivity, and any other alibis of social scientific method; further, he wanted to use the issue to "create the conditions for a total, indeed, a paroxysmic exercise."[10] This rejection of method and scientific pretention has been extended along Guattarian lines in the deconstruction of the figure of the "native informant."[11] The decentring of scientificity entails the rejection of the logic of the survey; push beyond the psychoanalytic sameness fixation; and getting in step with social liberation movements, beyond classical union-based militancy. For

Guattari, the problem of militancy is its inability to connect with social liberation movements. This was the task that CERFI attempted to ameliorate by engaging the expressive desires of the FHAR and the MFL (Mouvement de libération des femmes) during this period. This did not mean that Guattari was hyper-valorizing the figure of the gay activist: "Incidentally, for the deaf: the gay, no more than the schizo, is not of himself a revolutionary—the revolutionary of modern times!"[12]

Guattari considered the potential of what a gay activist could become; such becoming would constitute a critique of sexuality as such, to the degree that homosexuality "concerned all normal sexual life." In this expanded field, "homosexuality would be, thus, not only an element in the life of each and everyone, but involved in any number of social phenomena, such as hierarchy and bureaucracy."[13] This would not require an ethnographic study of a minority, but a non-uniform becoming in which opportunities would be pursued and tendencies mined across the social field. In the process, for Guattari homosexuality becomes trans-sexuality: "From this perspective, the struggle for the liberation of homosexuality becomes an integral part of the struggle for social liberation."[14] Minoritarian becoming has three principles: finding what is foreign in the familiar, and then carrying it off; everything minor is political (*Recherches* was not competing with the sex shops in pedaling pornography); and create a truly collective assemblage of enunciation. The implications of this collectively were put on view before the court. Guattari explained: "We dispensed here with the notions of an author and a work. When the examining judge asked me, for example, who had written this or that article, supposing I would even answer, I was not able to do so. . . . Even the layout was done collectively."[15] The refusal of individuation resisted the demands of the legal system and put into play the indiscernibility of becoming that ran between those involved in the issue's production. This becoming was an objective feature that made it impossible for Guattari to link single names with tasks and outcomes. Of course, since Guattari was listed on the masthead as director, he was readily identifiable. Guattari found himself facing a day in court. His lifelong passion for the work of Kafka was about to be put on trial in a becoming Joseph K. The "ridiculous side" of the charge began with his return to his flat on rue Condé from an overseas trip. The door was padlocked, and few patients sat on the stairs waiting for their consultations. Upon entering, Guattari's flat had been trashed by the police during the execution of dozens of warrants for the seizure of all copies of *Recherches* 12, despite the fact that it had been available for sale in bookstores around Paris for several weeks. Guattari wrote: "When I protested these proceedings to the examining judge, I must say that he remained largely perplexed. I thought then that there had been a mistake and that the case would be adjourned *sine die*."[16] No such indefinite adjournment would be offered. It may be recalled from Kafka's *The Trail* that certain drawbacks, the prevention of actual acquittal, most certainly, are entailed by preventing the trial from progressing towards the accused's sentencing.[17] Limbo of a sort was described in these very terms by Deleuze, but with reference to the passage from disciplinary to control societies: an endless postponement to which Guattari's case did not accede. Guattari failed to convince the perplexed judge who was stuck in the disciplinary society. Hence, the fine of 600FF.

The other side of this Kafkaesque predicament is, perhaps, just as serious. The journal issue was "indefensible," Guattari believed, as long as the representational logic of the court was granted. It was a matter of convenience that Guattari was held responsible. The court and counsel conveniently decided upon a signifying semiology, a bad theatre of representation, that specified in advance a regime of signs from which there would be no deviation. Guattari summarized:

What does the fact of holding someone responsible for something signify?

- I am responsible, I represent *Recherches*;
- You represent the law;
- Members of Parliament represent the people;
- The President of the Republic, France;
- Universities, knowledge;
- Gays, perversion.
- *Recherches* wishes to have done with this sort of representation, with all the bad theatre to which officials and institutions resort.[18]

Guattari did not distinguish between different kinds of content in number 12. He cited a range of examples that included the sexual misery of youth, masturbation, and two racial themes: "the way in which different immigrant groups from North Africa live their homosexuality," and "the racist fantasies which are sometimes invoked in relations of sexual dependency."[19] The publication did not answer to any pre-established category: it did not answer to a specific discipline or national professional organization; nor was it undertaken in terms of a legitimated methodology. That it let some gays and straights communicate directly their experiences "without precautions and without supporting documentation" made it dangerous. The shock issued from the absence of interpretive grids and the ambience of a deterritorializing semiosis. Guattari also took some abuse from disgruntled contributors.

GAME ON

Recherches 12 began with a game. There are six players: arabe, petit garcon, femme, enseignant, travesty, pédé. The board is numbered 1 through 30 from start to finish along a segmented, snaking penis. The rules of the game dictate movement forwards and backwards. Land on segment one—"Les arabes et nous," which corresponds to the journal's first article— and you are directed to "sip a mint tea until you have rolled a six," which is another article, "Les arabes et les blancs." Or, if you find yourself on segment sixteen, then you are directed to "have an arab fuck you and keep his cock in your ass until either one of you rolls a five"; the fifth article is "l'autre côté des ténébres." And so on, with a range of substitutions, trips to the hospital, indications of sadism and masochism, and even the fate of having to read most of the journal in order to continue. The game form was up front: Jeu de l'oie or Snakes and Laders, with instructions.

> The game is played by six persons corresponding to the six detachable pieces beside the board and two copies of the issue. On each roll of the dice, consult the Rules of the Game for the number upon which you have landed. Between turns, read the article in the second copy corresponding to your position on the board.[20]

This editorial contrivance allows readers to adopt a number of identities, and therefore there are at least six ways to approach the issue. It is a matter of the roll of the dice with which a reader begins to read an article.

ARAB AND BERBER

This reader begins with one of several political statements in support of indigenous North Africans, "Vivent nos amants de Berbérie." "Long live our Berber lovers" is a detachable pictorial tableau of young North African men assembled for a group photo, and it may be used, it is suggested, as an alternate cover for the journal. The supporting text is a manifesto and declaration of love that begins with the recognition that Berbers are not reducible to Arabs. In fact, Berbers have been oppressed for centuries, and their struggle continues today: "Arabs destroy their language and culture." To state these matters is taboo, but we do not know for whom. A few historical facts are mentioned: "The first great rebellion of North Africans against colonial oppression was the war of Rif. The first experience of freedom we want to acknowledge here was the République berbère des Rifains, founded in 1921 by Mohamed Abdelkrim Alkhaltabi." The text continues:

> We, the homosexuals who have found a voice in this issue of Recherches are in solidarity with their struggle. Because we have sexual relations with them. Because their liberation will also be our liberation. Long live our friends from Rif, Atlas, the Aurès, and the Kabylie! Long live Berbérie! Long live our Berber lovers![21]

The facts line up: the Riffian (Berber) Republican State was declared by Morroccan tribal leader Abd el-Krim in 1921 in a war against the Spanish (eventually surrendering to Spanish and French troops in 1926–1927). That el-Krim, a heroic precursor of anti-colonial struggles, instituted sharia law, mixing it with tribal traditions at odds with Islamic prescriptions, is not mentioned for the obvious reason that homosexuality would have likely been condemned. This makes the declaration of love an intense provocation. As the declaration is not signed, as opposed to the statement in support of a French schoolteacher fired for being gay, it creates ambiguity beyond the obvious fact that the only voice given to the unidentified loved ones by their lovers is pictorial.

The declaration is, nevertheless, grounded in a fundamental focal point of French-North African relations that underlines the role of language. Arabic and Berber are the two major language groups in the Maghreb. Language proved to be a key point of division, since both Arabs and Berbers were largely Sunni Muslims, but with different tribal traditions thrown into the mix, not discounting numerous dialects, traditions, and hybridities. It was Albert Camus who preferred in his political writings of the late 1950s to link the future of Algeria with the French rather than any "empire of Islam" and Arab nationalist-imperialism.[22] There may be other relevant distinctions at play that inform us about social and political realities: urban Arab versus rural Berber and veiled Arab versus unveiled Berber women. As Fanon subtly explained, this latter distinction was used by the colonizing French to emphasize the positive aspects of Berber identity against the so-called opacity of Arabic women, despite the fact that Berber women in urban settings may be veiled as well.[23] The politics of language under colonial rule can be an expression of a typical divide and conquer approach,[24] in which co-optable aspects of cultural identity are praised, and resistant aspects are criticized, criminalized, and re-categorized as foreign. The colonial curriculum rendered Arabic a foreign language and even the post-colonial psycho-existentialist problematic favoured French as the language of the elite, of the writer, thinker, and modern citizen. Jacques Derrida once exclaimed, in reflecting on his linguistic choices as a French Algerian lycéen, that Arabic was an option permitted but also interdicted: "Arabic, an optional foreign language in Algeria!"[25] In Algeria, the post-colonial linguistic policy of Arabization stumbled on the colonial legacy since Arabic (classical versus spoken dialects) had to be "recovered" and elevated to the official language, after 1962.[26] But if a certain Arabic became the official language, where did this leave Kabyle and other Berber tongues? Whither French? On the side of multilingualism, Fanon wrote stirringly of the radio station The Voice of Fighting Algeria in the anti-colonialist struggle and the significance of the use of Arabic, Kabyle, and French, which "had the advantage of developing and strengthening the unity of the people" in the cities and in the countryside.[27] The term Kabyle is thought to be misused when it describes a linguistic territory from which political consequences such as separatism are drawn, by those far removed from the territory; in this sense it is a political projection.[28]

Is the colonial legacy exacerbated by flagging the Arab oppression of Berbers in a declaration of love? Pierre Bourdieu once observed, after remarking on a series of obvious differences, that "it would be dangerous to exaggerate the opposition between Arabs and Berbers. Between these two ways of life there are frequent transitions and deeply rooted affinities."[29] Indeed, such phenomena manifest themselves differently in Algeria and Morocco, across different periods.[30] Do these considerations render unstable the declaration "Long Live Our Berber Lovers!" since it fails to address the official post-revolution Arabization (linguistic) and then Islamicization (religious erasure of civil society) in Algeria and the Berber resistances within long colonial shadows? In a way this declaration is actually prescient since it would not be until the late 1980s that the spectre of an accelerated Islamism would help to articulate the predicament of linguistic minorities, especially the Kabyle political elite who were Francophones and profited from colonial favouritism and/or capitalized on the failures of decolonization.[31] And what is the taboo? A queered Algerian independence?

MINORITARIAN BECOMINGS

Guattari's basic orientation with regard to sexuality and racism may be surmised in an interview published two years after the Three Billion Perverts affair. He explained that "all disruptive semiotization involves a disruptive sexualization. Thus it is not necessary, in my view, to pose the question of homosexual writers, but rather to search for what is homosexual, at any rate, in a great writer, even if in other respects, s/he is heterosexual."[32] The excavation of minoritarian becoming, the becoming homosexual of the heterosexual writer, has its parallel in Guattari's tactics of anti-racism. Circa 1983 he wrote: "All nations require immigrants and the relations to alterity are posed through their arrival. I am claiming that a nation's vitality corresponds to its capacity to engage itself in all the components of a becoming immigrant."[33] The becoming immigrant of everyone is a refusal of racism in a rather bleak neo-liberal period in which opportunities for subjectivation were limited and tightly scripted through failures of the socialist government and re-emergence of dangerous archaisms and fictions that quickly filled the void, for example, the "France is France" of the Poujadists all the way to Le Pen and beyond.

Becoming immigrant was for Guattari a tactic for refusing uniformity and the resulting anguish. Becoming minoritarian, whether gay and/or immigrant in a becoming *beur*, may be soundly criticized as sterile if it actually reduces particularity and fails to deliver on the passages into the cracks, or in any ways inhibits the release of components, the assemblage of which build new solidarities and opportunities, at least for a practical modification of racist alignments. A becoming gay Berber would not entail a Gallic embrace or liberal-minded statement of sympathy but would burrow into the majoritarian dichotomy Arab/Berber in order to find detachable components in a transformative process that could give expression to hybridity, exchange, and alterity in lines of escape. The valorization of Berbers must reckon with a partial becoming Arab and Gallic that would reveal paradoxical elements—perhaps the absence of a transnational Berberism entails a rapprochement with Islamism?

RACIST DESIRE

The controversial transcription of a discussion between P. 22., G. 32, and M. 24, "Les arabes et nous," is quite ordinary in its prejudice towards an Arabic bloc that is barely differentiated and only vaguely identified. The conversation is peppered throughout with negative stereotypes about stealing, lazy, lying, greedy people, tempered at times with self-recognition that such things are not the unique qualities of a particular people. This is no politics of fucking: it is either politics or fucking. At one point M. reflects: "When I was a militant, we would explain that it was a matter of descending into the working class in order to have political relations with young workers. Basically, our requirement was to establish with them a relation of seduction, and cruise them for the organization. I just couldn't accept that. Whereas with the Arabs, whether at the hotel or elsewhere, it's true that our relations were not hidden behind political cruising."[34] This is the moment at which Deleuze (assuming he was the author of the unsigned "Sex-Pol en acte" article) dug into the text. He wrote: "This remark is understood to be that of a lapsed former militant who has substituted homosexual activity for political action, making the former the litmus test."[35] What interested Deleuze was not so much the many scattered examples of 'racism or racist desire expressed by the interlocutors, but the magical appearance of a "diffuse and mobile" racism informed by a basic sexism attributed to those Arabs who do not speak. In a way, things go from bad to worse: "la bête Arabe" (to whom G. is happy to deliver himself) may himself be racist towards "us" (G. and his friends) it is claimed, because "for them [Arabs], the homosexual relation is the same as their relation to women in which there is great contempt, and a taste for domination."[36] And for Deleuze, this was just one displacement among many in which Oedipal traps were set by the interlocutors themselves. Such traps included the distinction between Europeans (parents) and Arabs (husbands), with disdain for the former functioning, snapped Deleuze, as an incest prohibition, while the animalization motif served as a focal point of racist desire. Deleuze even ventures a symptomatic reading of a telephone call that interrupts the discussion at one point as "the sign of Oedipus and Cain." Gay conjugality is Oedipal when it crystallizes a micro-fascist trap for desire set by coupledom and perhaps even bewitched by rights (marriage). By repeatedly trumping the discussion with Oedipus, Deleuze seems to be shutting down discussion, but he also uses it to make sure the message is loud and clear: clear out, de-couple, take flight. If you lubricate a homosexual desiring machine with Oedipus you get a variant of heterosexuality.

ACADEMIC CALL AND RESPONSE

"Sex-Pol en acte" is not the only response to "Les arabes et nous." The "beautiful cocks" lubricated by saliva rather than vaseline—the latter is so Saint Germain, so Roland Barthes—extolled by G., despite the alleged serial sameness of Arabic men complained about by L., are not really the issue in "Le sexe 'arabe.'" As contentious as "Les arabes et nous" is, the author of "Le sexe 'arabe'" believes, it is acceptable if it provokes discussion, with the proviso that it takes place among a small group of like-minded people. In fact, there is more than one proviso: always refer to "Arabs" in scare quotes and invoke in this qualification the Arab/Berber distinction as the men at issue are Berbers, more or less Arabized and Islamicized, but in a political context in which "the real name of the Maghreb is Berbérie (Barbary)." The socio-sexual context is also significant. The author underlines the same distinction that Deleuze saw as Oedipal: it is easier to cruise "Arab" than European men, both in Europe and in North Africa. Why? Because, as knowledgeable members of FHAR will attest, that is, for those Arabophiles, Europeans live their homosexuality "pathologically," while "Arabs" live theirs "problem-free" and "guilt-free." There is a constant recourse to a qualified referent, "Arabs," who are without certain qualities. Projection of a qualified existence is the violence of colonialist representation.

The whole discussion is vaguely sociological and proto-ethnographic, to the extent that responses are sought from "Arab" students in Paris to "Les arabes et nous," but nothing much comes back beyond fears of Zionist exploitation of racist desire to fan the flames of anti-Arab French rightist discourse. This study (and the scare quotes would come in handy here once again) took place in a Parisian university milieu among Maghrebian students whose sexuality was fundamentally bisexual owing to the character of homosexuality in Islamic countries, apparently. By the time these students graduate, they will have broken with the "collective cultural fact" of their bi-curiousity, and thus separated off their homosexuality, for the sake of normalized desire for a European opposite-sex partner. University life inculcates normopathic desire.

It is probably not worth disputing these so-called findings. Their truth or falsehood is not at issue. How is this academic call and response played out as it fills the pages of the journal? The effect is alienation, as M. explains in a brief exchange with G. embedded in a series of texts under the heading "Les arabes et les 'blancs.'" M. is a straight white male, non-university-based writer, a "white-hetero-bourgeois" among "imaginary Arabs." The editorial committee, in rejecting his contribution as "too literary," showed its true face: "A section was done on cruising without cruisers, another on Arabs without Arabs, and only the thinkers of homosexuality can speak about homosexuality." Identity politics? The *blanc* sits among the *blanks* at the heart of a journal in which the editors publish themselves, and it is necessary to "sublimate," M. complains, before Guattari using the politically correct "salad" of theoretical jargon. Is this sour grapes or the excavation of a syndrome? No doubt there is a crowd of subjects expulsed from the issue. But personalizing the rejection of one's contribution misrecognizes the collective character of the undertaking, while identifying the implicit rules of the games. There is no point in molarizing the collective process by insisting on being represented, as if any individual could account for all the elisions, and bringing to such a process only qualifications.

POLITICAL IMPASSE

Three Billion Perverts is a masterpiece of political impasse, implosive sexuality, and legal transgression. Perhaps it should be stated, along with the author of the delirious and interminable contribution "Les culs énergumènes," that in the end when all is said about "Les arabes et nous" it truly wedges readers between "the ivory cock and the ivory tower."[37] Three Billion Perverts appeared only a year after Hocquenghem's book *Homosexual Desire*,[38] a foundational text of queer studies before the letter, and the other a neglected period piece. The queering of Deleuze and Guattari studies can find its own original points of reference in this issue, and there is no shortage of lingering notoriety attached to the recovery operation. My reading does not attempt to present an overview. There is more work to be done on that point. Rather, I worked through some of the problems associated with the figure of the Arab as it circulated throughout the text because it was on this point that desire and revolution seemed to part ways, although some effort was expended to put them back together again. There is little doubt for the author of "Les culs" that any reader of "Les arabes et nous" would classify it as a "pathological episode" between "phalluses without penises and penises without phalluses,"[39] that is, between Us with editorial privileges intact, and the "Arabs" who are without a number of real and imagined attributes. My selection of the figure of the Arab is not random; it is a transversal jumble of lines exposing the soft tissues to critical scrutiny. With all of its problems, such a figure has the virtue of probing the worst attitudes, blunders, and repressed values circulating in the journal's pages and through its collective producers. The strategy reaches for a dense socio-sexual-political description that provides a context for the debates which retain some features of the period and the tenor of the specific undertaking within all of the workings of CERFI. There are many other markers of historical context stirring in the background, of course, and these include the oil crisis, Yom Kippur War, Vietnam, and the Charter of the Agrarian Revolution in Algeria.[40] While in principle every issue of *Recherches* has a lesson to communicate about the formation of institutional matter into substance, Three Billion Perverts occupies a special place for it is the most notorious issue in Guattari's estimation. By focusing on it, this chapter signals that specific episodes, political and personal junctures, despite their somewhat old-fashioned appearance, may serve as valuable entry points for organizing research into the impact of Guattari's projects on the social field. The role of a journal and its collective production cannot be underestimated in the formation of intellectual life.

NOTES

1. Félix Guattari, "Raymond and the Hispano Group," in *Psychoanalysis and Transversality*, trans. A. Hodges, Los Angeles: Semiotext(e), 2015, pp. 352–53.
2. Anne Querrien, "La Borde, Guattari and Left Movements in France, 1965–81: Interview by Constantin V. Boundas," *Deleuze Studies* 10/3 (2016): 407.
3. Félix Guattari, "Three Billion Perverts on the Stand," in *The Guattari Reader*, ed. G. Genosko, Oxford: Blackwell, 1996, p. 192.
4. Anne Querrien, "CERFI 1965–1987," www.criticalsecret.com/n8/quer/1fr (2002).
5. Félix Guattari, "A Liberation of Desire: An Interview with George Stambolian," in *The Guattari Reader*, ed. G. Genosko, Oxford: Blackwell, 1996, p. 204.
6. Michael Moon, "New Introduction," in *Homosexual Desire*, ed. G. Hocquenghem, Durham, NC: Duke University Press, 1993, pp. 12–15.
7. Gilles Deleuze, "Letter to a Harsh Critic," in *Negotiations*, New York: Columbia University, 1995, pp. 3–12.
8. Frantz Fanon, *Black Skin, White Masks*, trans. C. L. Markmann, New York: Grove Press, 1967, pp. 155–56.
9. François Tosquelles, "Frantz Fanon et la psychothérapie institutionnelle," *Eres: Sud/Nord* 1/22 (2007): 71–78.
10. "Three Billion Perverts On the Stand," p. 186.

11. G. C. Spivak, *A Critique of Postcolonial Reason: Toward a History of the Vanishing Present*, Cambridge, MA: Harvard University Press, 1999, p. 6.

12. Ibid.

13. Ibid., p. 187.

14. Ibid.

15. Ibid., p. 191.

16. Ibid., p. 190.

17. Franz Kafka, *The Trial*, trans. W. and E. Muir, New York: Schocken, 1969, pp. 160–61.

18. Ibid., pp. 188–89.

19. Ibid., pp. 190–91.

20. Unsigned (1973), *Recherches* 12 (March 1973): 4.

21. Text on the recto of the aforementioned detachable poster.

22. Albert Camus, "Algerian Reports," in *Resistance, Rebellion, and Death*, trans. J. O'Brien, New York: Alfred A. Knopf, 1966, p. 124.

23. Frantz Fanon, *Studies in a Dying Colonialism*, trans. H. Chevalier, New York: Monthly Review Press, 1965, p. 36, n. 1 and David M. Hart, "The Tribe in Modern Morocco: Two Case Studies," in *Arabs and Berbers: From Tribe to Nation in North Africa*, ed. E. Gellner and C. Micaud, London: Duckworth, 1972, p. 26ff.

24. William B. Quandt, "The Berbers in the Algerian Political Elite," in *Arabs and Berbers*, London: Duckworth, 1972, p. 286.

25. C. Malabou and J. Derrida, "Of Algeria," in *Counterpath: Travelling with Jacques Derrida*, Stanford: Stanford University Press, 2004, p. 81.

26. Philip C. Naylor, *France and Algeria: A History of Decolonisation and Transformation*, Gainesville: University Press of Florida, 2000, pp. 63–64; Edward Said, *Culture and Imperialism*, New York: Vintage, 1993, p. 267.

27. Fanon, *Studies in a Dying Colonialism*, p. 84.

28. J. Favret, "Traditionalism through Ultra-Modernism," in *Arabs and Berbers*, London: Duckworth, 1972, p. 321.

29. Pierre Bourdieu, *The Algerians*, trans. Alan C. M. Ross, Boston: Beacon Press, 1962, p. xiii.

30. On this point see Paul Rabinow, *Symbolic Domination: Cultural Form and Historical Change in Morocco*, Chicago, IL: University of Chicago Press, 1975.

31. Naylor, *France and Algeria*, pp. 180–81.

32. Félix Guattari, "Une sexualisation en rupture," *La Quinzaine littéraire* 215 (1975): 15.

33. Félix Guattari, "On a le racisme qu'on mérite," in *Les Années D'Hiver 1980–1985*, Paris: Bernard Barrault, 1986, 40.

34. Multiple unidentified authors, "Les arabes et nous," p. 19.

35. Deleuze, "Sex-Pol en acte," p. 29.

36. "Les arabes et nous," p. 17.

37. "Les culs énergumènes," p. 230.

38. Guy Hocquenghem, *Homosexual Desire*, trans. Daniela Dangoor, Durham, NC: Duke University Press, 1993. Originally published 1972.

39. Ibid., p. 229.

40. J. Ruedy, *Modern Algeria*, Bloomington: Indiana University Press, 1992, p. 222ff.

Chapter 13

For a Transdisciplinary Metamethodology

As a theorist of transdisciplinarity, run-of-the-mill academic multidisciplinary clusters were of little use to Guattari since they were indelibly stamped with the paradox of the between: subject to an institutional orthodoxy that allowed them to be valorized from an already-established disciplinary perspective of expertise as exciting places to visit. Guattari poked fun at interdisciplinarity in its limited sense and referred to it as an *abracadabra* word deployed cynically by many pretenders. However, he made several significant attempts to theorize a meta-method adequate to the passage from inter- to trans-disciplinarity in his co-written report (with Sergio Vilar), "De la pluri-disciplinarité à la transdisciplinarité en passant pas les OBJETS COMPLEXES qui composent L'OBJET-MONDE et son HYPERCOMPLEXITÉ L'INTERDÉPENDANTE."[1]

As a non-university trained psychoanalyst, Guattari acquired his knowledge of transdisciplinary theory from his youthful practices in organization building, beginning in the youth hostelling movement, a mentorship from institutional pedagogue Fernand Oury, and the tutelage of Jean Oury in institutional analysis at La Borde that involved the establishment of intra-hospital patients' committees. Guattari learned early that there were always other ways of doings things, even though the same old barriers could be thrown up again and again.

For Guattari, the movement from interdisciplinarity, with all of its compromises, towards transdisciplinarity, was both necessary and inevitable. This movement was an internal ecological force whose very existence necessarily transformed how interrelations between living systems, social structures, and psychical processes could be conceived. Such movement was evident, thought Guattari, in the IT revolution because its objects composed a world of interdependent hypercomplexity irreducible to unidimensional evaluation, by the market or by predictive, objective science. Hypercomplexity requires the transformation of method as such. Guattari's preferred term transdisciplinary was a call to rethink the kind of research that involved science, society, politics, ethics, and aesthetics through the development of a metamethod adequate to a new field of relationships; here, adequacy ensures precarious, uncertainty, and creativity over fixity, universality, and preset articulations. Meta- in this usage is about not one but all methods and does not seek to consolidate or generalize or integrate them in any way but, instead, to criticize the reductive practice of modelling: a meta-method is "an instrument for deciphering modelling systems in diverse domains."[2] Problems of organization directly entail problems of method beyond the compromise of merely transporting one method from one domain to another. This correlation of theory construction and organizational research practices in a specific institution was at work in Max Horkheimer's directorship of the Frankfurt Institute for Social Research, circa 1933. His sense of social research, cooperatively integrating the social scientific perspectives of members of the Frankfurt Circle, including economics, philosophy, psychoanalysis, literature, music, and so on, was not towards the creation of a superdiscipline but, rather, following the lead of the object (contemporary society) and developing a new method on that basis.[3]

THEORY AND ORGANIZATION

Theory development and organizational change are mutually supporting aspects of schizoanalysis: "Schizoanalysis, rather than moving in the direction of reductionist modelizations which simplify the complex, will work towards its complexification, its processual enrichment, towards the consistency of its virtual lines of bifurcation and differentiation, in short towards its ontological heterogeneity."[4] Schizoanalysis is a practice of critical metamodelling. Its ontology is pragmatic as it is oriented towards discerning potential for the auto-modelling of subjectivity: "[Schizoanalysis] is a metamodelization. It tries to understand how it is that you got where you are? 'What is your model to you?' It does not work?—Then, I don't know, one tries to work together. One must see if one can make a graft of other models."[5] In order to respond to events that show potential for giving to patients the opportunity to remodel themselves, reorganizing their field of references and taking up new materials of expression, a cartographic rhizome of this process might include a graft of models. Such cross-assemblage hatchings are encouraged by institutional procedures that respect and provide opportunities for self-positing trajectories and processes of singularization. Guattari's task of putting into place the non-linear schedule of work rotation at La Borde, supported by a range of internal and external clubs, committees, commissions, performances, and so on, is a good example of how he cross-hatched fluxes of temporalities, duties, rotations, money, matters, and signs towards the creation of dynamic, unfinished, diagrams. Automodelization is given access to new fluxes to create new lived subjective territories built around shifting collective alignments and assemblages of enunciation.

"There is no general pedagogy relative to the constitution of a living transdiscipinarity," Guattari wrote.[6] None of his group endeavours, beginning in 1965 with Fédération des groups d'études et de recherches institutionnelles (FGERI) and later CERFI, were static models of organization. He thought of FGERI as nothing less than a proto-transdisciplinary experimental research group that was a "*detour*" around the false problems posed by entrenched disciplines.[7] But Guattari did not romanticize FGERI:

> The FGERI was rather extraordinary: no funding, no grants and even so there were more than a hundred people, from very different backgrounds, who would meet in order to deepen the theme of widening the scope of analysis, moving it beyond the limits of the couch and the psychoanalytic structuralism that had begun to install itself in a despotic way around Lacanianism. The negative aspect was that this technique of "brainstorming" could become an alibi for doing nothing.[8]

FGERI had a specialized analytic focus but sought new lines of escape from rigid interpretive grids. By the time CERFI appeared, funding became a factor in which projects were undertaken, vouchsafed by Foucault's participation, and how their outcomes would be disseminated, including reports such as Guattari's *Lines of Flight*.[9] Why Guattari's name alone appears as author remains unclear, although it is not unrelated to his role as director of *Recherches*, in the Three Billion Perverts imbroglio.

In the jointly written UNESCO paper, "From Interdisciplinarity to Transdisciplinarity," Guattari offers a vision of the tasks of metamethodology beyond the postmodern condition of the rule of paralogy and dissensus. Guattari's engagement with the concept of dissensus needs to be carefully disimbricated from that of Lyotard in *The Postmodern Condition*.[10] Lyotard, like Guattari, had to reckon with the fallout from the post-1968 popular promotion of "interdisciplinary studies" in the form of team-based brainstorming, social science tokenism in science grants, the innovation agenda, and the rhetoric of excellence, under the growing influence of the market in all research cultures. Both Guattari and Lyotard would have agreed that consensus had become a problem. Guattari criticized the displacement of the capacity to create consensus around certain issues by political parties, unions, and other democratic associations onto mass media and advertising. Mass consensus that is created in terms of passive and largely politically distracted responses to commercial inducements not only weakened true debate but is "an avoidance of authentically dissensual problematics."[11] This is where Guattari parted company with Lyotard: dissensus was not the new end of dialogue, but merely a "transitory phase of the state of media" out of which something new will emerge. Genuine dissensus cannot be achieved under current conditions in which new media is used by corporations to further their shallow interests, and the absence of effective bodies to investigate and act on media manipulation, corruption, and collusion. New media, information technology, and artificial intelligence together require the development and deployment of progressive ethical perspectives paired with an ecological sensitivity to planetary concerns.

For Guattari and Vilar, "the organization of human culture by disciplines belongs to the past, although to a certain degree it is a necessary point of departure in the advance towards domains of knowledge that involve new practices and changing styles of individual and collective life."[12] Within typical university structures, specialist-trained academics often remain ignorant of one another's work. Disciplines bicker over resources, and the arts and humanities are financially strangled by the financial flows of the applied sciences and professions. There continues to be much fanfare about interdisciplinarity as a novel combinatory, but few breakthroughs have occurred at the level of method. Thus, the task becomes the elaboration of a genuine metamethod that would upset existing power-knowledge configurations. The rethinking of method would challenge the status quos of knowledge production. The authors elaborated eight conditions:

1. Call into question every discipline's ability to understand the globality within which it finds itself;
2. Adopt a humble attitude in the face of the immense field of knowledge of the real;
3. Open one's own assemblages towards diverse fields of dialogue, both consensual and dissensual, and other forms of mutual exchange;
4. Do not abandon specialization for the sake of an ideology but rather proceed irreversibly by fluctuation and bifurcation towards transdisciplinarity, each discipline according to its own speed and willingness to make sacrifices or suffer "amputations";
5. Certain theoretical approaches will need to be deconstructed, but hopefully not in an anarchic way so that existing disciplines may see the confluence of concepts and problems from a new theoretico-pragmatic perspective;
6. The creation of numerous cross references is not heresy but has always existed to some degree;
7. From a critical interdisciplinary perspective, scientific positions of self-sufficiency and omnipotence will be subject to definitive critique;

8. Intradisciplinary graspings of the virtualities of heterogeneous, evolving fields will have repercussions for the movement towards transdisciplinarity.[13]

None of these points can be isolated from more global cultural, political, institutional, and technological changes that a critical thought in elaboration needs to recognize. Guattari and Vilar suppose that researchers will be predisposed to adopt a transdisciplinary perspective, even at first from within their own disciplines, if they understand that the objects of study are multidimensional and hypercomplex. No one, of course, wants to fear punishment or professional diminishment if they pursue openness and answer the call to familiarize themselves with concepts from other disciplines and learn how to work with them. In this way certain fundamental traits of hypercomplex objects, for example, the rise and centrality of data processing, may come to be known relative to cultural utilizations, social features that presuppose gender, race, and class issues, a variety of micro- and macro-perspectives that are crossed by diverse universes of value, including economic factors in local, regional, national, and global contexts; technico-scientific developments; and ecological implications. A metamethod would identify stabilities and instabilities, contingencies, vulnerabilities, and irreversibilities, and then map the transitions, transformations, and effects of complex objects theoretically and empirically, as they undergo changes based on imbalances between their elements, and the conditions with which they interact, and the forces that promote and inhibit their development.

It is both a weakness and a strength that much of what Guattari and Vilar wrote was attitudinal and concerned a perceived mental ecology of specialists. It seemed to impose a need for action onto the sciences and the recourse to potentialities grasped intradisciplinarily. At times they seem to think that the technological convergences that will overcome static, siloed thought, as well as a certain quality of globality, will simply favour transdisciplinarity, which seems in this respect inevitable. This immanentist evolutionary perspective has been developed by Pierre Lévy who sees technological evolution tending, in Guattarian terms, towards a molecular revolution led by genetics, nanotechnology, digitization, and self-organization. Lévy's term for transdisciplinarity is knowledge organized along cosmopedic lines; this is made possible by technological complexification (computerization) that facilitates the multidimensional combination of many semiotics whose mapping activities are ongoing. Importantly, cosmopedia is based on a principle of "non-separation" and Lévy figures it as a "quilt," where the "dissolution of differences between specializations" will take place across porous borders.[14]

A Guattarian metamethod is far from a metanarrative. It is akin to a continuous process of assisted automodelization that attempts to find its own consistency. A metamethod is not an abstraction because it requires putting into place the organizational means for its collective realization. The study groups and collaborative journal projects were not merely about production outcomes, but of investigating how transdisciplinarity takes place, answering the question of how does one assemble a workable collectivity that will function as a counter-current against all the fallback positions, become aware of its own blockages and self-mutilations, as well as find ways to realize its potential, risking itself in the face of others—for make no mistake about it, developing a metamethod is a great risk as it invokes "creative uncertainty"[15] against demands for quantifiable results.

WHITHER CERFI: TRANSDISCIPLINARY PROJECTS

For Guattari, transdisciplinarity projects can be neither productively framed in terms of their inadequacies, for instance, in terms of their inability to integrate all of the factors at play, and thus as failed efforts at wholeness, nor dismissed as luxuries permitted in times of affluence. Experimental transdisciplinary auto-production gives shape to institutional microspaces and produces substances, some well formed but others less well formed, that are actualized through technological media. For instance, for Armand and Michèle Mattelart, the question of transdisciplinarity mutually imbricates technology and microinstitutional auto-formation, but within a university milieu and in relation to a journal, *Communications*, first published in 1961 under the auspices of Georges Friedmann in the Centre d'études des communications de masse.[16] The object of the Centre was the link between technology and massification, rejecting the term mass communication as conceptually insufficient to account for emerging processes. The centre and its journal are born through this questioning, and it extends to a hesitancy about the objects it will address, and to the methods used to address them: deflecting the content analysis that was popular in communications research. *Communications* published a yearly activities report of its members, a fairly typical academic annual report. In 1974 the Centre changed its name to Centre for Transdisciplinary Studies, and its three directors were presented as head of research streams (sociology—Edgar Morin; anthropology—Georges Friedmann; semiology—Roland Barthes). Whether this streaming in the form of a specialist multiplicity betrayed the transdisciplinary mission at the moment it was named remains unresolved. As the 1970s rolled onward and the institutional site of the journal shifted from its original site of Ecole pratique to the renamed Ecole des hautes études en sciences sociales, and mass communications receded into the background as the masters of structuralism came to dominate the institution and journal, the project would whither with the passing of Friedmann in 1978 and Barthes in 1980. The Centre for Transdisciplinary Studies would be thoroughly integrated into the Centre national de la recherche scientifique (CNRS) as Morin rose in its ranks (the Edgar Morin Centre attracted CNRS funding within the Institute for the Anthropology of Contemporary Societies in the Ecole des hautes études, a transdisciplinary space for training graduate students that superseded Freidmann's Centre). Guattari would fulminate against the CNRSization of research, that is, big social science, state-funded and -directed grants programmes.

Returning to the example of CERFI, this freelance research group managed to solidify a core membership in affective communion around the production of collective objects, specifically, funded projects leading to the production of specials topics journal issues of *Recherches*. CERFI was an extra-academic assemblage that acquired funding through civil research contracts under the budget of the French Ministry of Research. It provided salaries to its members and financed projects. These were not so many individual contracts, as François Fourguet recalls, but covered the entire group of twenty core members for four or five years.[17] The hypercomplex object under study was the state itself. Eventually CERFI was edged out by professional academic bodies as budgets shrank, governments changed, and research became more university-focused, favouring Centres like Friedmann's. This began to occur around 1975. The state's strategy was to co-opt CERFI members, a move that largely failed. The radicals who had prepared Three Billion Perverts no longer had a place, and new members were not so interested in the causes of old radicals. The book publishing wing, Encres, appeared in 1977, and some of the special issues of *Recherches* were printed as books by Editions 10/18. Even Guattari began to take his distance, and he relinquished his directorship in 1981.[18] CERFI was no longer in the picture.

It is not possible to separate the role that journals play in the formation of microinstitutional matters from the extended network of collective equipment, those "machines that produce the conditions of possibility for all capitalist economic infrastructure,"[19] which programme mutually imbricated molecular semiotic powers and molar political frames and relations. Flows of funding can be and are manipulated, research teams can be programmed, and the most transversal assemblages can be reoriented to either vertical or horizontal coordinates. For Guattari, "collective equipment is not just walls, offices, circulations, transmissions of orders and information, but also and above all, a modeling of attitudes, of rituals of submission that are imposed across multiple semiotic components."[20] In the reports for CERFI grants, Guattari was elaborating the collective equipment that both made the writing possible and sought to curb its influence, by explaining how the network reached into the social unconscious by means of facefication (the faces of bureaucrats) and the refrains they pronounce (cycles of grant application results). Citing Foucault's Groupe d'information sur les prisons as an example, the emergence of an analytic-militant assemblage that successfully intervenes in the social unconscious and cuts across collective equipment occurs through the refinements of its collective enunciations, not taken literally of course, and thus reduced to the pages it published. Everyone knows how success breeds jealousy among others, as Querrien observed with regard to CERFI.[21] Yet journals and the research and study groups that produce them remain for Guattari a pragmatic component in the elaboration of a situational rhizome of collective enunciation.

NOTES

1. Félix Guattari and Sergio Vilar, "De la pluri-disciplinarité à la transdisciplinarité en passant pas les OBJETS COMPLEXES qui composent L'OBJET-MONDE et son HYPERCOMPLEXITÉ L'INTERDÉPENDANTE," (1992). Barcelona-Paris. Fonds Félix Guattari ET05–13. IMEC.
2. Guattari, *Schizoanalytic Cartographies*, p. 17.
3. See Helmut Dubiel, *Theory and Politics: Studies in the Development of Critical Theory*, trans. B. Gregg, Cambridge: The MIT Press, 1985, p. 129ff.
4. Guattari, *Chaosmosis*, p. 61.
5. Guattari, *The Guattari Reader*, pp. 132–33.
6. "Les fondements éthico-politique de l'interdisciplinarité," Handwritten text. Dated April 1991. FFG. ET20–24, p. 15.
7. See Guattari, "L'intervention institutionnelle." Typescript of an interview, published in 1980 by Payot in its Petite Bibliothèque series number 382 under the same title of the essay. FFG ET09–26.
8. Guattari, *Chaosophy*, p. 28.
9. Parts of the manuscript appeared in *Recherches*, but are gathered in *Lines of Flight*. It was originally a report to the funding agency, Ministère de 'léquipement.
10. Lyotard, *The Postmodern Condition*, pp. 52–53.
11. Félix Guattari, "Pour une éthique des medias," *Le Monde* (6 nov. 1992): 2.
12. "From Interdisciplinarity to Transdisciplinariy," p. 3.
13. Ibid., pp. 6–9.
14. Pierre Lévy, *Collective Intelligence*, trans. R. Bononno, Cambridge, MA: Perseus, 1997, pp. 216–17.
15. Guattari, *Chaosmosis*, p. 134.
16. Armand and Michèle Mattelart, See *Rethinking Media Theory: Signposts and New Directions*, trans. James A. Cohen and M. Urquidi, Minneapolis: University of Minnesota Press, 1992, p. 20.
17. F. Fourquet, "Histoire du CERFI," *Multitudes* (2007): 2. http://www.multitudes.net/Histoire-du-CERFI/
18. Dosse, *Intersecting Lives*, pp. 280–81.
19. Guattari, *Lines of Flight*, p. 12.
20. Ibid., p. 50.
21. "La Borde, Guattari, Left Movements," p. 407.

Afterword

Post-Media Singularities

Janell Watson

Félix Guattari remains relevant to social science research today because, wary of reducing complex objects by applying general paradigms, he invented metamodelling, a schizoanalytic cartography that maps singular psychic and social phenomena, treating them as singularities rather than as instantiations of a syndrome, a model, or a structure. Even though a psychic or social formation may share many characteristics with other such entities, the schizoanalyst treats each instance as its own unique, singular assemblage of heterogeneous elements. This means that the researcher must construct new maps and model for each analysis, even as the assemblage itself continues to generate its own singular mappings. It's not this or that concept—transversality, machine, chaosmosis, ecosophy, and so on—that makes an approach Guattarian, but rather the emphasis on the particularities of a situation, event, or assemblage, always presumed to be transindividual, evolving, and contingent. Writing simultaneously as methodologist and practitioner of schizoanalytic social science, in this essay collection Gary Genosko demonstrates "the possibilities of modeling for singularization,"[1] taking full advantage of Guattari's complex tools for making maps and repurposing models that not only plot but also create assemblages, human and nonhuman, discursive and non-discursive, virtual and actual, possible and real. The post-media era that Guattari foresaw in the 1980s has arrived, for better and for worse. In what follows, I borrow from both Guattari and Genosko to describe the current post-media era as an age of singularization, algorithmic coding, and suprahuman hypercomplexity.

Long before the launch of the World Wide Web, Guattari advocated replacing the abstract structures of prevailing social science models with what he was calling machines, and which he and Deleuze would recast as assemblages. Unlike the notion of structure, which expresses a generality, the machine enacts "a repetition of the particular."[2] Repetitions of the particular can get stuck in a loop, or instead cross thresholds of singularity that enable them to take off in new directions, producing large transformations from small events, effectuating molar changes by molecular means. Guattari thus understands singularity as an attribute of real existents, as well as a bifurcation capable of transforming a complex system. He was an avid follower of the emerging scientific theories of information, chaos, fractals, fuzzy sets, and open systems, but metamodelling and schizoanalytic cartography enabled him to apply these new sciences of complexity to social phenomena without succumbing to the illusion that human relations can be mathematized. Complexity theorists such as James Clerk Maxwell, Norbert Wiener, and René Thom thought of human societies as complex systems, but to directly applying models from physics and mathematics to social phenomena is to run up against the problem of taking abstract theory into the real world.[3] Guattari's notion of the "aesthetic paradigm" addressed this disconnect between theoretical abstraction and the asperities of real life, but rather than succumbing to eclectic methodological impressionism, he instead drew upon the sciences of uncertainty while acknowledging their limits. Rather than seeking mathematical consistency, as did Thom with his catastrophe theory, the aesthetic paradigm strives for existential consistency, since anything that actually exists must attain enough cohesion and coherence to persist as an entity. Michel Serres, historian and philosopher of the sciences and mathematics of complexity, observes that advances in these fields "allow us to perceive the singularity of individuals or cultures, without renouncing scientific and conceptual generalization."[4] The aesthetic paradigms of schizoanalytic cartography navigate this passage between the singularity of the real and the abstract generalities of science.

Meanwhile, abstractions—software, algorithms, data structures, and so on—control more and more of the world's social, economic, and institutional machines. This historical shift impacts not only industrial production but also the production of subjectivities, social collectivities, and science itself. Data at once enables post-media technologies and offers governments, industry, and cybercriminals a new means of surveillance, control, and exploitation. Most information gathered from the public remains officially accessible only to governments, corporations, and academic researchers, though the latter are not guaranteed access. Genosko explores the tangled complexities of data collection, access, and use in his chapter on the "informatic striation" of indigenous peoples by government agencies who use various types of code (e.g., identity numbers) to organize and manage cultural practices he describes as "smooth," which is to say uncoded. He observes that "striation has the aim of identifying and (in)dividuating otherwise unidentifiable persons," but that the striating databases cataloguing indigenous individuals may set off "a new smoothing operation in the ease with which files and data sets are compared, contrasted, and combined in novel ways."[5] Genosko provides fascinating real-world examples of resingularizing, resignifying reappropriations of data on the part of the groups whose smoothness had been striated. Smoothness does not necessarily indicate liberatory nomadic singularization.

Even though the World Wide Web was still in its infancy when he died in 1992, Guattari wrote of an interactive post-media era before its full emergence, offering conceptual mappings for understanding what is now our current age of pervasive digitization, interactive media, and big data. Thanks to networked information technology, the post-media era has indeed democratized media production, in the sense that users have more access than ever to tools of producing and sharing texts, images, and video. However, although the prefix "post" implies a historical succession, Guattari warned that mass media would not disappear even after a broader public gains access to interactive post-media. Genosko observes that for Guattari, "the shift from mass into post-media would not be sequential and definitive but co-existent, contestatory, and messy."[6] In both journalism and entertainment, the productions of mass media corporations continue to dominate. Moreover, personal participation in the web is funnelled through corporate entities like Google, Facebook, YouTube, and Wordpress. Data gathered from these platforms are now routinely used by law enforcement, marketing, and finance. As a result, true singularization remains rare. Genosko wisely warns his readers to be wary of "infocapital's capacity to provide pseudo-singularization."[7]

Achieving singularization depends less on gadgets than on socio-politics and semiotics. As Guattari himself put it, "We cannot expect positive repercussions from new technologies unless these technologies are adopted by way of individual and collective creative practices."[8] Access to the tools of interactive media in no way guarantees singularizing creativity, nor is digital technology always necessary. Analog cultures and institutions have not disappeared, and likewise benefit from singularizing cartographies, as Genosko demonstrates in his report on an alternative high school organized around designing, building, and marketing skateboards. The students' capacity for the "rhizomatic resistance" characteristic of skateboard culture was redirected towards their rebellious low-tech DIY entrepreneurialism. The founders and teachers of the school deployed transversal tactics, like those Guattari developed at La Borde, in order to navigate school board curriculum and accreditation requirements.[9]

A crucial contribution to social research in the post-media era remains Guattari's politically aware semiotics, which astutely differentiates among sign, symbol, signal, and code, creating what Genosko describes as "a novel semiosis adapted to the age of the algorithm."[10] The strictly linguistic semiotics of his Saussurean and Chomskyian contemporaries seems sadly dated in comparison. Information technology greatly expands the scope of coding, for better and for worse. Coding, data, and information are not always bad, despite the negative examples of controlling codes throughout capitalism and schizophrenia.[11] After all, the interactive tools of post-media creativity rely on code to produce and disseminate many types of cultural production. Proliferating code can only produce subjectivating striation when deployed for the ends of domination or exploitation, although even apparatuses of disciplinary striation sometimes escape the control of those who created them, taking off on their own singularizing lines of flight.

Guattari spent his adult life studying, operating, and writing about machinic assemblages such as hospitals, militant groups, adolescence, capitalism, and the unconscious. These same machines have since undergone further encoding by processes of digitization that now permeate both living and inert bodies at the molecular level. Genosko shows that Guattari's "immanentist metamethodology" to be "adequate to the hypercomplex objects of the contemporary universe of things."[12] Guattari's "transdisciplinary metamethodology"[13] enables social researchers to embrace the full complexity and global scope of human-nonhuman assemblages such as climate change, world markets, water supplies, energy grids, transnational terror, piracy, organized crime, species endangerment, and human population growth.[14] Supra-human assemblages such as these impact even the most local social formations. Government, industry, and finance dominate them, but no one entity fully controls them. Nonetheless, Guattari would not despair. Molecular revolution can always pursue points of singularity, no matter how large the system. As Genosko puts it, "the human-machine assemblage" of the post-media age "is at once the site of capitalist exploitation . . . and the promise of new collective formations that can act against capitalist subjectivations."[15] To be effective, these new collective formations must be singular and can be constructed only with the help of schizoanalytic cartographies which simultaneously create and map. Given the ever-expanding role of digital mapmaking and computer modelling in the post-media world, this may require the help of schizoanalytic computing, a yet-to-be-invented technology that I am imagining as the harbinger of a new era that I would call post-algorithmic.

NOTES

1. "Micropolitics of Hope" in *The Reinvention of Social Practices*, p. 164.
2. Félix Guattari, *Psychoanalysis and Transversality: Texts and Interviews 1955–1971*, trans. Ames Hodges, Los Angeles: Semiotext(e), 2015, p. 322.
3. See the introduction to Guattari's *The Machinic Unconscious: Essays in Schizoanalysis*, trans. Taylor Adkins, Los Angeles: Semiotext(e), 2010.

4. Michel Serres and Sven Ortoli, *Pantopie: de Hermès à petite poucette : Entretiens avec Martin Legros et Sven Ortoli*, Paris: Editions le Pommier, 2014, p. 109.

5. "Informatic Striation in Indigenous Canada and Australia," p. 23.

6. "Promises of the Post-Media Era," p. 45.

7. "Promises of the Post-Media Era," p. 54.

8. "Toward an Ethics of the Media," trans. Janell Watson, *Polygraph* 14 (2002): 3.

9. "Transversality of the Oasis Skateboard Factory Alternative School."

10. "The Search for Non-Meaning," p. 185.

11. "The Search for Non-meaning."

12. Introduction to Part IV, "Search for a Method," p. 169.

13. "For a Transdisciplinary Metamethodology."

14. Other names for planet-spanning human-nonhuman assemblages include actor networks, vibrant matter, and hyperobjects, as theorized by Bruno Latour, Jane Bennett, and Timothy Morton, respectively.

15. "The Search for Non-Meaning," p. 185.

Index

About the Author

Gary Genosko is professor of communication and digital media studies at the University of Ontario Institute of Technology. His many publications include *The Guattari Reader* (1996), *Félix Guattari: An Aberrant Introduction* (2002), *Félix Guattari: A Critical Introduction* (2009) and *Machinic Eros: Félix Guattari's Writings on Japan* (2015).

www.ingramcontent.com/pod-product-compliance
Lightning Source LLC
LaVergne TN
LVHW101447200926
848483LV00001B/70
9781786605054